Sarada Ranganathan Endowment for Library Science Series. 4

NEW EDUCATION AND SCHOOL LIBRARY

Experience of Half a Century

New Education and School Library

S R Ranganathan
National Research Professor in Library Science

Assisted By
P Jayarajan
Research Assistant to
National Research Professor in Library Science

SARADA RANGANATHAN ENDOWMENT
FOR LIBRARY SCIENCE
Bangalore-560 078

Shiyali Ramamrita Ranganathan (1892-1972).
Parappurath Jayarajan (1945 -)

Reprinted 1989
Reprint 2006

2,J1
N73

ISBN: 81-7000-467-5

Ess Ess
Rs.875/-

Published By:
Ess Ess Publications
4837/24, Ansari Road,
Darya Ganj,
New Delhi-110 002
Ph.No. 23260807, 51563444, Fax: 51563334
E-mail: info@essessreference.com
url: www.essessreference.com

For:
Sarada Ranganathan Endowment for Library Science
702, 'Upstairs',
42nd Cross, III Block,
Rajajinagar,
Bangalore-560 010.
Ph.No. 23305109
E-mail: srels@vsnl.com

Printed in India at: Printline, New Delhi

TO

PANCHU AND JAGANNATHAN

THE FIVE LAWS OF LIBRARY SCIENCE

1 **Books are for use**

2 **Every reader his/her book**

3 **Every book its reader**

4 **Save the time of the reader**

5 **A library is a growing organism**

"To carry knowledge to the doors
of those that lack it and to
educate all to perceive the right!
Even to give away the whole earth
cannot equal that form of service."

— MANU

"If it is necessary,
omit one bridge over the river,
go round a little there,
and throw one arch at least over the
darker gulf of ignorance which surrounds us."

— HENRY DAVID THOREAU

CONTENTS

Part A Preliminaries

Chap	AA	Conspectus	15
	AB	Foreword to Edition 1 (1942) by Sir John Sargent	16
	AC	Pre-library Days in Schools and Colleges	19
	AD	Genesis of the Book	21

PART B/E WHY OF SCHOOL LIBRARY

Part B Why of School Library: Lines of Approach

Chap	BA	Answer Based on Authority	27
	BB	Answer Based on Tradition	29
	BC	Answer Based on Imitation	30
	BD	Answer Based on *A Priori* Method	32

Part C Why of School Library: From the Angle of Curriculum

Chap	CA	Teleology of Education	35
	CB	Education for a Changing World	36
	CC	Education for an Accelerated Change in the Universe of Ideas	38
	CD	Factors Leading to Overloaded Curriculum	41
	CE	A Way Out of Overloaded Curriculum	43
	CF	From Oral Communication to Socialisation of Books	47
	CG	From Camel Theory to New Education	51
	CH	New Education and Library Scene in Elementary School	54
	CJ	New Education and Library Scene in High School	56

PART D WHY OF SCHOOL LIBRARY: FROM THE ANGLE OF EDUCATION

Chap DA	Humanism and Universal Education	61
DB	Arrest of the Progress in Educational Techniques in the Early Awakened Countries of the West	64
DC	Arrest of Progress in Educational Techniques in India Today	67
DD	Lines of Solution	69
DE	Problem of Lower Quartiles in the Intellectual Scale	70
DF	Unconscious Hit	73
DG	John Dewey and Individual Instruction	75
DH	Emergence of School Library and New Education	79
DJ	Library Hour and New Education	81

PART E WHY OF SCHOOL LIBRARY: FROM THE ANGLE OF THE PROCESS OF EDUCATION

EA	Inherence and Becoming	87
EB	Education as "Becoming": Some Case Studies	90
EC	Education as "Becoming": Some Opinions	92
ED	Passivity *vs* Activity	95
EE	Global Experience	100
EF	New Education and Pedagogical Consequences	103
EG	The Look of School Library	105
EH	Sum-up: Inequalities and Equalities	108

PART F/J WHAT OF SCHOOL LIBRARY

PART F WHAT OF SCHOOL LIBRARY: CONSTITUENTS OF A LIBRARY

Chap FA	Evolution of the Concept of School Library	113

	FB	Current Definition of the Term 'Library'	115
	FC	New Outlook on School Library	116
	PART G	WHAT OF SCHOOL LIBRARY: BIBLIOGRAPHICAL FACTOR	
Chap	GA	Range of Books in a School Library	119
	GB	Range of Subjects in a School Library	123
	GC	Range of Standards of Books in a School Library	125
	GD	Illustrations in Books	127
	GE	Physical Make-up of Books	128
	GF	Fugitive Reading Materials in a School Library	129
	GG	Extension Work	131
	PART H	WHAT OF SCHOOL LIBRARY: HUMAN CONSTITUENT	
Chap	HA	Three Human Constituents of a School Library	137
	HB	Human Constituent: Students	139
	HC	Retention of Students as Customers	142
	HD	Teachers: The Human Constituent of a School Library	146
	HE	Library Staff: The Human Constituent of a School Library	148
	HF	Qualification for a School Librarian	151
	HG	Status and Scale of Salary of School Library Staff	153
	HH	Grouping of Schools for Library Services: Both Necessary and Sufficient	157
	PART J	WHAT OF SCHOOL LIBRARY: MATERIAL CONSTITUENT	
Chap	JA	General Features of School Library Building	163
	JB	Specification for Library Building, Fittings and Furniture	166

PART K/N HOW OF SCHOOL LIBRARY

PART K HOW OF SCHOOL LIBRARY: OBJECTIVES OF SCHOOL LIBRARY WORK

Chap	KA	School Library to Create Library Habit in Students	173
	KB	School Library to Create Library Civics in Students	176
	KC	Objectives of School Library: From the Angle of Students	180

PART L HOW OF SCHOOL LIBRARY: MEANS

Chap	LA	Fallacies	185
	LB	Handicaps	
	LC	Student's Preparatory Work in the Library	189
	LD	Student's Parallel Reading	190
	LE	Student's Follow-up Work	192
	LF	Extra-mural Stimulus	194
	LG	Story-Hour for the Young Students	196
	LH	Fact Finding	197
	LJ	Reading for Information and Pleasure: A Sample	202
	LK	Inspirational Book	206
	LL	Learning of Library Habit	209

PART M HOW OF SCHOOL LIBRARY: STUDENT'S WORK

Chap	MA	Need for Keeping Diary	213
	MB	Fact Finding Diary	217
	MC	Recreative Reading Diary	219
	MD	Inspirational Reading Diary	220
	ME	Fact Finding: How to Make it Pleasurable	221
	MF	Recreational Reading: How to Make it Profitable	224
	MG	Inspirational Reading: How to Make it Pleasurable	226
	MH	School Library: The Training Ground for Responsible Citizenship	228

Chap	MJ	Promotion of Public-Mindedness	229
	MK	Consideration for Others	230
	ML	Queue System	233
	MM	Public and Private Hygiene	235
	MN	Fire Prevention	237
	MP	Personal Manners	238
	MQ	Student's Work While Attending Library Lessons	240
	MR	Notes-taking Work	246
	MS	Bibliography Building Work	247

PART N HOW OF SCHOOL LIBRARY: ACHIEVEMENT TEST

Chap	NA	Fact Finding	251
	NB	Recreative Reading	254
	NC	Inspirational Reading	256
	ND	Library Habit	257
	NE	Notes-taking	263
	NF	Bibliography Building	264

PART P/R PRESENT DIFFICULTIES

PART P PRESENT DIFFICULTY: BOOK FAMINE

Chap	PA	Medium of Expression	269
	PB	Choice of Words	273
	PC	Sentence and Style	275
	PD	Futility of Translation and Adaptation	276
	PE	Need for Indigenous Books for Students	278
	PF	History of Students' Books in English	279
	PG	Book Industry in India	283
	PH	A Tentative Solution	285

PART Q PRESENT DIFFICULTY: MANAGERIAL APATHY

Chap	QA	Technical Staff	289
	QB	Space and Equipment	291
	QC	Finance	292

PART R PRESENT DIFFICULTY: PEDAGOGICAL INERTIA

Chap	RA	Role of State Government	295
	RB	Role of Management	297
	RC	Role of Teachers' Association	298

PART S/Y LIBRARY TECHNIQUES

PART S FIVE LAWS OF LIBRARY SCIENCE

Chap	SA	Five Laws of Library Science: The Foundation of Library work	303
	SB	Role of Five Laws of Library Science	304

PART T REFERENCE SERVICE

Chap	TA	Definition of Reference Service	307
	TB	Qualities Necessary for Initiation Work	308
	TC	Apprenticeship Method of Initiation	309
	TD	Practical Guidance as a Method for Initiation	310
	TE	Formal Lesson as a Method of Initiation	311
	TF	A Sample of Two Concentric Cycles	312
	TG	Service to Individual Students	316
	TH	Service to the Class	318
	TJ	Social Role of Reference Service	320
	TK	Cultivation of Mental Resources of a Community: Schematic Representation	322
	TL	Reference Service: The Hub of Library Work	323

PART U CIRCULATION WORK

Chap	UA	Rules of a School Library	327
	UB	Modernising Circulation Method	334
	UC	Ticket Work for Student-Member	336
	UD	Ticket Work for Teacher-Member	340
	UE	Ticket Work for Outside Member	343
	UF	Book-card Members-ticket Method of Circulation	345

Chap	UG	Work at the Entrance Point of the Counter	346
	UH	Work at the Exit Point of the Counter	351
	UJ	Charged Tray Work	357
	UK	Work of Renewal of Loan	360
	UL	Bespeaking Work	362
		PART V LIBRARY CLASSIFICATION	
Chap	VA	Scheme for Library Classification	367
	VB	Decimal Classification	369
	VC	Colon Classification	371
	VD	Main Subjects and Partial Comprehensions in Colon Classification	373
	VE	Steps in Classifying	376
	VF	Schedule of Anteriorising Common Isolates	378
	VG	Schedule of Space Isolates	379
	VH	Schedule of Language Isolates	386
	VJ	Schedule of Time Isolates	388
	VK	Schedule of Select Ready-Made Class Numbers	389
	VL	Examples of Anteriorising Common Isolates	408
	VM	Book Number	411
		PART W LIBRARY CATALOGUE	415
Chap	WA	Physical Form of Library Catalogue and Library Hand	417
	WB	Library Catalogue Freed from the Function of Stock Register	419
	WC	Main Entry	422
		WD/WJ *Added Entry*	
	WD	Cross Reference Entry or Subject Analytical Entry	424
		WE/WJ *Alphabetical Index Entry*	
		WE/WG *Index Entry*	
	WE	Author Index Entry	427
	WF	Editor Index Entry	428

Chap WG	Series Index Entry	429
	WH/WJ *General Added Entries*	
WH	Class Index Entry	430
WJ	Editor of Series Entry	434
WK	Tracing Section	435
	PART X MAINTENANCE WORK	
Chap XA	Functions of Maintenance Section	439
XB	Collection Formation	440
XC	Preparation of Book	444
XD	Stack-room Guide	448
XE	New Books Added to the Library	451
XF	Volumes Returned After Use	454
XG	Shelf-Rectification and Stock-Verification	456
XH	Binding	460
	PART Y OTHER WORK	
Chap YA	Book Selection Work	467
YB	Book Order Work	471
YC	Periodical Publications Work	473
YD	Accession Work	476
YE	School Library Finance	477
	Bibliography	479
	Index	482

PART A

PRELIMINARIES

CHAPTER AA

CONSPECTUS

0 This book is based on the experience of the author during the last 50 years.

1 The book consists of 162 Chapters grouped into 23 parts.

2 The two other Chapters of this Part describe the necessity for library service in schools and its possible place in education.

3 Parts B to E take the reader through the highways and byways of educational theory. They throw all the activities and work of a school in a perspective showing the prepotent place to be given to a school library.

4 Parts F to J examine the resources to be had in a school library. Further, they picture the interrelation among the library staff, the teachers, and the taught; and end with a description of a school library building.

5 Parts K to N examine the work of each student in the library. They correlate the school library work with the methods of New Education; and end with illustrative achievement tests.

6 Parts P to R examine the present difficulties of the school libraries of India. They suggest possible lines of remedy.

7 Parts T to Y describe "School Library Practice." Chapters VK and VL give a brief schedule of ready-made Colon Class Numbers, suited to books commonly found in school libraries. For the benefit of teachers it also gives Class Numbers for select subjects on Education and Library Science. Part W gives brief cataloguing rules and model entries. Chapter F3 outlines library lessons arranged in two cycles for the Concentric Method of teaching. There are descriptions of the routines of circulation work and library rules, shelf arrangement, binding, book ordering and accessioning, periodical publication work, and school library finance.

8 The numbering of the parts, chapters and sections is on a decimal basis. A decimal point is to be understood at the beginning of the number of each Chapter and Section. If this is done mentally, the sequence of the numbers of the Chapters and of Sections will appear to be natural.

FOREWORD TO EDITION 1 (1942)

Sir John Sargent, *Educational Commissioner, Government of India*

1 Competence of the Author to Write this Book

S R Ranganathan needs no introduction to the reading public of India. Few people in this or any other country have devoted more thought or study to library technique than he has done. Even those not accepting all his conclusions nor adopting his methods, will, I am sure, acknowledge the debt under which his industry and erudition have placed them.

2 Status of the Library Profession

No one loving books and regarding the appreciation of them as one of the main hall-marks of a civilised society, will despise the craft of the librarian. It is an encouraging sign that the status due to this learned profession is beginning at last to receive the recognition, hitherto withheld from it for some mysterious reason. The extent to which this most desirable change has been due to Ranganathan's untiring efforts, other people can judge even better than I can.

3 Ranganathan's Vision of the Functions of a Library

My gratitude to Ranganathan, and I am sure that of a great many people who like myself cannot claim to be experts in Library Science, arises not so much from his contributions to the techniques of assembling and distributing a large number of books as from the fact that he never allows what I may perhaps almost irreverently describe as professional details to obscure his vision of the essential value and function of a library. To him all the complicated business of accessioning, indexing, cataloguing and distributing, however important and even controversial the issues involved in it may be, remains always subordinate to the fundamental aim of getting as many books into as many hands and their contents into as many heads as possible.

4 Importance of the Library

It must always be true of libraries intended for the benefit of students or the general public, as distinct from private collections, that the best will be the one with the smallest proportion of its books on its shelves at any given time. For, in this modern age, the store of accumulated human experience is so vast that in spite of the manifold media for publicity and inter-communication the great bulk of it can only be transmitted through the written word; and a library is the essential channel by which the wisdom of the past can be brought to aid or to satisfy the needs of the present. Nearly four hundred years ago a wise man writing in praise of books pointed out that anyone who neglected their help and trusted solely to his own experience for the acquisition of knowledge would be dead long before he had attained even to the rudiments of it.

5 Means to World Peace

In his new book to which this is, I fear, a most inadequate Foreword, Ranganathan turns to an aspect of his main subject which has never been more important than it is today. Many people for many years have expressed their dissatisfaction with the Indian system of education. Apart from its general inadequacy to fit a country of 400 millions [550 millions in 1972] to take its proper place in a society of civilised and peace-loving nations they have pointed out that only too often for all its materialistic objectives it fails to be practical and for all its academic emphasis it misses the inspiration of true learning. In spite, however, of many past disappointments and of the widespread inertia and pessimism which these have produced one need not be a visionary to nourish the hope that out of the tribulations through which we are now passing the realisation may come at no far distant date that a tithe of the cost of destroying men in war, if wisely and persistently applied to improving their condition in peace, might in the fullness of time remove the causes of war altogether.

6 School Library: A Live Workshop

Once the necessity for providing India with a comprehensive

public system of education is recognised and its implications, financial and otherwise, are boldly faced, those responsible for providing and equipping schools and colleges will at last be in the happy position of being able to consider what these institutions ought to have rather than what they must do without. Then, it is to be hoped, every school even in the lower stages of education will be in possession of a library which deserves to be called in Ranganathan's words "a live workshop."

7 Library: The Hub of Educational Institution

There are even now many well-equipped libraries. But, through an imperfect appreciation of their possibilities, by those managing or using them they fail to produce their full cultural influence. To teach the proper significance of reading and writing is one of the main aims of education. In order to write well it is necessary to have read well and there is hardly any branch of study, even the most practical, which does not bring us sooner or later to the use of books. How to extract from them, ruthlessly yet reverently, the last ounce of value is therefore one of the things which every teacher should know and every student should learn. The library should be literally and figuratively the hub of every educational institution and the librarian should be the guide, philosopher, and friend of all its inhabitants. This book aims at explaining how the whole curriculum can be made to radiate and indeed can be irradiated from this hub.

8 Educational Theory and its Translation into Practice

It contains much educational theory but it does not despise even the smallest details which may help in translating theory into practiee. I should much like to comment on some of the opinions and suggestions found in the following pages. But, writers of Forewords must resist the temptation to usurp the function of reviewers. I will therefore content myself with commending this book to all workers in the field of education, and particularly to those refusing to allow the contemplation of "what is" to blind their eyes to the vision of "what might be".

CHAPTER AC

PRE-LIBRARY DAYS IN SCHOOLS AND COLLEGES

1 Dissatisfaction with the Absence of a Functional Library

This book is based on the experience gained as a teacher and as a librarian. From July 1917 to December 1923, I was teaching successively the students of the School Final course, of the Intermediate Course, and of the Pass and the Honours Courses of the University of Madras. The first course covered Mathematics and Physics; and the other Courses covered Mathematics only. This experience as a teacher led me to realise that the potency of a well-equipped library in,

1 Stimulating the self-educability of each student; and

2 Helping each student to develop along his own lines, at his own speed, to his own fullness.

This realisation came to me very pointedly, because it threw some light on some unexpressed dissatisfaction felt by me throughout my student career. Even during the course in the Teachers' College, Saidapet, library did not figure either in the teaching given or in actual use. A picture of the attitude towards library work in educational institutions, prevalent in those days is illustrated by an incident experienced by me in 1920.

2 Anecdote about the Lack of Faith in the Use of a Library

In July 1920, I was transferred from the Government College, Mangalore to the Government College, Coimbatore. The latter College did not have a library suited to student-centred, library-centred teaching. Therefore, I gave to the Principal a list of essential books to be bought by the library. This was returned to me with the remarks "Extravagant." Then I had the certitude and fearlessness of a youth. I wrote back, "I should not be held responsible for the results in the University examination, if forced to teach without the books requisitioned." I now realise the rashness of thisact of mine and its possible danger in a Governmental institution!

3 At Long Last the College Provides for a Library

One day the Principal sent for me.

Principal.— Why do you want so many books?

S R R.— For the use of the students.

Principal.— Do you really think that your students are going to use them all?

S R R.— Yes, certainly.

Principal.— If so, each of your students will become a "Ramanujam"!

S R R.— Why not?

Principal.—You are thinking of the students of Mangalore. The students here are a poor lot. You can't make much out of them.

S R R.— According to my faith with the aid of the books the students of even this College will go up.

Principal.— You are too optimistic. Anyhow, I shall sanction your list of books this year as a special case.

4 Attributing to the Teacher the Phenomenal Success in the University Examination

The year came to an end. I had been transferred from that College. I went to the Principal to say "Good-bye."

Principal.— The Director of Education was here a few days ago. He congratulated the College on the excellent results in Group I — Mathematics being one of its subjects. 17 out of 19 passed; 10 gaining distinction in your subject. Above all, the First in the University was one of your students! I told the Director, "This should not be taken as the standard for future years. For Ranganathan would be no longer with us!"

5 Phenomenal Success due to the Integration of Library Work and Class Room Work

S R R.— But the library will still be with you and your students can use it fully. This phenomenal success is largely traceable particularly to the integration of students' work in the library and class room work. I am sure that this can and will be continued by my successor.

CHAPTER AD

GENESIS OF THE BOOK

1 A Surprise Invitation from the Teachers' College to Give a Course of Lectures on "School Libraries"

Little did I dream in 1920 about my being transferred, within three years thereafter, to develop the Madras University Library almost from scratch. Five years after becoming University Librarian, the Principal of the Teachers' College asked me to give a course of lectures on "School Libraries" to the teachers under training. This was a God-sent. This new interest, in developing the library of a school as the hub of all educational processes practised in the school, naturally gave me immense satisfaction.

2 One Hour of Discussion on each Friday during the Second Term of each Academic Year

In response to the request of the Principal, I discussed the function of the library in a school, with the graduate teachers under training, one hour each Friday all through the second term of each academic year. The Principal himself attended the course. This gesture on his part made the students take the Course on School Library Work with some seriousness and willingness. This was encouraging. Some of the students appeared to have shared with their senior teachers in their respective schools the value attached by them to the course.

3 The Director of Education Makes Library Hour Compulsory in Schools

Some of the students of the Course given in the Teachers' College began to develop interest in setting apart, for the students doing work in the library, atleast one hour in a week in the time-table of each class. This idea was reinforced by the public relation work on the subject done by the Madras Library Association. The result: By 1933, the Director of Education issued Proceedings making Library Hour compulsory in schools.

4 Request from Headmasters

In 1934, the Senate of the University of Madras accepted a resolution of the Headmaster of a high school asking for the University arranging for a suitable training for the teachers in conducting library work in schools. In view of the University requiring about a year to give effect to the resolution, with the consent of the University of Madras, the Madras Library Association arranged for a course of twenty lectures to be delivered by me during the Christmas vacations of 1933 and 1934. (*See* Sec LA 2).

5 Source for this Book

On the recommendation of the Director of Education, an appreciable number of teachers were admitted to the Course. The Director himself attended a few talks of the course. This gesture on his part added value to the Course.

During 1935 to 1937, the Course was conducted by the University of Madras. The experience gained in conducting these Courses has been embodied in this book.

6 Genesis for the Request of the Headmaster

At the request of the Director of Education, I had prepared in 1933, a draft form for the library diary of a student. The Director had asked each Inspector of Schools to include in his Inspection Report a short account on Student's School Library Work. The student's Library Diary contained the item "The new words the student would like to use." This admitted of simple numerical measure. Most of the Inspectors reported that the Library Work by the students was poor. This report was based on the very small number of the new words mentioned in the Diaries. The headmasters realised the fault of this simple method of judging the quality of school library work. They protested against this to the Director of Education and to myself. Finally, one of the headmasters asked the University of Madras to give a course of lectures in school library work. This was the genesis for the four years of course given to the teachers of schools.

PART B

WHY OF SCHOOL LIBRARY : LINES OF APPROACH

PART B/E

WHY OF SCHOOL LIBRARY

CHAPTER BA

ANSWER BASED ON AUTHORITY

1 Four Lines of Approach

The questions "Why should there be a library in each school?" and "Why should there be provision for a library hour in the time-table of each class?" are fundamental ones. They are also pertinent ones. Therefore, we should first seek to answer these questions. As a preliminary measure, we shall examine these questions from four different angles:

1 Is there any well known and compelling authority in the theory of education, for the provision of library work by each student, as part of his course;

2 Is there any educational tradition developed in course of time, about the necessity for the work of each student in the class room, being correlated with and followed up by the work of the student in the school library;

3 Has school library work by each student been in vogue in other countries — particularly the countries said to be in an advanced state of development? If so, is it necessary and useful for us to imitate them; and

4 Does an intensive consideration of the theory of education point to the need for library work by each student as a useful and necessary adjunct to his class room work.

2 Answer Based on Authority

21 Authority from Revealed Books

One of the forces influencing and regulating human ideas and action is Authority. The Authority may date even from Prehistoric times. It may be found in the sacred (revealed) books of different religions — forming the earliest institutions regulating human attitude and conduct. It would be an interesting subject for research to find out the sanction, if any, in revealed encyclopaedic books such as the Vedas, the Yi-King, the Tripitakas, the Talmud, the Bible, the Koran, or the Granth-Saheb, for library hours in educational institutions. But, it is doubtful, if such an ancient sanction could be given sufficient weight in the context of today.

22 Authority from Powerful Personality

Authority of many kinds are traceable to the direction of powerful historic personalities of the past or even of today. The Authority emanating from a person is likely to go out of context even more quickly than Authority from Pre-historic sources.

23 Authority from Corporate Body

In modern times, characterised by democracy, Authority often emanates not so much from an individual as from a corporate body made of several individuals. Generally speaking, a corporate body *qua* corporate body has a much larger expectation of life than an individual. Therefore, in course of time, the members of a corporate body will be replaced by others. A time will soon come when the corporate body lays down directions different from the old ones. In fact, the changes in the directions given may be too frequent to be followed up in practice. The supreme corporate body is, no doubt, the Government of the State. It may give its direction about School Library Work, through its Director of Education. This also is liable to frequent change. The direction of a Government may not be understood and implemented alike by all. Here is an example. About 50 years ago, the Government of Madras wished to lower the curricular load for examination. Therefore, it introduced the so called "B Group subjects" to be studied by students, not for examination purposes but for general information. But, with in two decades, the system died unnoticed and unhonoured, as a result of neither the schools nor the teachers approving or understanding the educational philosophy behind the scheme.

CHAPTER BB

ANSWER BASED ON TRADITION

1 Tradition of the Last Two Centuries

The present Tradition of our schools originated with Wood's Despatch on Education to the Directors of the East India Company early in the nineteenth century. During that time we had no printed books for use in schools. We did not have even text books. Indeed, the production of school text books was just then being initiated by the Vernacular Book Society established by the British Government. Thus, the Tradition of school library could not have started at that time. Perhaps, a century later some English books — not only of the text book kind but also of the near-text book kind — came to be produced in India or were imported from UK in small quantities. Some schools bought copies of some of them and locked them up in cup-boards, and kept them in small rooms. They were seldom brought into use by students. This Tradition continued till very recently in most schools. Perhaps it is being continued even today in some schools.

2 Tradition Two Centuries Earlier

Before the nineteenth century, no Tradition about school library or its use by students could have been started — or atleast appreciably practised — in any country of the world. For, books other than text books were not printed for students' use. It was only due to the pioneering enterprise of John Newbery, a few general books for students were published in the English language, during the second half of the eighteenth century (*See* Sec PF2). Their number did not increase nor were their subjects sufficiently varied till late in the nineteenth century, to form functional libraries in schools fit to be correlated with class room work.

3 Failure of Tradition

Thus generally speaking there has been hardly any Tradition to give sanction to the establishment of school libraries and to correlate the students work in school libraries with their work in the class room.

CHAPTER BC

ANSWER BASED ON IMITATION

1 Individual Imitation and Social Imitation

According to some, "Imitation" is the strongest force influencing human affairs and conduct. According to Gabriel Tarde, the force of Imitation plays an overwhelming part in shaping, not only the affairs of an individual, but also of the community as a whole (70). In other words, Social Imitation is as effective as Individual Imitation.

2 Social Imitation

Will the force of Imitation be of any help in the introduction of library work by students in schools? "Yes, to some extent. Social imitation has begun only during the last three decades." In educational matters, we have been largely imitating UK and USA. It is common in our educational circles to say, "We transplant into our country, educational ideas and practices developed in those countries a generation earlier, but only just about the time of those countries giving them up as not worth-pursuing." But, in the case of school library hour, those countries have begun to devote their full attention only after World War II. They are still developing the idea with full faith in its usefulness.

3 Great Attention Paid to School Library in UK and USA

During the last two decades, great attention is being paid to the problems of schools libraries in UK and USA — particularly to the best way of correlating students library work with their work in the class room. This can be easily inferred, from the increasing space devoted to school library problems in their educational periodicals. Another evidence is the large number of books on school library work, being produced in those countries. Further, UK has its School Libraries Association and USA has its School Libraries Division of the American Library Association.

4 Contra-Arguments

Some cynics say, "There are many dangers in yielding to the force of Imitation. Imitation is blind. It is of no use for one community to imitate another, without satisfying oneself about the conditions in the two communities being similar." Assuming *ex-cathedra* about the conditions in India being dissimilar from those of UK and USA, the cynics assert about the wisdom of India in imitating UK and USA in school library matters.

5 Support of the Phlegmatic Old to the Cynical Young

The phlegmatic old people would support the cynic by argument such as, "The temperament of the Indian boys is so different from the temperament of the Western boys. The Western boys are for activity, adventure, and enterprise in everything. Hence the freedom of the library hour is quite appropriate to the Western Schools. But the Indian boys are temperamentally for a passive quietitude. They are more eager to be led and to be told rather than to lead and to explore." These opinions are reinforced by them by an abuse of the "Tropical Sun." According to them, this temperamental difference is brought about by the severe Tropical Sun!

6 The Danger of Incomplete and Little Knowledge

The arguments mentioned in Sec BC5 is traceable to incomplete and little knowledge. They forget that the best world-output of ideas and action of about 1,500 years ago, were put forth by the great Indian thinkers living in the severely Tropical Banaras and its neighbourhood. They also forget the sociological law of the rise and fall of nations. They do not understand that the Indian community having been, during the last few centuries, in a state of cultural exhaustion and intellectual in-action. (*See* Chap DC1). They also forget the Indian community having begun to move up the ascending phase of the current cultural cycle. Evidently, they have not had any opportunity to observe our latest generation — creatures of Independent India — becoming rich in originality, able in leadership, and bubbling with activity. Let us forget these pseudo-arguments. UK and USA are worth imitating. But, we are also now fit to decide the issue by *a priori* methods.

CHAPTER BD

ANSWER BASED ON 'A PRIORI' METHOD

1 Unreliability of "Authority," "Tradition," and "Imitation"

The three methods, used respectively in Chapter BA, BB and BC, to determine the issue of the need and usefulness or otherwise of each school in our country having a school library working in close collaboration with classroom work, implies leaving the decision in the hands of some others:

1 The Method of Authority would leave the decision in the hands of some unknown and unknowable being or an individual or a bureaucracy, taking it away altogether from the hands of the educational and library professions of today;

2 The Method of Tradition would surrender the act of judgement to the generations long dead and totally unfamiliar with the context of today; and

3 The Method of Imitation would transfer the responsibility of judgement to some foreign community, without a reliable knowledge of our country's educational and library context. But in case of the practice of the foreign community being a current one, there will be a good chance of its being of use to us in our own thinking.

2 Thinking it out for Ourselves

By now, our country is shaking off its cultural rest and intellectual in-action. Last year we completed the Silver Jubilee Year of our Independence. Many young minds are ready and fit to face our problems and solve them ourselves. The problem of school library and its relation with classroom work is one such problem. Our teaching and library professions have already put forth young persons devoting their thought to these problems. We can therefore fight out own battle in our own way. In this process, we need not ignore anything of value found in the contributions of Authority, Tradition, and Imitation. We can arrive at an eclectic decision.

PART C

WHY OF SCHOOL LIBRARY: FROM THE ANGLE OF CURRICULUM

CHAPTER CA

TELEOLOGY OF EDUCATION

1 Three Lines of Pursuit

We can pursue the mentined in chapter BD problem from the angle of the following three factors:

1 The Curriculum;
2 The Educand; and
3 The Process of education.

2 Purpose of Education

In the direct study of the problem of school library, we should first clarify our ideas about "Education" itself. We shall do this with the aid of Teleology — the conscious purpose, according to Bosanquet (77). The purpose of education has been an ever-widening one. Each age has criticized as narrow the purpose generally believed in during that age. The forward among them have suggested their own Utopian purpose. Later ages have found these to be narrow practicable and formulated their own Utopian purpose.

3 Examples of Changing Purposes of Education

The following are some examples of the purposes of education emphasised in different ages:

1 Plato (427–347 BC) : Fitting the individual to community life.

2 Sir Thomas Moore (1478–1535): Giving a grind in classics.

3 Lord Bacon (1561–1626) : Advancement of science.

4 John Dewey (1859–1952): Transmission of the acquired powers to the new generation in order to secure the continued existence and growth of the community (20).

5 George S Counts (1889) : Induction of the maturing individual into the life of the group, including the dead as well as the living (67).

6 S R Ranganathan (1892–1972) : Releasing and exercising the creative ability of each member of the community in his own field and in his own measure.

CHAPTER CB

EDUCATION FOR A CHANGING WORLD

1 Curricular Load

The curriculum has to take into account, the variety of facts, information, and ideas, to be transmitted without forgetting the brain-capacity of the students to stand the strain of its transmission. The progressive expansion of the curriculum went on for long without much thought being devoted to the brain-capacity of the students, until reaching the breaking point. Still, the additions to the facts, information, and ideas to be transmitted, went on growing at an ever increasing rate; nor could they be ignored. This phenomenon calls for consideration while on the way of examining the "why of school libraries and library hours in schools." This consideration may be centred round three factors:

1 Rate of change in the volume of facts, information, and ideas;

2 Limit to the holding capacity of the brain; and

3 Over-loaded curriculum, a chronic feature.

2 Rate of Change in the Universe of Ideas

The culture of no non-regenerating human group is static. It has to be ever progressing; for, the needs and conditions of life are ever changing. The rate of change is now becoming appallingly high. This is due to the rapid succession of great inventions; their effects speedily reach the level of our daily life. To meet their inevitable incidence, we should keep ourselves constantly informed, educated, and re-educated at the peril of our otherwise going to the wall. We are utterly oblivious of the enormous weight of nearly half a ton of air carried by us on our head every moment of our existence. So also, many of us do not realise the impact of the enormous downpour of inventions being experienced by us. Here is a rough list of the major inventions of a single generation — inventions that have already come to affect our daily life:

1892 Automatic telephone patented.
1894 Typhoid anti-toxin and diphtheric anti-toxin introduced.
1895 X-Rays discovered.
Principles of the motorcar patented.
1896 Steam turbine patented.
First cinema show.
1897 Electrons identified.
1898 Radium discovered.
1899 Long distance telephone invented.
'Sugar' prune developed.
1900 Gasoline motor invented.
Submarine invented.
1901 Wireless signals flashed across the Atlantic.
1902 Active emanations of radium discovered.
1903 Ford car patented.
First flight of 120 feet in 12 seconds.
1904 Fessenden's plan of radio-wave production patented.
1905 Theory of Relativity announced.
1906 Crystal detector patented.
1907 Vitamin hypothesis postulated.
1908 Two and a half miles of continuous flying.
1909 Installation of wireless in steamship.
1910 Ionic medication invented.
1911 Hydro-air plane invented.
1912 Talking pictures invented.
1913 Tungsten filament patented.
1914 Military tank invented.
1915 Continental telephone installed.
1916 Browning machine gun invented.
1917 Submarine detector invented.
1918 First Air-mail service begun.

3 Static Curriculum Ruled out

This staggering succession of inventions has profoundly affected our concept of the purpose of education and consequently the curriculum of schools. The curriculum is no longer exhausted by the three R's. It is no longer learning to till the same hands with the same ploughs at the same season as our fathers and grandfathers did. It cannot be gone through merely by committing to memory once for all the peptonised wisdom of the past ages.

CHAPTER CC

EDUCATION FOR ACCELERATED CHANGE IN UNIVERSE OF IDEAS

1 Change Has to Give Place to Acceleration

It is not merely the absolute change that counts. It is the rate of change. We want to get a grasp of not only the rate of change but also rate of change of the rate of change or the acceleration, as used in mathematics. Let us take one or two fundamental factors of civilisation and examine their rate of change.

2 Illustration of Accelerated Change

21 Accelerated speed of Transport

Let us forget for the time being the *Pushpakavimana,* the air vehicle, used by Rama. Let us also forget Hanuman capable of flying from the Himalayas to Sri Lanka within a day. About 1,000,000 years ago Rama could send a letter from Ayodhya to his ally Vibhishana at Sri Lanka just as quickly as the Viceroy of our grandfathers' days in the nineteenth century after Christ, could send his letters to the Governor of Sri Lanka. The roads were no better in the one case than in the other and conveyances, no faster. But see what has happened since our grandfathers' days. First the steam engine of the nineteenth century quadrupled the speed; then the superheater of the twentieth century quadrupled it again and increased the speed to fifty or sixty miles per hour. More recently the motor has come to compete with the superheater; while in still more recent years, the aeroplane has increased the average speed to three figures, and its speed has become greater than that of sound.

22 Accelerated Communication of News

Trace again the rate at which telegraph, telephone, wireless, television, teletyping and broadcasting have come in rapid succession. Examine again the rate at which the art of writing and the art of reproducing writing have been changing during recent years. About forty years ago, the editor of the *Hindu* could not put into their daily, the information received just on the day of publication. But to-day, even information got as late as 5 pm comes out in print at 6 pm and what is more 30,000 copies come out within half an hour, printed, folded, and packed, quite easily. What these mean can perhaps best be seen by comparing the newspaper of our grandfathers' days with the *Hindu* of to-day.

23 Future Acceleration May be greater

One need not multiply instances of the kind to give an idea of the acceleration at which the world is changing. We have given a fairly long list of such instances in the previous Section. The world threatens to change still more rapidly in future, perhaps, in the geometric ratio.

3 Unanticipative Growth

It is no longer sufficient for the school to confine its aims to supplement the teaching of the three R's by the loading of the students' memory with the maximum possible amount of facts, ideas, and information, however up-to-date. At the present rapid rate of change of the world, facts, ideas, and information, go out of date even within a year. New ones appear in the horizon with a rapidity unthought of in the past. They could not be anticipated even by the most far-sighted teachers.

4 Capacity to Pick up New Facts, Ideas, and Information After Leaving School

Thus the equipment gained by the student while at school proves to be too inadequate in the battle of life. To face the world successfully, the old knowledge of facts ideas, and information, is no longer sufficient. New ones have to be picked up, new methods have to be adopted, and a new outlook is to be developed, after leaving school. This phenomenon exists in every craft and profession.

5 Illustrations

51 Legal Profession

Nobody can thrive in any of the professions, merely with the stock of facts ideas, and information, acquired while at school. Can any advocate mint his money with the mere stock of the ideas learnt at the law college, without reading books from day to day to know the latest case law and the numerous new acts added after his leaving the college.

52 Teaching Profession

Imagine the effect of a teacher teaching his students only the facts ideas, and information, taught by his own teacher, in the very way of his teaching, without learning new ones by his own continuous reading.

The lawyer will not get any brief and the teacher would unfit his students to modern life.

CHAPTER CD

FACTORS LEADING TO OVERLOADED CURRICULUM

1 A Dilemma

On the one side we have an ever-increasing mass of facts, ideas, and information. On the other hand, the capacity of our memory to retain facts, ideas, and information is very limited and the capacity of the brain to supplement rote memory by rational memory is even more limited in most people (*See* Sec CF7). It is impossible even for the cleverest person to know and to remember a thousandth part — nay, even a billionth part — of the facts, ideas, and information accumulated and available. But yet, any of us may have to know and use some of them at any time. This is a perennial dilemma.

2 The Dilemma and the School Curriculum

The dilemma descends heavily on the design of a curriculum of studies in schools. The inherent reaction of self-defence makes the students resist any heavy curriculum beyond the capacity of their brain and memory. But, family ambition — and occasionally even a student's ambition egged on by family — leads to overloading of curriculum. This dilemma at the school level and its one-sided solution against the inherent resistance by students, cause much damage to the self-confidence and the natural capacity of the student. Cases are not unknown of this forced solution of the dilemma having resulted in occasional insanity or even suicide among some students.

3 Sociological Factor and Overloading of Curriculum

A sociological factor urges over-loading of curriculum. In the present formative stage of India, after a few centuries of intellectual in-action, the sociological factor forces intensification of education. This is parallel to a similar happening in UK about a few centuries ago — during the period of Industrial Revolution. But, in those days UK had a great chance for spreading itself out into thinly populated countries in rest phase, and making them its colonies. This made the people of UK take intensification of education in small dozes. But, today there is no spot in the world for the expansion of India. Therefore the inexorable force of the instinct for self-preservation is leading to an aggressive intensification of education in all spheres of life. This naturally tends to increase curricular load.

4 Pedagogical Factor and Overloading of Curriculum

The traditional pedagogical solution of the dilemma has generally been to ignore the angle of students and uphold increasing the curricular load. A good example of this tendency can be got by a comparison of the Matriculation Curriculum of the mid-nineteenth century with the curriculum for the Secondary School Leaving Certificate of today.

5 Anecdote of a Meeting of the Madras Teachers' Guild

The pedagogical preference to increase the load of curriculum is well brought out by the following anecdote. In 1929, a meeting of the Madras Teachers' Guild was held to consider the revision of the school curriculum. In that meeting, each participating teacher played the role of a specialist in his subject. They harangued for adding substantively new ideas to the syllabus in their subject. With all vehemence and sincerity each specialist predicted disaster to the future of the nation by failure in adding to the contents of the syllabus in his subject! At the stage of voting, each specialist voted for the additional load proposed for every subject in self-defence. For, each wanted the others to reciprocate by voting for adding to the contents of the syllabus of his own subject. This was done spontaneously and not by any pre-meditated plan. Mine was a solitary voice. I said, "Brother teachers, our voting reminds me of Hamlet without the Prince. I wish we could also get the vote of the students. For, all these additions to the curricular load would over-strain their brains and over-load their memories beyond their capacity."

6 How to Stop Increase of Curricular Load

Any further loading of the curriculum should be given up. The curriculum should be reconstructed on newer principles. To do so we require a new outlook. It can be got by a sharp analysis of the objectives of education.

CHAPTER CE

A WAY OUT OF OVER-LOADED CURRICULUM

1 Postulate 1: Induction into Current knowledge

Postulate 1 in the new out look is, "Each student should be inducted in the use of current facts, ideas, and information, tailored to his needs and capacity." To make progress possible, students should be given the fundamental ideas and essential facts and information. Further more, each student must have some grasp of the essential factors involved in his specific type of work and other occupations. No doubt, the greater their extent, the better the students are fitted for life. There are many things, the student need not know at present; they need not be carried in their memory even from now.

2 Postulate 2: Education for a Changing Future

The prescription by Postulate 1 is not, however, sufficient. Therefore Postulate 2 introduces a new out look. It is, "Replace 'no change' by 'change' ". What is the effect of this Postulate of Change. The factors guiding us in the technique of education are to be decided in the light of the terms such as 'change,' 'Rapid Change,' 'Increasingly Rapid Change,' and 'Unknown Future.' The method of education must help our students in acquiring a dynamic outlook, habit, and attitude, enabling them to steer their course amidst change. No longer can one generation presume to know the precise new problems likely to be met with by the next one. To meet such a future, one can at best train the students in the general and flexible techniques likely to serve them in facing the unknown problems of the future. We cannot do this by giving pre-digested facts, by cramming them with information, and by drilling them in skills, determined solely by the passing social and material conditions.

3 Postulate 3: Internal Memory and Externalised Memory

The Postulates 1 and 2 lead us to Postulate 3. It is, "Divide facts, ideas, and information into two varieties —

1 those to be carried in memory (in Internal Memory); and

2 those to be found out when necessary from Reference Books ("Externalised Memory").

The quantity of facts, ideas, and information to be found out is an immense one. Without experience and guidance it is not easy to find out all the facts, ideas, and information required. In spite of there being difficulty to find out, if not totally inaccessible, a large part of the ground has been thoroughly surveyed, "mapped" and embodied in Reference Books — "Externalised Memory." (*See* Sec CF6). In addition to developing Internal Memory, education should also train students to become adepts in the use of reference books, as the "Externalised Memory." This training is mostly got by students in their school library work. Then in addition to their being better equipped for normal work, they will be also saving time by locating information from Reference Books.

4 Anecdote 1: Without Training in the Use of Reference Books

One day a university graduate was helping me in writing out the addresses of certain of the lecturers in the colleges affiliated to the University of Madras. The rough notes, furnished to him, contained only the names of the colleges such as, St Christopher's, Government Brennen, Victoria, etc, without the name of their respective places. At the end of the day, I found many of the covers without the station written. I naturally fretted. But he said, "I do not know the information." All the while, a copy of the University Calendar was within his reach. This graduate was not an idler. He was quite industrious. He is really typical of many of the graduates turned out by our educational system without their even being told about the existence of reference books.

5 Anecdote 2: Ignorance of Encyclopaedia Britannica

In this anecdote it was a graduate of the University of Madras, an adult middle-aged man and a City Father. Worried by the ever perplexing, unsolvable problem of the Madras water-supply, he stepped into the library one day and asked for some book on "Water Purification." We did not have any book on the subject and, more than that, we did not have even a set of the Encyclopaedia Britannica. This fact, itself, is a measure of the scant regard of our library even for basic reference books. I directed him to a sister-library under the same roof having a set of the Encyclopaedia. But the location of the Encyclopaedia in that library is another indication of the scant regard of that library for reference books. The volumes were put in the third gallery. I was looking from a distance. My friend was frequently going from his seat to the counter and back with a volume in his hand. A little later, the counter clerk — an "old veteran in the art of scaring away readers — got into a temper, and said something in a loud voice. Then I approached them. Our graduate friend did not know the existence of an index volume to the Encyclopaedia, nor did he know of the alphabetical arrangement of the article. Hence he began to ask first for the first volume and, not finding the article on "Water Purification" in it, asked for the second volume, and so on. I need not repeat the whole story leading to the veteran clerk's noisy words.

6 General Inference

The legitimate general inference from the two anecdotes given in the preceding sections is, "Neither our schools nor our colleges train our students in the use of reference books, not to speak of the general use of libraries." This is a measure of the idea about education prevailing a few decades ago.

7 Postulate 4: Formal Education for Life-long Self-Education

A student knowing only a few things taught while at school, and being not taught how to find out additional information from published materials, is sent out into the world only half-equipped. This leads us to Postulate 4, "School education should involve not merely the three time-honoured R's but should involve also the fourth R — Reference Method." Students should receive equal instruction and practice in the use of the chief sources of facts, ideas and information in the elements of the methods of research-in-little" — that is, finding out ideas by one's own effort. If the term 'Research' is too high-sounding, I would call it 'Tiny Research.' If even that is high sounding, we may call it 'Reference Method.'

To put it in plainer terms, we must develop in the students the capacity to find facts, ideas, and information promptly and accurately as and when required. The outlook on education should no longer confine the aim of education to the cramming of a tiny brain with more than what it can hold of the vast universe of facts, ideas, and information. According to the new outlook, work at the formal school should be mainly for educating the student for life-long self-education, with the aid of materials published from time to time.

8 Postulate 5: The Term 'Book' Transcends the Term 'Text Book'

The new outlook on education has its repercussion on the conception of "Book" in its relation to students. Before the advent of the new outlook the term 'Book' meant only "prescribed Text Book" and even came to mean "manuscripts containing the notes dictated by teachers." 'Teaching' meant "Dictation of select notes," including the "Dictation of punctuation marks"! But the new outlook has released the connotation of the term 'Book' from such narrow limitations. Books for students and books for adults are now required to include also:

1 Informative books, including ready reference books;

2 Recreative books, including books on positive ideas thrown into the traditional recreative literary forms of drama and fiction; and

3 Inspirational books.

The "division of books" into the above three categories has led to Postulate 5, "The term 'book' transcends the term 'Text Book.'

CHAPTER CF

FROM ORAL COMMUNICATION TO SOCIALISATION OF BOOKS

1 Recent Entry of Library into School Education

The delay in the acceptance of the need to give a place to library in the complex of school education is due to the relative recency of books as a means of communication. Books have been socialised, as a means of communication only within less than two centuries. Education has been democratized even later. This period of time is almost negligible in the long stretch of time taken by the evolution of education for communicating ideas from one generation to another.

2 Oral Communication

In the most ancient days, known — in the Vedic period of India — education was through oral communication for, writing had not come into vogue so early as that. In oral education, India is said to have reached a high-water mark. The teachers achieved the unbelievable feat of carrying all the Vedas, all the Smritis, all the Poems, and even the Dictionaries in their memory. Even now, we come across occasionally persons with such a memory capacity. One of my friend's T Sundarachari, an advocate by profession, was a prodigious example of this kind. So it should have been in every other community.

3 Invention of Writing

The credit for the invention of writing goes, according to some, to the Indian Community. After the invention of writing, a movement should have set in to redo the technique of education. Education through reading should have made a small beginning in minimising total dependence of education on oral instruction. The invention of writing would have begun to revolutionise the equipment of the school. Sand trays with the forefinger as the stylus to write with, was perhaps the first stage in the revolution. I myself had used this primitive first equipment of a school during the last three months of 1897 on being put to school. By slow degrees, other surfaces and other forms of stylus came into vogue. The new invention, manuscript books, would have been admitted. Thereafter, atleast some of the time of the students might have been diverted from hearing and memorising to writing and reading.

4 Invention of Paper

The next great epoch was that of the invention of paper by the Muslims of the ninth or the tenth century, and according to some even earlier by the Chinese. This invention led to the production of written books on a progressively large scale, in a convenient and plastic form. This intensified the change in the technique of education. Part of the time of a student was spent in making manuscripts for his own use. Calligraphy slowly reached its high water mark. Increase in the manuscripts, considerably modified the techniques of formal education. In particular, a student was given some time to learn for himself.

5 Invention of Printing

Perhaps the invention of a far-reaching influence on educational methods was that of printing. This increased the speed of multiplication of copies of books, by mechanical means. This invention is said to have become popular from the fifteenth century. And yet, this invention took a few centuries to have its fullest repercussion on the techniques of education.

6 Invention of Ready Reference Books

From the angle of the need for re-thinking about the purpose and the method of education, the invention of ready reference books, about 200 years ago, carries the palm. Their essential quality is their use as "Externalised Memory." (*See* Sec CE3). We are now living in the age of Directories, Encyclopaedias, and Yearbooks. There are many other structural varieties of reference books. We have many of them in each of many subjects. The following table gives an idea of their variety of forms about 30 years ago (63):

Atlas ..		81
Bibliographical periodical and abstracting periodical ..	161	
Bibliography of subjects ..	520	
Bibliography of persons ..	188	
Bibliography of bibliographies ..	27	
Biography (total) ..		896
Bibliographical dictionary and who's who ..		42
Concordance ..		80
Dictionary, general ..	336	
Dictionary, special — that is of terms peculiar to special subjects ..	92	
Dictionary (total) ..		428
Encyclopaedia ..		164
Formulae ..		21
Gazetteer ..		27
Guide ..		52
Leading cases ..		18
List ..		21
Statistics ..		17
Tables ..		153
Yearbooks, directories, and calendars ..		148

The number of such reference books in the world today goes far into four digits. The publishing trade is bringing these reference books up to date from time to time.

7 An Anachronism in School Practice

A school becomes an anachronism if it,

1 Merely brings to the notice of the students the existence of ready reference books;

2 Does not give the students practice — amply living practice — in the use of ready reference books; and

3 Does not induce in its students, the spirit of self-reliance and the desire for self-education.

Recently, however, in several countries, the initiation of the students in the use of ready reference books has been taken up as one of the necessary functions of the school. This new function has transformed the technique of education in unthought-of ways. The transformation has been brought about with eagerness. For, it has given a new solution to the conflict between the acceleration of the coming in of the facts, ideas, and information and the limited capacity of memory (*See* Chap CD)

8 India and Externalised Memory

It is not fair to carry on the work at school, as if ready reference books were not invented. Ready reference books should be recognised as Externalised Memory. India should be second to none in the world in harnessing this new invention of Externalised Memory. For, we are the descendants of those famous, for having harnessed ordinary memory to educational purposes to an unparalleled degree.

9 Socialisation of Books

Another consequence of the sequence of inventions, mentioned in the preceding sections, in provides newer and newer facilities for the transmission of the community's new facts, informations, and experience to everybody. With the production of printed books on all subjects in large numbers and at small cost, books can now be socialised for the free use of every body. They are being socialised in "Public Libraries". The establishment of public libraries too has had considerable effect in hastening the changes in the technique of education initiated by the invention of ready reference books. School education should accustom students to take advantage of the socialisation of books, throughout their life.

CHAPTER CG

FROM CAMEL THEORY TO NEW EDUCATION

1 Consolidated Postulate 6 About the Function of a School

The substance of the five Postulates formulated in Chap CF may be consolidated into the single Postulate: "Educating for a changing world means imparting to the students the basic and current facts, ideas, and information, and habituating them the methods of finding out from books and periodicals other facts, ideas, and information, as and when, getting developed and needed."

2 Camel Theory of Education Ousted out

The Consolidated Postulate 6 will oust out the Camel theory of Education. According to this Theory, Education means imparting to all students of the class, through a one-way talk, all conceivable facts, ideas, and information likely to be required by them at any time in their journey to the end of their life. Many of these will not be within the comprehension of the students. They can only be received and stored in their memory — rote memory. This is similar to the belief about a Camel starting on a long desert journey filling its hump with all the food necessary till the end of the journey. In following this Theory, Education would mean dictation of notes (*See* Sec CE8).

3 New Education: Ushered in

The consolidated Postulate 6 would usher in "New Education." New Education would change the whole outlook on education and its methods. In particular:

1 Students would not be kept passively receptive.

2 No student would be able to be thinking of something else, though apparently listening to the teacher's words.

3 Each student would be made the chief actor in the arena.

4 The curiosity of each student would be kindled instead of being smothered by his being thrown into a passive mood devoid of much interest in the words reaching his ears.

5 The enquiring and exploring attitude would be roused up in each student only in the measure of his interest.

6 Teaching the methods of "Finding out" would be half the task of educating.

7 The only way to teach a method would be providing opportunities for applying it.

8 Situations should be created for each student or each small group of students to "Find out" facts, ideas, and information, by themselves from the library.

9 After the rousing of curiosity in the class room the students should be thrown amidst the books in the library.

10 In the library itself the librarian and the teacher should make the necessary plan for helping the students to enjoy their work in the library and benefit from it.

11 The librarian and the teacher should:

1 Guide the students to find their way about so as to reach "their books" to the satisfaction of Law 2 of Library Science — Every reader his book — and Law 3 — Every book its reader;

2 Train the students in taking relevant notes from the books; and

3 Teach them to weave these notes into a whole so as to form the fact, idea, or the information, sought.

4 Memory Testing: The Wrong Way of Examination

The "New Education" would bring a change in the objective and in the technique of examination now in vogue. Examination need no longer mean solely "squeezing the sponge of the memory of a student." This makes an ambitious student to over-work his memory to the point of making himself unfit for creative work. Cases of students standing first in the public examination but becoming failures and gloomy misanthropes in later life are many. Surely the educational world can not be so bankrupt as to be unable to invent an examination system free from the tragic results mentioned above.

5 Examination with Books

The aim of examination should be to find out the capacity

of a student to conduct himself successfully in situations in life. In an examination with such an aim questions are not confined to testing those memory — either internal memory or the externalised memory stored in books in a readily available form; on the other hand, testing the capacity of the student to think in his own original way.

In the case of those requiring the use of facts or of formulae printed in books, the students are allowed to look them up in books. I have myself conducted this new type of examination. I have also seen this in common use in some of the countries of Europe. The new examination even admits of assessing the relative capacity of students by bringing in six or seven of them at a time and the examiner and the student engaging themselves in a vigorous discussion in pursuing some proposition falling within the scope of the course of studies taken by the students.

CHAPTER CH

NEW EDUCATION AND LIBRARY SCENE IN ELEMENTARY SCHOOL

1 General Feature

The library of an elementary school adopting New Education will be a live work-shop. The students will be running about. A small group of students will be sitting at a round table engaged in discussion without much noise. The teacher and the librarian being here there and everywhere guiding the students. There will be no regimentation of a static variety with sepulchral silence.

2 The Library Room

The library will be a gay little room, with books arranged in a classified sequence in open book racks. The books on a shelf plank may be in moderate disarray suggesting frequent handling by students. There will be low chairs and tables to suit the students. There will be also puranic pictures, historic portraits, maps of the human land as well as the fairy land, and diagrams of topical interest, all along the walls and/or in special stands.

3 A Typical Library Scene

The 11 o'clock bell goes. The distant pattering of the tiny feet of children reaches the ears of the librarian. He throws down the work on hand and rushes to the entrance with a few bunches of flowers. Gopu, Sanku and Yogu get the bunches. For, their library diaries had been declared to be the best for the month. They are taken into the librarian's enclosure to help him in discharging the books returned by their classmates. They are beaming with satisfaction in getting this privilege.

In two minutes, the class is found spreadout all through the library. Some are browsing at their favourite shelves; some are turning through the pages of their favourite magazines; some are doubled over a set of pictures spread over the table by their leader. A child hurries over the noiseless floor and asks the librarian for the best book on "Railways." Another child wants pictures of "Bombers and Fighters." A third child wants his little notes to be looked through by the librarian.

4 Story Corner

There are still a restless few not yet settled down. They are collected by the librarian to the "Story corner," the gangway between the western wall and a parallel book-shelf. The story is finished and the children rush to the shelf to find books on that story. All is quiet thereafter.

5 The Class Leaving the Library

The leader strikes the gong. Chairs are replaced. Each child has a book under its arm. They form in line to leave the library. Gopu, Sanku, and Yogu again get into the counter to help the librarian in charging work. There is the march past. The librarian has some funny personal remark to make about each child as it steps out of the wicket gate. They all leave the library in hilarious laughter. They all love to come back next week.

CHAPTER CJ

NEW EDUCATION AND LIBRARY SCENE IN HIGH SCHOOL

1 General Feature

A suite of rooms. A spacious reading room. Its northern side forms the stack-room. The room in the east is the students' conference room, with a magic lantern and its equipment. The room in the west is the teachers' study room. The tables and the chairs are higher. Some of the books in the racks are just what we may expect to find in the adult's library. These is the same busy hum and a similar division of duties between the librarian and the student-helpers as in the Elementary School Library.

2 A Typical Library Scene

A forward group is engaged in the conference room to organise for a project. Some students are working on special assignments. Some browse among the shelves on personal quests other than cross-word puzzles! The organizing hand of the librarian is in evidence everywhere. A student is rummaging the file of pamphlets and clippings. A student messenger comes from the Fourth Form for the promised lantern slides or cinema reels on "Sugar Cane" for the use of his class.

3 Library Ethics Gets Fostered

A student in the library rushes to the circulation assistant.

Student.—Three pages of this beautiful book are missing. I want to impeach the unknown vandal at the next group conference!

Librarian.—God bless you for your righteous anger! With efforts like yours, our little community will soon be rid of all such vandals.

4 Special Services by the Library

Now comes the Mathematics teacher.

'Can you lay your hands on a few pictures of mathematicians"?. The cabinet of picture index reveals an exhaustive list of the requirement. Immediately the books containing the pictures are sent over to the class room with book marks at approprate pages.

A group of students in charge of the decoration of the library for the "Dasara" come in to discuss their plan with the librarian.

5 Order and Disorder

There is a discipline running through all the bustle of the crowd of students in the library. It is not a forced discipline. It is self-imposed or group-imposed. It is the result of an organised school citizenship. Attendance is optional, but the rooms are always full. Hence, there is need for the scheduling ahead of the conference room. Throughout there is a spirit of helpfulness, sympathy, and give and take. It is truly the heart of the school, stimulating currents go out of it into every corner of the school.

6 Wish

May God hasten the day of minimising, if not elminating, the harmful inner forces in our adults—*Kama* (Desire), *Krodha* (Anger), *Lobha* (Covetousness), *Moha* (Illusion), *Mada* (Excitement) and *Matsarya* (Envy).

Then they will be in a position to take a selfless and farsighted and social view of things. Thereafter, they will bestow on our new generation the right educational and library opportunities and facilities, worthy of Independent India.

PART D

WHY OF SCHOOL LIBRARY: FROM THE ANGLE OF EDUCATION

CHAPTER DA

HUMANISM AND UNIVERSAL EDUCATION

1 Beginnings of Universal Education

According to Walter Lippman, Humanism concerns itself with the progress of the individual from helpless infancy to self-governing maturity. Humanism is a system, mode or attitude of thought or action centering upon distinctively human interests or values. A thorough-going shift in human values occured in the latter part of the eighteenth century. The shift was initiated in France. This shift was from the old mode of adjusting all social institutions and changes to the advantage of a small small class of the community, to that of equality to all. One consequence of this shift was making education Universal — Education for all and not merely for the chosen few.

2 Regimentation *vs* Equality

During its first manifestation in France, inexperience led to a superficial interpretation of the term 'Equality'. In the educational sphere, the term 'Equality' was taken in its absolute and formal sense and not in its intrinsic and relative sense. This was like interpreting the term 'Equality' in respect of an individual's garment as absolute equality in all its dimensions, and not as a garment with its dimensions closely fitting his body. This is typified by the Report made to Matthew Arnold by the Chief of Education in France in the following words: "All the students in all the schools would be studying at this moment, such and such a lesson in the official text book in geography". Here, regimentation was taken to be "Equality" — blinded by equality in suitability to individual.

3 Sociological Pressure

This wrong interpretation of the term 'Equality' went on for some years. After some time, sociological pressure brought its inappropriateness prominently to the surface. The following table shows the relative time-lag and intensity in the sociological pressure, in USA, UK and in the old undivided Madras Province:

31 TABLE OF PERCENTAGE OF NUMBER OF STUDENTS IN SCHOOLS TO NUMBER OF PERSONS OF SCHOOL GOING AGE

Year	USA	UK	Old Undivided Madras Province
1851	35.8	19.3	0.1
1861	36.7	21.9	0.7
1871	57.0	29.5	1.9
1881	65.5	61.4	5.5
1891	68.6	72.2	6.7
1901	71.9	75.2	7.3
1911	73.5	79.3	12.2
1921	77.8	78.5	16.8
1931	81.3	88.4	25.2

32 FACTORS FOR CONSIDERATION

Several points in the table, call for notice:

1 Sudden jumps;

2 Probable distribution; and

3 Need for change of technique.

4 Inevitability of Mass Teaching

In USA and UK the percentage shot up suddenly in the 1860's and the 1870's respectively. The educational organisation was not prepared for such a steep rise in the number of students. The predisposing cause for this steep rise was the urge to implement the demand for Universal Education made by humanism. But the immediate cause had been the incidence of the principle of equality in the political plane and the consequent widenting of the franchise. At present, India prints in the ballot paper, a distinctive picture to represent each of the political parties competing in the election. Each voter is provided with a rubber stmp with a cross (X) mark. He is asked to put the mark on the picture represented by the party preferred by him. Thus, it is not necessary for a voter to be literate. But, this mechanical device did not suggest itself to UK at the time of the Universal Franchise Act. It was therefore necessary for a voter to read the names of the candidates. To meet this exigency, elementary education was made universal all of a sudden. The unpreparedness of the schools to meet the new crowd of students, led to the watering down of education to that of teaching the three R's. This restricted view of education made it possible to have a large class and teach the students *en masse*. Education degenerated to enabling a student to sign his own name and to read the names of others. Thus, the individual student was "lost" not ony amidst those sitting in his own class room, but also amidst the entirely of his contemporaries in the whole nation. Mass teaching with a vengeance indeed! Also a mockery of the demand of humanism in education.

ARREST OF PROGRESS IN EDUCATIONAL TECHNIQUES IN THE EARLY AWAKENED COUNTRIES OF THE WEST

1 Sociological Phenomenon and the Development of Teaching Technique

Let us consider the distribution of self-educability among the students of the community. Let us in fact consider the frequency-distribution of self-educability. An assumption we make at this stage. The probability for a student to get enrolled in a school, when education is not compulsory will be proportional to his self-educability. This would lead us to an inference of great significance in the development of teaching technique. The above assumption taken with the table in Sec DA31 leads us to the inference that till about the middle of the last century, it was mostly the uppermost quartiles in the intellectual scale that entered schools in USA and UK. This sociological phenomenon had two inertial effects on the development of teaching technique:

1 That due to homogeneous classes; and
2 That due to an illusion.

2 Effect of Homogeneous Class

A class drawn from a narrow strip of the frequency distribution is bound to be homogeneous. The homogeneity is likely to be particularly high in a class made of the uppermost quartiles in the intellectual scale. This hides the defects in the mass method of teaching. The success was due to homogeneity of a class of students of high self-educability inspite of mass method of one-way teaching. On account of this the mass method was believed to be efficient, and it was continued. This false evaluation in the early nineteenth century led the lay authorities, caught up in the difficult situation caused by the sudden onslaught of a crowd into the schools, not only to clutch at it but also to extend it by executive orders amounting to the point of over-centralisation and mechanisation of teaching.

3 Effect of Illusion

What is worse is the illusion created by the uppermost quartiles alone being in a class. Any technique and even no technique will do in their case. They are all highly self-educable. Even the slightest external aid is sufficient to stimulate them. "Genius will sprout even from a dung heap," according to a well known saying.

To vary the figure, among the topmost in the intellectual scale, the nucleal element containing his personality in a potential form awaiting a suitable stimulus to receive education along lines suitable to him—is, extensive and almost reaches the surface. In viewing teaching technique as bombardment of the nucleal element, so as to release it to progressive manifestation, even a random shot has a great chance of proving effective in the case of the gifted. It is not necessary, in the case of a class of the uppermost quartiles, to explore for the nucleal element of each student individually, to find its location fairly closely, and then direct the bombardment of the teaching technique on it, repeatedly readjusting it from moment to moment in the light of the experience gained by the previous efforts. On the contrary, even a general mode of bombardment not adjusted to any student in particular — really amounting to random bombardment — is likely to hit on and excite the nucleal element only of the uppermost quartiles. In other words, mass methods appeared to prove effective in the early nineteenth century. In fact a faulty mass method or even no method would have been effective. But the halo of success, really belonging to the intrinsic superior self-educability of the student was usurped by the mass method of teaching. This illusion was responsible for a feeling of complacency and the repression of a progressive outlook on the technique of teaching.

4 Average Student

However, the feeling of complacency could not last long. Towards the close of the nineteenth century, the inundation of the schools first by the two middle quartiles and eventually even by a good number of the lowermost quartiles shook the complacency.

Many students could not find much in the class room to engage them. The talk of the teacher — the main stay of the inherited mass method — had to be turned on the average student. But such a student was often non-existent. So the teacher's talk had to be turned on the imaginary average student. The actual students were either above the average or below it. The super-average felt bored as the talk was below them. The sub-average felt uninterested as the talk went over their head. The former became restless and engaged themselves in other occupations before the very eyes of the teacher. The milder among the latter went to sleep while the others became rebellious. Discipline was undermined, temper exploded frequently, and a look of concern came on everybody.

5 Failures

The end experience was more disheartening than the daily experience. At the end of the year, an increasing percentage of students had to be declared failures — not a very edifying state of affairs. This led to a statistical audit. It disclosed an appalling waste of educational effort. This gave a shock. This shock played some part in betraying the illusion originated in the nineteenth century.

6 Performance After Leaving School

The careers of ex-students were watched. Some of those branded "never-do-wells" by the schools did very well indeed in life; they looked brighter; they proved to be quite competent; some of them became even creative. All this happened because the nucleal element in their personality had been stimulated for progressive unfoldment by the bombardments turned on them by the experience gained on them after leaving school. But it had been left unstimulated while at school, because the nucleal element had very little extent and it was lying buried deep — very deep — and the impersonal random bombardment of the mass method of teaching had altogether missed it. This was the ultimate factor for consideration and it challenged the existing technique of teaching and called for a new technique.

CHAPTER DC

ARREST OF PROGRESS IN EDUCATIONAL TECHNIQUES IN INDIA TODAY

1 Late Awakening of India

Due to historical reasons, India had been in a state cultural exhaustion (Chap BC6) till recently. During this period it has been a dependent country. Its affairs were regulated by the ruling country. The latter was not interested in the improvement of its people. Therefore, there was no attempt to educate even all the students of the first quartile in the intellectual scale, Indeed, the literacy is even today as low as 30 per cent.

2 After Independence

The Constitution of India (1949) had the Directive Principle that Education should be made Universal. The state shall endeavour to provide, within a period of ten years from the commencement of the constitution, for free and compulsory education for all children until they complete the age of fourteen years. But India was still suffering under the illusion of the early nineteenth century of the West. It continues to believe in the adequacy of mass teaching to fit a student for life. Schools were multiplied in large numbers. Provision was not made to train teachers in necessary numbers. There was no attempt to realise the educational wastage involved in this sudden expansion. There is frustration all round. Education has degenerated into some "verbal notes dictation."

3 Illusion

Failing to recognise the facts mentioned in the preceding section, the term 'Universal Education' began to degenerate into a slogan, without any useful achievement. Thought stopped with satisfaction over the increasing numbers of schools and even more increasing number of students. At least now, after 25 years of political freedom, India should reexamine this question of 'Universal Education.'

4 Insufficiency of Attention

At present, every Education Minister merely quotes the number of schools and students. No thought is devoted by the Government to audit the amount of money being spent on 'Universal Education,' No thought is paid by the Government on the educational wastage involved thereby. The result is only some political advantage for the party in power, gained by displaying such misleading figures to the public.

5 Before the Golden Jubilee Year

Such has been the wasteful self-delusion by the time we have reached the Silver Jubilee Year of our political Independence. It is high time therefore for India to work out a realistic plan in detail to achieve profitable and true universal education before we reach the Golden Jubilee Year. This may be far away from the 10 years mentioned in our Constitution. But that provision in the Constitution was due to the lack of experience in organising education on a large scale in one of the largest countries of the world. It cannot hereafter afford to drift along with slogans. All concerned — from Ministers to the lower most teachers — should seriously consider this situation. They should take off their "coat," as it were, and work hard to make our universal education not merely nominal but also totally real.

CHAPTER DD

LINES OF SOLUTION

1 Statistical Study of the Problems

In the attempt to reform the technique of education, the first step taken was to study the standard deviation of distribution of self-educability in students. Self-educability was found to vary from very near zero to very near one. This led to a re-examination of the connotation of the term 'equality,' a concept thrown up to the forefront by the forces of the late eighteenth century.

2 View of Humanism

Does giving a seat to each student in the school exhaust the requirements of equality? Is it all the implication of democracy? Is it the ultimate end that the shift in human values demanded? Humanism said "No". Further it added:

1 Turn your thought upon distinctively human interests and values;

2 The epithet 'human' is not used merely in the collective sense, it lays an equal emphasis on the disjunctive sense as well.

The shift in human values chimed in:

1 Unsatisfactory institutional arrangements in education not only could be changed but should be changed; and

2 The waste in the educational system was there, not because of God's will or intention, but because man's lack of vision and his accepting it with indifference.

3 True Demand of Democracy

Democracy turned round and said:

1 Democracy means equal opportunity in education and not equality in a superficial or formal sense.

2 Equal opportunity demands not only admission into the school but also equal opportunity within the school to benefit by the school.

CHAPTER DE

PROBLEM OF LOWER QUARTILES IN THE INTELLECTUAL SCALE

1 Equal Opportunity for the Lower Quartiles

The student in the lower quartiles do not get equal opportunity in the mass teaching. They need to be watched individually; they need to be contacted personally; they need to be treated with sympathy; they need their individual differences to be understood and they need to be guided accordingly. Let us illustrate.

2 Illustration 1

In 1917, the first year of my teaching, in the very first class met by me, there was a sad looking boy. His father was a poor fisherman. The boy showed every sign of anxiety to learn. But he could not. Some of his classmates were brilliant; and they in later life became high court judges, surgeon generals, and chief engineers. Perhaps such a company induced in him an inferiority complex. My mentioning his case to a colleague of the same community made him laugh hilariously. He remarked, "He is a dunce, why do you worry yourself about him?" I asked "Have we given him a fair chance?". "Chance for him!" he ejaculated, "The best chance we can give him is to send him out of the school and ask him to assist his father in fishing." I got excited by this naive remark from a senior colleague and observed "Then we won't be doing our duty. We need not be here at all." He was disgusted by this remark and snubbed me with the words "New broom!"

The student was a problem to me. I tried various methods to make him cheerful and communicative. But he knew about his being put down as a dunce by most of his teachers. This weighed him down. Once I had to demonstrate to the class the need for taking several readings in measuring anything and taking their average. I gave a yard-stick to each of the nine students of the class and asked them to measure three different objects such as:

1 length of the demonstration table in the class room;

2 length of a bench; and
3 the height of a door.

The readings of the different students were entered on the black-board. The students were surprised to see the different readings got by the different students. At first, each student swore by his own reading. Finally it was elicited from them that the average of their nine readings was a more reliable measure. This was agreed to, after some discussion. Then the class proceeded to strike the average for each of the three objects. But now the so-called dunce stood up. His eyes were gleaming. He had something to say. I was glad of the opportunity. The height of the door was about eight feet. The best of the students, later judge in the High Court, was unusually short in the class. He had measured the height of the door as seven feet and one inch. The dunce said, "Sir, that reading is obviously absurd. It should be left out of account while striking the average." The top-students of the class, sneering at his impudence in standing up, were humiliated, and particularly the author of the wrong measurement jeered at him for his impudence remark about the reading of the best student in the class. I then asked the student first to find the average of all the nine readings of the height of the door, and then of the eight readings omitting the one challenged by the so-called "Dunce." The great differences between the two averages made the so-called superior students "Wise." A brightness developed in the face of the "Dunce." From that day, he gradually gained confidence. The other students, also began to show respect to him. Ultimately he became the headmaster of a school!

3 Illustration 2

The headmaster of a school was deeply interested in the progress of individual students. He had a band of loyal colleagues. There was one student least responsive to all the methods tried in various classes. The teachers were all asked to pay special attention to him and to make a report the moment his response became visible in any class.

It was a drawing class. The teacher drew a square and asked the class the place for keeping a single flower. Most of the students pointed to the centre. Then two flowers were given. Then many hesitated. The boy branded unresponsive went from his seat to the board and marked the two ends of a diagonal. But he would not speak. The matter was reported to the headmaster. That gave a clue to him. He was waiting for a reporting of that kind. The student was given further opportunities in design and drawing. On finding that his silent response was respected and approved in most cases, he felt encouraged. He began to make progress not only in the drawing class but also in the geometry class. In due course he developed more cheer and courage and became more sociable and communicative. Books came to have a new meaning to him, and he improved by leaps and bounds by reading them. Ultimately he became an eminent architect

CHAPTER DF

UNCONSCIOUS, HIT

1 Personality of the Teacher

Some times, all conscious attempts fail. Hence we have to act on the principle of "the more, the merrier." By contacting the student intimately in varied situations, we may increase the chance to hit their nucleal element. So little is ever achieved by verbal transmission. A true teacher fulfils himself more effectively through that intangible influence emanating from his personality and transforms the students and throws them into the most favourable mood for the creative unfoldment of their own personalities.

2 Illustration

Here is the testimony of Dr A Allen Brockington, a headmaster, having had the privilege of teaching the renowned physicist Sir Arthur Eddington. Brockington gives a vivid picture of the unexpected ways a teacher influencing a student (13):

"One day I was wandering back to the place of the 'heavies' when I saw a major of artillery whose walk I recognised vaguely. He accosted me with "Hello, Sir" and looking more closely I knew him. He was an old pupil of mine. I walked with him to his battery and we had a scratch meal together. He said he was enjoying every moment and told me that I was taking this war (last Great War) too seriously.

"Isn't it serious?"

"Yes, of course, but I don't believe in taking seriously anything for which you are not responsible. I remember how you used to laugh. One of the things at school I remember best...We both laughed then, but you laughed more than I did."

I have not looked upon myself as a laughing person and he 'remembered that best.'

"What led you to that belief ?"

"What belief ?"

"In not taking seriously anything for which you are not responsible!"

"You did!"

"I am sure I never said so."

"Oh, no! But I learnt it from you all the same."

He learnt it from me!

The net result of my influence on him was something I had not thought of — a belief or conviction that I felt sure I did not hold. How is anyone taught anything? The imparting of information, the instruction in technique, these are temporary matters; the communication of beliefs is diffierent. And here, before me, stood a man whom I had known as a boy, and the belief that governed him was due to me, and it was a belief that I should have denied for myself. The effect of the belief was to enable him to enjoy his job. It was more; he showed himself as one of the most alert, conscientious fearless of men. The very morning of our meeting, he had returned from performing a task which earned him the military cross. And if you please. the fact I have laughed with him at school has led to this belief of his!

3 Deliberate Attempt is Necessary

We cannot afford to depend solely upon chance hits on the nucleal element of the personality of a student. We should, on the other hand, endeavour to help the stimulation of the nucleal element in a deliberate manner. Each student will have to be watched and helped individually. Then, the student can be helped sooner or later. Here is a picture of the nucleal element:

"There is an inmost centre in us all,
Where truth abides in fulness; and around,
Wall upon wall, the gross flesh hems it in,
This perfect, clear perception — which is truth,
A baffling and perverting carnal mesh
Binds it, and makes all error: and to know
Rather consists in opening out a way
Whence the imprisoned splendour may escape,
Than in effecting entry for a light
Supposed to be without" (14).

4 Need for Changing Mass Method of Teaching

The pedagogy of individual differences must replace the prevalent mass method. Otherwise the student will leave his mind behind, and bring his body alone into the school. The result: The teacher's efforts become futile.

CHAPTER DG

JOHN DEWEY AND INDIVIDUAL INSTRUCTION

1 John Dewey

The principle of equality first manifested itself, as the pedagogy of individual differences, in USA. John Dewey played the part of John the Baptist for this manifestation. His *School and society* records its genesis.

2 *School and Society* of John Dewey

The *School and society* of John Dewey is now a public document. It first saw the light of day in 1899. In ten years, the educational profession of the English-speaking world absorbed about 15,000 copies of it. It is an epoch-making book. It sets out, in a charming way, the pedagogical consequences of the modified manifestation of the principle of equality as intrinsic or relative equality. It was not a mere theoretical book, spinning abstract ideas. It was all based on concrete experience and experimentation.

3 University Elementary School

The experience was picked up and the experimentation conducted in the University Elementary School, began in a small house in the Fifty-seventh street, Chicago, with fifteen children in the first week of January, 1896. This school eventually promoted the idea of "New Education."

4 Other Experimental Schools

The New School inspired the establishment of many similar experimental schools: In their turn, they have originated various modes of individual instruction — the supervised study, the project method, and the contract technique. The experience in these schools appears to have begun to radiate from the personality of John Dewey. For it seems to have been sensed by the dealer in a school supply stores and it made him say "You want something at which the children may work; these are all for listening."

5 Pedagogical Consequences

The dealer's remark clinches the pedagogical consequences. Those in the uppermost quartile could be educated by any technique. Making them listen amidst a mass of students would be sufficient to stimulate their nucleal element leading to the progressive release of their self-educability. But with the lower quartiles, the mere act of listening would be inadequate. They must be made to do various other types of work. They must have the liberty to progress at their own speed and along their own individual lines. They need also intimate personal contact by the teacher to discover the most specific means of stimulating the nucleal element in their personality and thereby releasing their self-educability.

6 The Humane Quality of John Dewey

61 John Dewey's Interest in Younger Men

I spent about eight months in USA from June 1950. For sometime, I was living in the Hostel of the Columbia University. During that period, I very much wished to meet John Dewey. But, I could not find his name in the Telephone Directory. I was disappointed. But one evening, Kirk Patrick invited me for a dinner. He had just then retired from the Department of Education of the Columbia University. About 25 years earlier, as one of the Secretaries of the Madras Teachers' Guild, I had met him during his visit to Madras. To my agreeable surprise, on my reaching his flat, he said, "John Dewey wants to meet you. Why do you not go to him? He has already crossed 90 years." I was delighted to hear this. I replied, "I had been longing to visit the Professor, but I did not find his name in the telephone directory." Kirk Patrick said, "Yes, it is true. The daily number of his "Pilgrims" is far too great for his own body to stand. Therefore, he has not inserted his name in the telephone directory. But he is on the telephone. Here is his number. Fix an appointment and call on him." I was overwhelmed with joy to have the opportunity.

62 His Generosity

The next day I was in his room. To my surprise, he had on his table a copy of my *School and college libraries.*

Dewey.— Your country has marched over others in the practice of "New Education."

S R R.— No, Sir. Many teachers there do not even know this name.

Dewey.— But the first half of your book contains vivid pictures of the New Education.

S R R.— They are merely expressions of my wish.

Dewey.— Is that all? Even as a wish, I value your book.

He was old enough to be my father. And I was a foreigner. I took his words of encouragement as a measure of his unusual humane quality.

7 Personality of John Dewey

The very moment of my entering his room, an unusual thrill came over me — a thrill usually experienced on entering into the sanctum sanctorum of Lord Venkatachlapathi in the Tirupathi temple. His face irradiated all love. The gleams from his eyes eyes were charming. I felt transformed. Such was the personality of the greatest educationist of our present century.

8 Child-Like Simplicity of John Dewey

In the course of our conversation, John Dewey said, "Your great Prime Minister Nehru visited us last year or so. My University conferred a Honorary Doctorate on him. I was invited to the dinner given in his honour. I had the proudest moment of my life at that occasion. For, at the table, I was allowed to sit just to the right of this great man. He was an embodiment of sincerity of purpose." While narrating this experience, John Dewey picked up from his drawer a small leather pouch. He took out of it a newspaper cutting. He told me, "Read it, it is one of the treasures I possess. It contains a short report of the experience of a pressman at the Airport at Stockholm." The summary of the report was as follows:

"The Press-man met Mrs Roosevelt in the airport.

It was the Presidential Election year in USA.

Press-man.— Whom did you like to have as the new President?

Mrs Roosevelt.— Mrs Vijayalakshmi Pandit.

Press-man.— Why? She is not an American.

Mrs Roosevelt.— It does not matter. She has lived with us for some years. She has the brain of a man, and the charm of a lady!"

This child-like simplicity, surviving even after the ninetieth year, threw a flood of light on the concept of New Education. He had recognized from the very beginning the open-mindedness, the individuality, the way of thinking, and the curiosity, common in every child. For John Dewey, Education is the process of helping — at any rate of not obstructing the development of the personality of each person in his own way, along his own lines, towards his own fullness.

CHAPTER DH

EMERGENCE OF SCHOOL LIBRARY AND NEW EDUCATION

1 New Education and Library

What is the bearing of the "New Education" on the "Why of School Library"? Let John Dewey himself answer — rather, let Dewey's diagrammatic representation of the New School (21) answer it. The diagram is reproduced below:

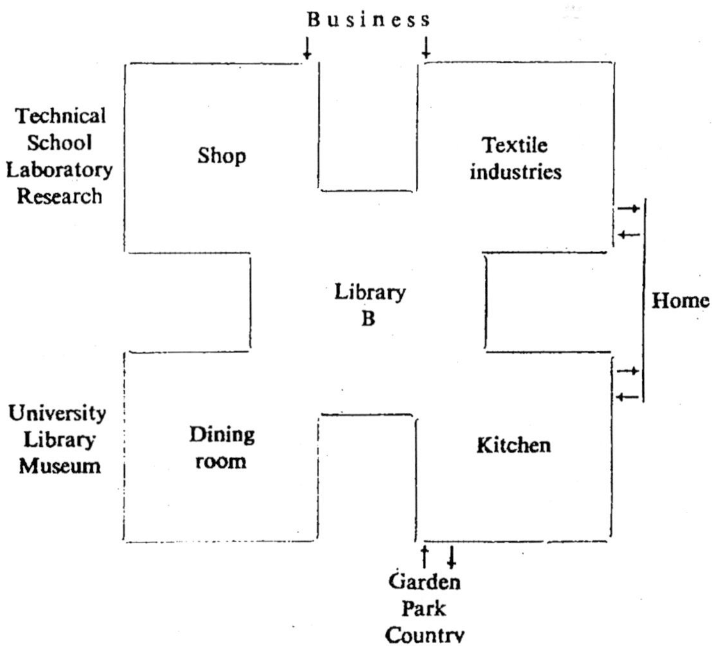

2 Role of Library in New Education

By way of elucidating the charts Dewey adds that the square in the centre marked "Library" is the place for the students to bring their individual and varied experiences, the problems and the questions, and to discuss and pursue them so that new light may be thrown on them — particularly new light from the experience of others, the accumulated wisdom of the world garnered, arranged and displayed in the library. Here is the organic relation of theory and practice. This relation is essential for the

1 Stimulation of the nucleal element in each student;

2 The student not simply doing things, but living the idea;

3 The student getting from the start some intellectual conception entering into his practice and enriching it; while

4 Every idea finds, directly or indirectly, some application in experience and has some effect on life.

This fixes the position of the book or reading in education and of the school library or library hour in the school. The details of the interaction of the school library, the class-room experience, and the extra-mural experience are described in Part K. In this connection the extra-mural factors marked in the back-ground and the fore-ground of Dewey's chart need to be specially noted.

3 Effect of New Education on Library Collection

The pedagogy of individual differences or the insistence of democracy on equal opportunity would point to some obvious inferences regarding the library collection of the school. The differentiation of reading matrials must be parallel to the differences of the students themselves, their "individuating particularities" in the words of William Blake. Variety in matter as well as in standard and style is indicated. No one can predict on what subjects or topics, books will stimulate the nucleal element in the personality of the different students. Hence the filling up of the entire spectrum of knowledge by worthwhile and attractive books is indicated. Again it is hard to define the form of exposition in books capable of stimulating the nucleal element in the personality of the different students. Hence the need for exposition of each topic in as many forms as possible is indicated. The implications of all these are worked out in detail in Part G. Further the collection will also have to vary from school of one area to school in another area with a different geographical and social environment. The avoidance of rigid centralisation of book-selection is indicated.

CHAPTER DJ

LIBRARY HOUR AND NEW EDUCATION

1 No Need for Formal Library Hour in a School Having Individual Method of Instruction

The freedom of the library hour is a great contrast to students from the restraint of the class hour of the traditional variety; and our class hours are still of the traditional variety of the pre-Dewey era and mass method of teaching still rules supreme in them. In schools having individual methods of instruction, there is no question of a formal library hour; nor is there much of a formal class hour. The library is an open house for the students; and he comes in at any moment of need to look up books either for information or for pleasure or for inspiration. This freedom of the library itself often provides the means of stimulating the nucleal element in the student.

2 Illustrations of Stimulation of Nucleal Element

Carr's *Synopsis* voluntarily picked up from a library was the means in the case of the world-famous mathematician S Ramanujan. Lyell's *Principles of geology,* voluntarily picked up from the London Library, stimulated the nucleal element in Harry Guier Seely. First Euclid, then Newton's *Principia,* and then scientific transactions, found in a heap of books captured by a pirate and presented to his local library, stimulated the nucleal element in the personality of Nathaniel Bowditch of the eighteenth century USA. This led him on steadily in the path of self-education and eventually enabled him to become famous in astronomy and write works to make navigation safe. Then there were no radio, no steam power, and the seas had not been properly charted. Bowditch remembered his debt to the library. He wanted everybody else to get a similar chance to get his own nucleal element stimulated and his self-educability released. Ultimately he succeeded in persuading the library of Boston Atheneum to adopt the lending system.

3 Stimulation of Nucleal Element in a School Having Mass Method of Instruction

In schools having mass method of teaching still hanging on, the library hour is perhaps the most suitable hour for individual attention. During that hour, the student is relieved of forced regimental marches and is allowed to feel at ease and take his own pace. During that one hour, his personality may look about for the specific idea, capable of stimulating his nucleal element of self-educability and thus releasing the creative forces in his personality. Perhaps, his nucleal element is tiny and lies deeply embedded. The teacher gets no opportunity in the class hour to probe for it and develop the specific technique needed for it. But he can find opportunities in the library to have the student all by himself and pay the necessary individual attention.

4 Library Hour in India

In India, the sociological force for releasing our educational organisation and teaching technique from the grips of inertia and stagnation is not forthcoming. This explains the indifference with which individual methods of instruction are tried and reported upon. Cynicism develops. It says: "Have we not succeeded with our time-honoured method — now dubbed mass method — in shaping a Ramanujan, a Raman, a Bose, a Vivekananda, and a Sapru?" Shaping indeed! Remember the great illusion. Did they get shaped by that method or in spite of it? Let it be again remembered that a genius will sprout even from a dung heap! This unprogressive and unresponsive attitude may lead to the danger of the library hour being converted into a formal class hour with the same old passive listening to words turned on the imaginary average student.

5 Appeal to the Teachers

Our teachers and our school librarians should agree that the principle of individual attention and individual development reigns supreme at least in the library. This means that the library hour should be an hour of high tension for the teachers. It requires great vigilance, great sympathy, and great activity. It should not be converted into a soft hour or an idle hour for themselves. The look of the library will show the effect given to this agreement.

6 A Travesty of Library Hour

In one year, the Department of History of the Presidency College, Madras, introduced the Library Hour. That Hour was to be spent by the students in the Library Room of the Department. One of the Assistant Professors was put in charge of that Hour. Once, I happened to pass along the side of that room, at the time of the Library Hour.

S R R.— Why were all of your students sitting in absolute silence with their eyes blinkered, as it were, with the palms of their hands? Was there any sad event being mourned by the class?

Asst Prof.— No. No sad event.

S R R.— I found them sitting in the same posture on my way back about half an hour later. How did the students develop so much fortitude to spend the whole hour in in-action and silence?

Asst Prof.— For a few days after the starting of the Library Hour, as per the instructions of the Professor, I brought the bunch of keys for the book cases and gave it to the students. The students began to open practically every book case. They pulled out all kinds of books.

S R R.— That is "the freedom of the library" as against the absolute restraint of the class room

Asst Prof.— Do you call it freedom? You must come and take my place during the Library Hour. Then you will find not "freedom," but "chaos and pandemonium." You should also stay after the Library Hour to replace the books in proper sequence.

S R R.— Is not all this enjoyable rather than boring? Do not the students brighten up and read to their satisfaction during the Library Hour?

Asst Prof.— Library Hour, I know, is your brain-child. You cannot help praising it. But we cannot help hating it.

PART E

WHY OF SCHOOL LIBRARY FROM THE ANGLE OF THE PROCESS OF EDUCATION

CHAPTER EA

INHERENCE AND BECOMING

1 The Process of Becoming

Certain features are intrinsic to the Process of Education irrespective of the curriculum and of the students. These features should be analysed, examined, and modified suitably. Indeed there is a pleasure in contemplating on any process; for it is the kinetic phase of any business; it is the phase presided over by Sakti, the Mother — the Power of transforming, enlivening and releasing creation (*See* Sec HE 5). At the Present, the Past and the Future meet and co-exist. It is not distracted by the look of the familiar of the past; nor is it shrouded in mystery as the unmanifest future. It keeps always on the edge of the manifest. It gives us the pleasure of anticipation. The pleasure of anticipation is greater than the pleasure of realisation. For there is more pleasure in travelling than in arriving. In the present the entire universe lies telescoped — the past, the present and the future. The potency of becoming is the potency of the process of becoming.

2 An Allegory

The potency of the process of becoming has been allegorised by a pretty puranic story of yore. A competition was arranged among the suitors of Ahalya, a legendary damsel of Indian tradition.

Judges.— The person coming out first in circumambulating the universe would have her hand.

All set about rushing through the space. But, Gautama did not show any such haste.

Gautama.— Gentlemen, I am here after completing the circumambulation.

Judges.— So soon? Let us wait till the others come back.

The other competitors returned after ages.

Judges.— Gautama has won.

Other competitors (in surprise).— How can it be? Gautama did not complete the prescribed test. He did not start before we did, nor did he overtake us. Surely, he has played same trickery?

Gautama.— My starting last is true. My not having overtaken the others is equally true.

Judges.— Then how do you justify your claim of having circumambulated the universe earlier than the others?

Gautama.— I completed the circumambulation in another way.

Judges.— What is that way?

Gautama.— I was still far behind the others. At that time, I was attracted by a cow big with calf. The expectant mother was radiant. In a minute the calf began to come out. I took advantage of the *Ubhayatomukhi* stage — double-faced stage. I walked around the cow at this stage and came back to you.

Narada.— Please remember an important passage in the *Mahabharata.* It reads, "When a cow is in the double-faced stage of nativity, it is deemed to be the Universe." There are also similar passages culled from the *Puranas.*

An applause of admiration went round the judges, the onlookers, and the very competitors themselves.

3 The Potency of the Process of Becoming

The whole universe stands telescoped in the process of 'becoming.' That accounts for its potency and charm. 'Becoming' is not a finite process. It is endless. As the poet says:

> "True end is not in the reaching of the limit, but in a completion which is endless" (69).

The process of education is the process of such a 'becoming'. In this process, the student seeks to become himself. He does so under a triangle of forces.

1 The biological force — the force of his living body including the glands, the nervous system, the gene, inherited from ancestors; and all other organs;

2 The environmental force — including the physical, social, and the psychic and including the school with its teachers, appliances and equipments; and

3 The forces of the vasana (the individuating particularities) the soul carries with it from birth to birth in its urge to

move onwards in its own evolution, during its journey through several embodiments.

4 Individuality of a Student

The last of the forces mentioned in Sec EA3 is not amenable to the so-called scientific measurement and manipulation; its very existence will be questioned in some orthodox educational cloisters. It is psychic in nature; it will be branded as something belonging to the occult. We can leave it at once, because it is not amenable to interference by educational agents. The biological force has already been recognised by orthodox science; it is being subjected to experimental study; but so far as the educational agents are concerned, it too cannot be interfered with, and so we may leave that too to a considerable extent. The individuality of a student is the name given to a factor, largely the resultant of the force of phylogeny and the force of vasana or psycheogeny.

5 Force of Environment

The field of educational agency is reduced to only one of the forces of the triangle — the force of environment. The environment is adjustable to some extent. The teacher's part in the process of education consists in its adjustment remembering himself being an element — vital element — within it. We have now to analyse this process in order to find out anything inherent in it. "How the individuality of the student and his environment — including the physical, the social, the institutional and the curricular parts of it — act and react on one another, and result in the growth of the student in his body, mind and soul — in the progressive blossoming of his personality?" This is to be examined and understood.

6 Factors for Consideration

The factors calling for consideration in the approach from the side of the process of education will be indicated by

1 The narration of the details of some typical case studies;

2 The study of the opinions of competent persons, both within the teaching profession and outside it; and

3 An attempt at general enunciation.

CHAPTER EB

EDUCATION AS "BECOMING": SOME CASE STUDIES

1 Truant Boy

My first problem will take us back by about forty years. I had then a classmate of mine — a daring and resourceful fellow. He enjoyed the company of friends and he was always cheerful. On several days, he would leave his home with books in his hand — to all appearance with the attitude of one going to school. But from 10 a m to 1 p m he would spend his time in utter solitude in one of the rooms of the temple tower — a place dreaded by us. He would join us punctually at 1 p m on our way home. This led his parents to take him to be returning from school as every other boy in their street.

2 Sleeping Class

Some years later, a famous professor taught us English prose at college. One of my uncles, a student of that college a generation before me, had given me glowing accounts of the reputation of that professor in teaching prose. But my dismay may now be a surprise to others. Hardly any of the students could resist falling asleep in his class. Still the professor went on, with his prose from day to day.

3 Routine Masters

Quite in keeping with these personal experiences of mine a very scathing remark is heard about some of our topmen who succeeded in the higher competitive examinations, and not only straightaway got into comfortable berths but also soon reached positions of responsibility and commanded great freedom and enormous opportunity for initiative. We have had this now for nearly a few generations. The scathing remark that has been flung at them is this: What is the permanent mark these first-rate men have left behind them? No doubt, they have run and established administrative machinery quite satisfactorily and become ideal routine masters. But have they succeeded in setting up more up-to-date administrative machinery in the place of the old ones inherited by them? Can they assert about the administrative machinery inherited by them having been perfect beyond improvement? Remember, every now and then the newer improved methods of running the office invented in foreign lands have been imported and thrust down their throat. No doubt they had been tame enough to learn to run the new machinery with equal efficiency. But the question is: "Why is it so few of the Indian FCS and ICS men have made their mark in inventive work?"

CHAPTER EC

EDUCATION AS "BECOMING": SOME OPINIONS

1 Frank Townshend

"They (people) begin to wonder whether all is well with our educational system" (74).

2 Ezra Pound

"Education is an onanism of the soul" (45) and "all repressive and uniforming education is an evil" (46).

3 Richard Burden Haldane

"School was indeed never an interesting period to me" (25).

4 Samuel Butler

"I have sometimes thought that, after all, the main use of a classical education consists in the check it gives to originality, and the way in which it prevents an inconvenient number of people from using their own eyes. That we will not be at the trouble of looking at things for ourselves if we can get any one to tell us what we ought to see, goes without saying, and it is the business of schools and universities to assist us in this respect. The theory of evolution teaches that any power not worked at pretty high pressure will deteriorate; originality and freedom from affectation are all very well in their way, but we can easily have too much of them and it is better that none should be either original or free from cant but those who insist on being so, no matter what hindrance obstruct, nor what incentives are offered them to see things through the regulation medium. To insist on seeing things for oneself is to be an. . .idiot; nor do I see any safer check against general vigour and clearness of thought, with consequent terseness of expression than that provided by the curricula of our universities and schools of public instruction. If a young man, in spite of every effort to fit him with blinkers, will insist on getting rid of them, he must do so at his own risk. Our public school and universities play the beneficent part in our social scheme that cattle do in forests: they browse the seedlings down and prevent the growth of all but the luckiest and sturdiest. Of course, if there are too many either cattle or schools, they browse so effectively" (16).

5 William Blake

Blake's detailed indictment is worth quoting in full:

THE SCHOOL BOY (9)

I love to rise in a summer morn
When the birds sing on every tree;
The distant huntsman winds his horn,
And the skylark sings with me.
O! what sweet company.

But to go to school in a summer morn,
O! it drives all joy away;
Under a cruel eye outworn,
The little ones spend the day
In sighing and dismay.

Ah! then at times I drooping sit,
And spend many an anxious hour,
Nor in my book can I take delight,
Nor sit in learning's bower,
Worn thro' with the dreary shower.

How can the bird that is born for joy
Sit in a cage and sing?
How can a child, when fears annoy,
But droop his tender wing,
And forget his youthful spring?

O! father and mother, if buds are nipp'd
And blossoms blown away,
And if the tender plants are stripp'd
Of their joy in the springing day,
By sorrow and care's dismay

How shall the summer arise in joy,
Or the summer fruits appear?
Or how shall we gather what griefs destroy,
Or bless the mellowing year,
When the blasts of winter appear?

6 An Experience in our Household

One afternoon, I happened to return home from the library at about 4 p.m. Our son, Chi Yogeshwar, six years old, was playing in the house.

S R R.— Why has the child come back so soon?

Mother.— He is afraid of going to the school.

S R R.— Yogeshwar, why are you afraid?

Yogeshwar.— Today, the teacher asked, "What are the uses of water?"

S R R.— It is a simple question. What is the trouble?

Yogeshwar.— I said, "for drinking, for cleaning the house, and for cleaning our clothes."

S R R.— You are all right.

Yogeshwar.— The teacher said, "Look into the book. Do you find 'washing clothes' among the uses of water?" I said, "No Sir." The teacher got angry with me saying, "You should not add anything to the statement in the book." I said, "But everyday, I do find water used for washing clothes in my house." Then the teacher added, "if you talk impertinently like this, I shall fleece your skin leaving only the bones." I said, "I am the only child of our parents. Please do not do so." But the teacher said, "You should not be so impertinent and insist upon repeating anything not found in the book."

S R R.— Were you afraid of this?

Yogeshwar.— Yes father. How can you lose me! I had to meet that teacher and make him a little wiser than before.

7 General Enunciation

The factors for consideration in the approach from the side of the process of education are as follows:

1 How to avoid students' hating coming to school?

2 How to make teaching interesting?

3 How to avoid suppression of creativeness in students particularly in the top ones?; and

4 How to avoid development of anti-social tendencies in students?

CHAPTER ED

PASSIVITY *VS* ACTIVITY

1 Opinions

We shall begin by recording some opinions:

1 Albert Einstein (in a convocation address to the University of the State of New York).—"Education is that which remains after one forgets all that one learnt in school" (66).

2 Gordon Melvin.—"The primary factor in the educative process is the child...Education does not exist for the teacher, or for the curriculum: but for the child" (40).

3 Oliver Wendel Holmes (In an extract from a letter dated 27-1-1925 to Dr John C H Wu).—"I am much interested and a little surprised at the subjects of your teaching. I don't doubt you do more than half in setting your class on fire. When you do that you do the best and the rarest thing that a teacher can do. I used to say that Emerson's great gift was that of imparting a ferment" (68).

4 Ryland Boorman.—"Over-organisation of personality is found in the attitude which leads older folks to say, 'This is the way we've always done it,' or 'We don't like these newfangled ways.' Is such cases, the reactions of the individual to the sum total of in-coming stimuli have become so rigid and set, that a decision against readjustment is almost a foregone conclusion... The disciplinary system of education which sought to drill into the child habits of various types were fairly effective in reducing him to this state of arrested development. This condition of personality is in mind when likening the child to clay which is to be modelled. The terms 'child training,' 'home training,' and 'religious training' represent to some extent the educational expression of this point of view" (12).

5 Kahlil Gibrah.—

"Your children are not your children.
They are the sons and daughters of Life's longing for itself.
They come thru' you but not from you,

And tho' they are with you yet they belong not to you,
You may give them your love but not your thoughts,
For they have their own thoughts.
You may house their bodies but not their souls,
For their souls dwell in the house of to-morrow which
You cannot visit, not even in your dreams.
You may strive to be like them, but seek not to make them like you.
For like goes not backward nor tarries with yesterday (24).

6 Frank Townshend.—

To you it is as if a child were an empty vessel, into which to pour perfection, to make a perfect man.
But a child is the product of universal energy; able to evolve of itself; growing up into life.
If therefore you allow children to form into perfect vessels; strong, beautiful, happy, healthy; in harmony with life;
There shall freely grow within them, a part of the spirit of all things; which is, in itself, perfection and truth.
But if you seek to mould and to form children.
You will but succeed in warping the vessel which life has made for itself;
and so restrict life's growth (76).

2 Passivity

Townshend has singled out the first fault disclosed by an analysis of the traditional process of education. The process had tended to be purely transmissive. The verbal transmission of an assortment of the intellectual deposits of the past demanded passivity on the part of the student — physical passivity, certainly, and mental passivity also quite often. Passivity dogged the students even outside the school. It was a concomitant of the presence of a teacher with his students in any setting whatever.

3 My Experience

Here is an illustration from my experience. Once I walked into the Madras museum. I saw a class of young students there. It was a guided excursion. There was a stuffed monkey in a life-like posture in a show case. Suddenly the whole class squatted on the floor and already they were doubled over their notebooks. The dictation of the teacher began: "The monkey has a black coat. It is holding to a branch of a tree with one of its hands" etc. Poor students! They were kept so busy writing with their heads turned down. They could not at all see the monkey! Guided excursion indeed!!

4 Need for Correction

Passivity leads to boredom; truancy and sleep were the two modes of escape. Some gifted teachers might relieve the mental boredom occasionally by a round of questions; some might manage to humour the students by making clowns of themselves — all sympathy to such professorial Charlie Chaplins! But in the last analysis, the conception of education is the same; the process is severely transmissive; the teacher is the most active member of the class. Benumbing passivity reigned supreme among the students. This needs correction.

5 Activity

Development in psychology shows the way. A child's salient characteristic is action and behaviour and not passive reception. The process of education should not work counter to this finding. Activity and not passivity should be its characteristic. It should make him perform freely the various activities of his life — including that of looking up the intellectual deposits of the past found in print. It should lead to helping, modifying, and conditioning the development of all his powers — physical, mental, and social. At the setting in of the momentum of this new phychology, the first step in change was a violent recoil from the subjects to be taught, to the student himself. Children's behaviour was analysed and atomised; Behaviourism said "the child is an aggregate of stimulus-response doublets! This view, no doubt, rescued the process of education from the grip of the sterile faculty-discipline notion. But, in its turn, it led to degenerating the process of education to the building up of specific skills, by the repetition of the necessary stimuli in isolation. The passive process made the teacher the medium of transmission to the exclusion of books and libraries. And this form of active process would at best make reading, one of the many specific skills, quite a skill standing by itself without any necessary relation to anything else. Further the urge of transmission caught hold of the activity process also, as effectively as the passivity process to the exclusion of the creative process.

6 Practical Geography

One can discriminate between a passive and an active learning of geography. The former is a process consisting of listening to lectures and memorising the facts found in a textbook. The latter is a procedure where the assimilation of the same materials is aided by illustrations, map drawing and other constructive work activities on the part of the students. In either case, ideas, judgement, and opinions are handed down — transmitted. The student does not take a creative part. He could not use them to his own enrichment by his own experience.

7 Fate of Graphs

Algebra was becoming unreal. There was a general agreement about the capacity of graphs to put everything right. It would make the students do something to make algebra realistic or its results vital. This would make the students active, so graphs were introduced into the curriculum of algebra. About 50 years ago, in the Madras University, University extension lectures were delivered to demonstrate their purpose in the curriculum. One or two questions on graphs came to be included in every examination paper in algebra. But the graphs became merely an additional load in the curriculum unrelated to algebra and unrelated to the students' life and, if at all, only related to adult life. It was, not built into the experience of the students. The students could afford to ignore it in the examination without the risk of failure. The graph sheets of the answer books became clean enough to be resold in the market!

8 Practical Geometry

So it was with practical geometry. It was made to lead to active education, but not to creative education. The propositions in theoretical geometry were then being taught in isolation from one another without being related with the experience of the student. The practical exercises in geometry also became isolated drills. They were not integrated with theory on the one side and the students experience on the other. It was again pure "transmission."

9 Practical Science

Take practical physics and practical chemistry — the same story. A sequence of isolated experiments and a splendid opportunity for creative education lost! The irony of it was this. In the sequence of the transmissive process chosen, the practical experiments were not even parallel to the sequence in the theoretical lessons. There was no correlation whatever between the two sequences. For example, student A would be given an experiment in Measuring Conductivity in Electricity months before the theory on it would be taught. On the other hand, student B would be asked to measure the density of air, months after "Density" was taught. In both the cases, the student had merely to follow a "work-sheet" in practical class. Practical work became an *ad hoc* extra load in the curriculum.

CHAPTER EE

GLOBAL EXPERIENCE

1 Global *vs* Atomised Experience

The reforms attempted in the earlier years of this century failed because of their being merely adding isolated atomised activities to the passive methods of transmission of unrelated aggregates of fossilised facts, ideas, and information; fossilised so far as the student went. For education to be really productive, its process must not be exclusively transmissive — with or without activity — it must also be creative. For it to be creative, the process must not be atomised but global; It must not be merely forced from outside, but also be generated from inside the student. It must not attempt merely to aggregate stimuli-response doublets, but it must also attempt to integrate them into related wholes and into the personality of the student. The process of education must not be exclusively guided by the Behaviouristic Psychology (*See* Sec ED5) but it must also draw a good deal from Field Psychology.

The process of education must admit of the experience of the student in synthesising all the subjects learnt and all the activities performed into one inter-related whole. The process must articulate every new experience with the integrated sum of the old ones; and it must also remodel the newly integrated sum of experience from moment to moment in order to meet new demands. Such a creative education does not totally eschew transmissive education; but it will use the same as a tool for certain types of experience. Creative education has also a place for memorising and for drill; but they have only subordinate places. Transmissive education based on atomised experience does not build up the "whole" student. Creative education based on global experience sensitises the student to the changing contemporary life and problems; it invokes in the student, the capacity for self-education, self-direction, and creative work. The process of education becomes the process of becoming (*See* Sec EA1). Anti-social tendencies can neither crop up not flourish in the presence of self-education, self-direction, and creative work. The process of becoming will scotch out all anti-social inducements and will radiate love, co-operation, and joy.

2 The Truant Explained

Had the process of education been made creative, based on the global experiences of students, and not being merely transmissive of isolated ideas — making the teachers glorified force-pumps — my classmate of about sixty years ago would not have turned truant (*See* Sec EB1). Situations would have arisen every day for his creative self-expression; he would not have been bored, his experience would have been globally enriched day by day. And his " becoming " would have been a source of joy to the teacher, the taught, and everybody else.

3 The Sleeping Class Explained

Had the professor correlated his teaching of prose to the experience of the student and attempted working it out with the students rather than on the students, the phenomenon of the sleeping class could not have occurred (*See* Sec EB2).

4 Routine Masters Explained

The conversion of our top intellectuals into routine masters and their stagnation in after-life were due to the process of their education not having been creative (*See* Sec EB4). It was the result of an *ex cathedra* attitude in teachers and the *ipse dixit* frame of mind in the students. This combination inhibits all urge to creative work. The futility of a purely transmissive process in education is revealed in great detail in the dialogue of Narada and Sanatkumara in the *Chandogya-Upanishad* (17).

5 A Vision

Here is a vision of the creative process of education through global experience, describing it and the result of it (75).

> Children are surrounded by a world in being;
> The outcome of every age and of every work of man, and of the earth;

By materials and tools, workshops and appliances;
Inventions and models, pictures and maps.
Everything that can be, is learnt by action and experience, from the use and the nature of thing,
Boys and girls together; they are always busy, always happy, alway free.
They build and make gardens, are carpenters and cooks;
They print and read, weave cloth and paint, and do all kinds of work.
Much of their life is passed camping in the open, playing in the sun, swimming and making journeys.
They create and control their own organisations;
They act and talk and sing and dance.
Every instruction and information that they seek is accessible to them;
Every experience of the past;
Every practice of the present;
All that they can imagine of the future.
And when children leave school, they know the needs of the earth;
They are aware of their own capabilities and limitations of their desires and dreams;
So that thereafter they are able to do the work they will,
With all their might.
The means to all knowledge is within their reach;
Truth is awakened in their hearts;
They put forth creative energy in joy and happiness,
In love with all the world."

CHAPTER EF

NEW EDUCATION AND PEDAGOGICAL CONSEQUENCES

1 The Emersonian Ferment

The first step in the process of global experience is the incidence of the Emersonian ferment. It may occur casually; but often the teacher will have to help its incidence. Fear, compulsion, and authority suppress rather than release the urge for global experience. They inhibit rather than stimulate creative impulses; they corrupt rather than purify the modes of discovery and sincerity. They induce the frustration complex rather than self-confidence in student. Passing of examination, as motivation, is futile at its best; at its worst it is trickery. Again another motivation in schools is the sense of personal ambition and desire for recognition. They very often lead to an unhealthy desire to be acknowledged as better than a fellow student. This egotistic attitude ultimately injures the individual and the group.

2 The True Ferment

The harmless, helpful and lasting motivation — the true Emersonian ferment — centres round interest of another kind. Not satisfied with the capacity of this word, Einstein improved it as "Divine Curiosity" (65). The Sanskrit language has a word for it – *Prema* (*See* Sec EF3). *Prema* or Divine Curiosity alone can pool the creative impulses in students and initiate the process of global experience as a means of education. This ferment is at the foundation of the laboratory movement and of the movement for live school libraries and library hours in schools. The ferment demands the school library to work effectively. The ferment is often supplied by the library itself. The cases of Ramanujan, Seely and Bowditch have already been mentioned (*See* Sec DJ2). The ferments of Einstein (27) Franklin (22) and Hardy (26) were also emanations from books. No doubt the class hour, if properly conducted, may be rich in ferments; so also the students have a great chance to come across their ferments in their life outside the school; and the probability of their coming across it, while with books in the library is also appreciable.

3 The working of the Ferment

The source of the ferment may be anything at the beginning. But sooner or later, it will make the students go into the school library in order to make the ferment work. It may be for finding precedents and models; or it may be for finding out facts and figures. It may be for verifying the new findings; or it may be to know the already recorded findings. It may be for inspiration; or it may be for relaxation, not of the kind leaving one botched, but one of elevating, recreating, and renovating kind. For students susceptible to ferments, the need for this superior kind of relaxation will be immense. Their global experience will need the library as often for relaxation as for information and inspiration.

Again the ferments suited to no two students may be alike. There is a specificity in the susceptibility of students to ferments. The centre of Divine Curiosity differs from student to student. The objects of *Prema* (*See* Sec EF2).— Divine Curiosity — are as varied as the faces of the students. As the ferment works, the demands of the students on the school library will be very varied. The true "Becoming" of even a single student will require the aid of a varied collection in the school library. For the true "Becoming" of hundreds of students it goes without saying that the variety in the library collection can know no limit.

4 Individual Way of Growing

Every one grows in his own way. Some by supporting political systems; some by religion; some by science; some by classics; some by social work; some by being vegetarians; some by industry; some by education; some by art; some many an other road. The school library should answer the needs of every one. Hence, the school library should cover the entire spectrum of knowledge. Surely the dictum of "Four copies of ten books chosen by the management" must go. We fail to enrich the student's environment with books of every kind and on every subject. As a result the student gets out of the school often undeveloped; and he becomes a victim of stagnation.

CHAPTER EG

THE LOOK OF SCHOOL LIBRARY

1 The Hum of Work in a School Library

The school library is a field for the global experience of many students: it should have the hum of a beehive with the difference, of its being not characterised by the monotony of work of a repetitive kind. For a student growing day by day — physically, mentally, and spiritually — there will always be fresh work to do in the school library. He will always be in a mood of alertness and awareness, not under external compulsion, but by inner necessity, nor will these factors be of the same colour or nature in the case of all the students. The disciplinary trouble due to idle minds will be foreign to the school library. This does not mean that death-like stillness will prevail. There will be action at high potential. The sleeping top rather than a lump of stone will be the correct analogue.

2 Charm of Diversity

Sometimes, the work of the students will be on diverse lines. Each will be doing his tiny research to satisfy his own curiosity. Some will be following up the problems picked up on the road side; some will be carrying out a contract originated in the class room; and some others will be deriving amusement from funny story books. One will be identifying butterflies; another will be copying out poems; and still another will be tracing out pictures and maps. A few will be exploring the files of clippings; a few will be making scrap books: and a few others will be helping the school librarian. A small group will be crowding round the librarian listening to a story. There will be diversity not only at any one moment. The hourly changes in the look of the school library will also be equally diverse. It will be ever full; but not with the same students. It will be ever in hum, but not of the same pitch. It will be ever charged with the radiance of the "Becoming" process, but the process will be at diverse stages at diverse hours.

3 Grace of Concerted Action

One feature of the diversity of work in a school library will be the moments of team work. Global experience needs also the leaven of team work. The diversity in the individuality of the students is no barrier to team work. In the nature of things the student's capacity in the play ground is as varied as in the class room and the school library. Team spirit can be fostered in the playground in spite of heterogeneity of physical aptitudes. There is no reason why it cannot be fostered in library hours in spite of heterogeneity of mental aptitudes and the interests at the moment. It is true that the traditional class room atmosphere has been responsible for a wrong view. The passivity of the class room does not offer opportunity for the students to share and correct each other's gifts and foibles. Anything in the class room often favours the induction of aristocratic attitude in the more gifted and a sense of inferiority complex in the less gifted. The two groups are repelled from each other. A spirit of exclusiveness creeps in and thrives. This fault, inherent in the class room atmosphere needs correction. Till the advent of the library hour, the sports ground had the monopoly of this job. But now the library hour offers another splendid opportunity. In progressive schools, the very class room method is being changed into project method for this purpose. Correction by project may not be practicable at present in the class room itself. Make at least the library hour an hour for co-operative effort by the student. Let there be openness and not secrecy in the library hour; let there be freedom and not restraint; and let there be mutual dependence and not mutual jealousy. The grace of concerted action in the school library is as enjoyable as the charm of its diversity

4 Socialisation

Global experience, initiated by ferments of a certain kind and working itself, up now and again into group activities in the school library, makes the student learn something profound — man owes his strength to his being living in intimate social relation, supplementing one another's abilities. He need not land himself in the fateful fascist pessimism that,

"Individualism is the negation of the fundamental unity which is at the root of Being; is the negation of that principle of duty which is the foundation of the moral world and the affirmation, in its stead, of the principle of rights — those rights which are the perennial spring of all human ills and evils. The search for a meaning of life leads to the realisation that what must be paramount for man is not the conception of his rights as individual, but the vision of his duties as a social being; that what is of supreme worth is not personal life, but the life of the nation; and that, finally, human life is at bottom not a vehicle of happiness but a bearer of sorrow" (43).

Planning the library hour gives ample opportunity for the development of correct social attitude, reconciling the individual and the society.

The investigation undertaken by student in the school library in response to Divine Curiosity or *Prema* (*See* Sec EF2) can be as varied as life itself. Thereafter, it can give as much opportunity for individual work as for collectivity socialising group work. The alternation of these kinds of opportunities will demonstrate that there is nothing intrinsically incompatible between the specific unfoldment of the personality of each individual and the due fulfilment of the life of the group, the nation and society at large. At the lower level, group work will develop basic conformity and habit formation. On the higher level, it should foster the qualities making individuality and independent personalities to fulfil the very need of the group. The school library can witness not only the 'becoming' of each student severally, but also at the development of the sense of the becoming 'all together.'

5 Rigvedic Passage

Well did the Rigvedic seers sing:

"Meet together, talk together, understand aright.

"Pray in common, achieve in common, let there be unity and understanding.

"Alike be your intentions, harmonious your feelings

"And concerted your thoughts so that there may be complete union among you."

CHAPTER EH

SUM-UP — INEQUALITIES AND EQUALITIES

After our wandering into the highways and byways of educational theory, we have arrived at certain findings. These can be expressed in the form of a few inequalities and equalities:

1 **Education** ≠ Memory training; but

= Training for use of externalised memory; requiring library work at school.

2 **Education** ≠ Mass lecturing; absorbing the same facts, ideas and information; and learning by all at uniform speed; but

= Individual instruction; varying the field of study with the individual; and learning by each at his own speed;
requiring library work at school.

3 **Education** ≠ A passive, partial, transmissive, inhibiting, anti-socialising process; but

= An active, global, experiential, creative, and socialising process;
requiring library work at school.

PART F/J

WHAT OF SCHOOL LIBRARY

PART F

WHAT OF SCHOOL LIBRARY

CONSTITUENTS OF A LIBRARY

CHAPTER FA

EVOLUTION OF THE CONCEPT OF SCHOOL LIBRARY

1 Library: Place for Writing Book

Going far back to the earliest use of the term 'library,' we land upon the obsolete meaning "a place where books are written." Surely, this concept of library does not lend itself to be pressed into schools.

2 Library: Place for Storing Book

Chaucer in his translation of Boethius (1374) has the following passage:

The walles of thy librarie aparayled and wrought with yuory and with glas,...in whiche I putte not whylom bokes, but I putte that that maketh bokes worthy of prys (18).

Here a library is just a place to house books. Therefore a school library is just a room for storing books. The term is used in this unhelpful meaning in the succeeding centuries right up to a century ago. This is evident from the following illustrative passage:

"1779. Camden's Letter's.— there saw his library; that is a room which contained his books.

1854. Collin's Hyde and seek.—Zack descended cautiously in the book parlour which was called a 'library' ".

3 Library: A Collection of Books

The term 'library' is frequently used to denote "a collection of books" — merely a collection as such. Users do not form a necessary part of such a library. The collection in some of the schools, one is obliged to confess, is often of such a nature. Such a collection might have been built up haphazardly or in a casual way by,

1 Accumulating rejected specimen copies of textbooks,

2 The motley of volumes discarded from collections built by adults in affluent circumstances and thrown away either because of the transfer of the owner to a distant place or because

of the lady of the house insisting upon the reclamation of the room occupied by the collection.

4 First Reference to Users

The definition recorded in the *New English dictionary* first made explicit reference to the users forming a factor in libraries. The volume published in 1901 defined a "library" as follows:

"A library is a public institution or establishment charged with the care of a collection of books and the duty of making them accessible to those who require use of them."

This definition appears, however, to make users a permissible but not an obligatory constituent.

5 Qualifications for School Librarian

The qualification of a person put in charge of a school library at the beginning of the present century is worth considering.

In my own school at Shiyali in the Tanjavur District of Tamil Nadu the stoutest and cruellest of the staff, nicknamed Mohammud of Ghazni in honour of the number of his unsuccessful attempts at matriculation, was marked out as the guardian angel of the library. And, he proved to be too zealous a guardian. It was late in the evening. The door of the Library was seen to be opened. This encouraged me to enter the library. The "Librarian" looked tired after the day's work. Without noticing it, I approached the "Librarian."

S R R.— I want a book for "extra-reading."

Librarian (Almost scorching me with his reddish eyes).— What you want?

S R R.— "*Pe-Pe-Peeps into many lands: Japan*, Sir"

Librarian.— How many marks did you get in the last quarterly?

S R R.— Fo-Forty-two out of fifty, Sir.

Librarian.— Go and get the remaining eight marks before you can think of "extra-reading."

Along with this injunction, the right hand fist of Mohammud of Ghazni descended on my head. I ran away and never returned to that Library again. This happened in 1905.

CHAPTER FB

CURRENT DEFINITION OF THE TERM 'LIBRARY'

1 Impact of World War II on Library

After World War II some changes came over the definition of the term 'Library,' In practically every department of human activity, the World War brought about many revolutions. The pre-War educational edifice of practically every country, was like a mud building without a roof. The illiteracy and incompetence of thousands of so-called "educated recruits" to the army served to disclose the huge waste of public money spent on compulsory educational system not backed by a compulsory library system. This led country after country to put a Library Act in its statute book, after the close of the World War.

2 New Function of Library

After the War, libraries began to multiply in great numbers in most of the countries. They were mostly created by legislation and were charged with the definite task of arresting the educational wastage disclosed by the War. Thereby, a third and a new function was assigned to libraries. This new function was that of converting every person in its neighbourhood into a habitual library-goer and reader of books.

3 Habit of Using Library

It is too much of a task to induce any new habit. So it is in inducing the habit of using a library. Any inculcation of habit including that of reading should be initiated in childhood. The educational method in schools should develop in each student the capacity and the desire to use library not only at school stage but all through life. To achieve this end, the School Library should work in close collaboration with class-room work. This is now accepted as an essential function of a School Library. In its new edition, the *New English dictionary* should include this as a necessary function of a library, in its definition of the term.

CHAPTER FC

NEW OUTLOOK ON SCHOOL LIBRARY

1 School Library: Training Ground for Nourishing Library Habit

The school library should be conceived as the training ground for nourishing library habit in each student by actual practice. The school librarian should devise various methods for attracting students to the library and making them read books with pleasure and profit.

2 Constituent of a Library

The new outlook on library in general and on school library in particular has led to the recognition and simultaneous development of three distinctive constituents of a library:

1 Bibliographical constituent;

2 Human constituent; and

3 Material constituent.

3 The Relation between the Three Constituents of a Library

There will be a school library only at certain moments. In such a warrant, all the three constituents mentioned in Sec FC2 co-existing would be brought into intimate relation with one another. Each constituent is necessary; but none by itself is sufficient to constitute a school library.

PART G

WHAT OF SCHOOL LIBRARY BIBLIOGRAPHICAL FACTOR

CHAPTER GA

RANGE OF BOOKS IN A SCHOOL LIBRARY

1 Variety of Books

The book resources of a school library could no longer be built up independently of the interests and the requirements of the students. Children are not different from adults in having potentiality for a variety of interests. They all would like to gather facts, ideas, and information on a variety of subjects. In collaboration with class-room work, the school library should make this potentiality an actuality. From this point of view, apart from the textbooks to be collected in a school library, books fall into five categories:

1 Reference books;

2 Normal form of books expounding ideas in diverse fields;

3 Descriptive and informative books, such as biographies, and travels;

4 Recreative books; and

5 Inspirational books.

A book must have the basic quality of meeting boys and girls at the point of some current interest of theirs. It should carry them further in their powers of perception, enjoyment, and ultimate broadening of powers. In other words it must be rich in interest. It must be abundant in every quality. It must keep the power of perception always keen and fresh. It must have the power of carrying the student with his willing co-operation into a world, outside his own experience. The building of the collection in the school library should do everything possible to make the environment rich — particularly, the intellectual environment. For this, the school library too should provide books just on the fringe of the current interest of the students, and also a little outside the fringe. In other words, the horizon of their interest should be capable of being continuously extended by the books available for them.

2 Reference Books

During the present century, even ready reference books have come into existence in the realm of books for the young. We have special cyclopaedias, dictionaries, directories, and year books, produced for the use of students. This is in addition to the old type of ready reference books such as atlases and linguistic dictionaries. The use of ready reference books has become almost indispensable in the life of the modern adult. So it is imperative to train students in their use. The result: A school library should be rich in students' ready reference books. Time is an important factor in such books. Therefore, a school library should not only go in for as complete a collection as possible of students reference books; but it should also promptly buy newer editions of all of them—if not each year, at least once in a small number of years. Old editions may be kept in the library for some years in order to enable the students, to sense the changes taking place. But after some years, one sound copy of each of the older editions should be kept in the dormitory collection of the central library of each federated system of school libraries (*See* Chap HH); the other copies should be weeded out.

3 Normal Form of Books Expounding Ideas in Diverse Fields

The collection of a school library should not be confined to mere textbooks. It should include a good representation of books of a general nature, written on all kinds of subjects. For some years now several authors and publishers specialise in students' books. These are written to suit the several standards of students. These general books will extend the horizon of interest of the students, far beyond the one restricted by mere textbooks. The general books for students should be sumptuously produced. Each book should fill the hands of the students sufficiently. It should not be a thick paper-covered stuff in order to make it cheap. The librarian should periodically form topical sequences of such normal books in correlation with class-room work.

4 Descriptive and Informative Books

Students' curiosity knows no bounds. They want information

on everything — from the stars and planets in the heaven, through the flying kingdom of animals, their abodes an habits, through all kinds of trees and plants, through the world of insects, through rivers, lakes, and oceans, to everything terrestrial — living or mechanical. In an informative book, the information should not be atomised as in a reference book. The school librarian should make an appropriate collection of informative books to satisfy the curiosity of the students. It does not matter whether the curiosity is roused in the class room or outside it.

5 Recreational Books

Next to informative books a school library has need for plenty of recreative books. Recreative books should not, however, be taken in the narrow sense of fiction. No doubt students like stories. But the stories need not necessarily be filled with fictitious or imaginary characters. Students assess recreative value even in books dealing with actual persons and situations. Travel books and biographies written with proper flair are likely to be enjoyed by students as recreative books. Moreover, we recognise in the world of students' books a peculiar combination of fact and fiction as being very popular; such books communicating facts not as a dry-as-dust narrative, but in the form of a story, are most welcome to students. Indeed there is hardly a subject which is not capable of being clothed in the form of a story for the enjoyment of students. We may even go a step further. In the fictional form of exposition, the author of the book is privileged to come before the screen and add his own statement. But in the dramatic form of exposition the whole subject gets evolved in the words of the characters. This dramatic form is very popular among students, particularly as it lends itself directly to their being enacted by them. Books of this kind are recreative in form and informative in content. We want plenty of such books in a school library. This is apart from ordinary fiction familiar to adults. We want stories of that category also in a school library.

6 Inspirational Books

A student of today becomes the adult of tomorrow. The

community of adults often contains persons needing more than information, general ideas, and recreation. They have something deeper in their personality. This makes them long for information about persons of a high order of spiritual experience — Mystics. The students at school should also be helped to find interest and value in the biographies of such persons with high mystic experience. Then, there is a chance for some of the adults of the community, to pursue the subject further. A community of adults, without value for things spiritual, will be a drab one without a sufficient number of persons of higher qualities, capable of drawing it to higher levels and deeper levels of living. Its scale of values will be too low. But, a community should have sources of elevating value. It is one of the functions of a school library to throw the seeds for such elevating values to sprout and develop in due course. Apart from biographies of mystics, books in Fine Arts, including those in "Literature" are sources of inspiration. Therefore, a school library should also build up an assortment of such books. Books in these subjects — particularly those in Fine Arts — have a great chance to develop the unmanifest capacity of students not only to enjoy fine arts but also to practise the subject. Such a practice will be a source of great enjoyment and joy in the later life of the students.

CHAPTER GB

RANGE OF SUBJECTS IN A SCHOOL LIBRARY

1 Curiosity of Students

The curiosity of students may be shallower than that of adults. But they are definitely greater in extension. All parents have enjoyed and felt baffled by the variety of questions put to them by their children. Sometimes, parents without patience even silence and snub the chiidren with abundant curiosity. The reason for this is often the inability of the parents to give answers to satisfy the curiosity of the children. The curiosity of such parents should have been inhibited long ago by the absence of any help — in the form of books or of human beings — to satisfy their curiosity. Fortunately, there is a tendency now to produce students' books capable of meeting much of the curiosity of the children.

2 Limitations of Finance

The limitations of finance will often lead to restrictions in book selection in a school library. But the limited finance should not be totally exhausted on textbooks and textbook-like conventional books. Each school library should allocate some money, from out of its annual book fund, to add books rich in their capacity to meet the curiosity of the students. Books to satisfy curiosity may be related to or suggested by:

1 The correlation of curriculum; or

2 The correlation with experience — cultural and scientific — picked up outside the school.

This experience may be purely local or one connected with several countries of the world.

3 Books on Side-Interests

The school library should have a variety of textbooks — not merely the prescribed ones — on every topic in the curriculum and of every standard. While teaching a subject in the class room, a resourceful teacher will suggest some subjects of side interest for study. The absence, in the library, of books on the side interests will have a chilling effect on the students. The librarian and the teacher should jointly select for the library, a good assortment of books on such side interests.

4 Correlation with Experience

All national occurrences, festivals, and events are shared by students. The adults allow most of them to pass off without devoting any thought to them. Perhaps, they never developed interest in them. Any interest developed in their student days might have been inhibited by their not having had any source of information. The interest of the students in them may be stimulated through their school magazines or even through the columns of the newspapers. Then the awareness and the eagerness to know the "why," the "what" and the "how" of them are not so easily repressed. The school library has a great responsibility in this matter. About the beginning of the present century, even university students showed no interest in understanding the significance of the "why," the "what," and the "how" of important local, national, or international events. I then used the daily newspapers of Madras to insert short articles on them saying that the University Library had some reading material on them. I also collected such materials and formed topical sequences of them in the very front row of the stack room. This produced the desired result. The school libraries of today should adopt a similar practice. A scanning of the books already in the library may disclose sufficient matter relevant to the events — local or otherwise. These books can be put in the topical sequence along with the list showing the related pages in the several books. The school library may also be led to buy a few books in connection with this specialised activity.

CHAPTER GC

RANGE OF STANDARDS OF BOOKS IN A SCHOOL LIBRARY

1 Intellectual Standard

Next to the range of subject matter covered, the intellectual standard of the books of a school library needs attention. The school days represent the period of fast intellectual growth in a student. This is a psychological fact. During these days, the transition from pure sensation to involved cognition, takes place. Attention slowly gets influenced by apperception and association. Abstraction steps into a larger and larger extent. Time relation consciousness gets established. The students gradually get accustomed to memory, imagination and intellect. They eventually begin to reflect on the experiences stored in memory, correlate them, try to discover relation of causes and effect among them, and in due course practise to think, to infer, and to judge. In fact, a student has just left infancy behind upon entering school, and is in deep adolescence before leaving it. This vast change comes within a period of five or six years. The result: A school library should have books on each subject at varying intellectual standards.

2 Linguistic Standard

Closely associated with intellectual development is the development of linguistic capacity. During the school period the student passes through a long range of linguistic capacity. In the earlier years, simple sentences and common nouns and words with but a sparing use of abstract nouns are the only ones capable of being absorbed in a participative way. By the time of leaving the school, he becomes fit to enjoy the writings of even the greatest masters in his language. He can follow complex sentences, long paragraphs, and involved chapters. He can read books containing words of abstraction and imagination. The result: On any given topic the school library should have books of every linguistic standard between the two extremes.

3 Quantitative Standard

Another psychological factor characterising the collection of books in a school library relates to fatigue. The incidence of fatigue varies with age. The duration for engaging oneself without discomfort in a particular piece of work, physical or mental, varies with age. Indeed, up to a point, it increases with age. A recognition of this factor is reflected in the provision of shorter periods and in the alternation of physical drill with formal teaching in the lower classes. This factor has certain implication on the book resources of a school library. We should have books of varying lengths on most of the topics — lengths not too much for the lowest psychological groups, lengths comfortable for students in the middle psychological groups, and lengths adequate enough for the highest psychological groups.

CHAPTER GD

ILLUSTRATIONS IN BOOKS

1 Effects of Illustration

The books in a school library should be rich in illustrations. Illustrations like pictures, sketch maps, and diagrams do much to enliven the text even in adult's books. The atmosphere of realism added by them will be more welcomed by students provided they amplify definite portions of the text and adjoin the relevant text. Naturally the proportion of pictures will be greatest in the books for the youngest.

2 Picture Books for Infants

Indeed at the very extreme, we have for infants picture books. They include pictures of things familiar to children. With their help, they first learn the names of things and then learn to read those names. In such a book the pictures should be clear and simple in treatment.

3 Books Without Illustration

The other extreme of absolute absence of pictures should not be tolerated in school library books. There is hardly any subject not lending itself to illustration.

4 Development of Techniques for Illustration

Now a days the illustrator's art has developed various techniques. The illustrations can be handsome, life-like, expressive of the intended theme and at the same time cheap.

5 The Nature of Illustration

The illustration should accord completely with the temper and atmosphere of the book. The day of merely pretty pictures is gone for the illustration of books.

CHAPTER GE

PHYSICAL MAKE-UP OF BOOKS

1 Book should Invite Students

The books of a school library should not be taken to mean thin, paper covered, wire-stitched books with miserable margins and flimsy paper; nor should they be too heavy and cumbersome. The physique of a school library book should be an invitation to the students. It must say "Turn my pages. I will fling wide to you the gates opening on far horizons of fact or fancy." A school library book should be outwardly attractive to draw the student to a closer examination of the contents. The cover decoration must not only suggest the theme of the book but also act as a stimulus. A School library book should have flexible bindings opening easily.

2 Strength of Book

Strength and durability combined with good form are desired. Paper of good quality is needed to avoid the absorption of dust. Margins should be wide: then only the open page would be attractive. Further it may admit of the necessary re-cutting when rebound.

3 Typography

The typography of school library books is of great importance. Large and beautiful type faces are wanted. We should not handicap students with small prints. The proportion of white and black in an open double page, must be soothing to the eye.

CHAPTER GF

FUGITIVE READING MATERIALS IN A SCHOOL LIBRARY

1 Fugitive Materials *vs* Durable Book

The layman often takes school library to consists of badly printed, and thin reading materials conveying macro ideas. According to him books in school libraries need not be well built books embodying ideas likely to be of value, for some years. But a school library should have both of these kinds of reading materials. In such a collection the former class of reading materials are weeded out much faster than the latter. Hence, they are called "Fugitive Materials."

2 Fugitive Materials are Necessary for Current Use

Fugitive materials are of many kinds but chiefly consists of pamphlets, folders, plans, pictures, posters, prints and clippings. Their acquisition is not as dependent on the funds of the school library as on the enterprise of its librarian. Even the smallest and the most poverty-stricken school library, may have its well assembled file of fugitive resources costing next to nothing but invaluable as sources of information and recreation for the students.

3 Pamphlets and Folders

In the *American book list,* a list of pamphlets and free material available appears every two months. The *Wilson library bulletin* occasionally publishes lists of educational pamphlets. The governments of several of the States of America publish and distribute valuable pamphlets on several topics. Some federal departments such as those of agriculture, commerce, and education issue free pamphlets and folders. Railway companies, shipping companies, and several industrial firms also publich illustrated folders. Many of these may be got for the mere asking for them. But their duration of usefulness is small. Time and money should not be spent in classifying and cataloguing them elaborately. They should be left on the shelves "Self-classified" and "Self-catalogued."

4 Pictures

A school library should have pictures on all possible topics to illustrate and supplement class work. Several governments have some remarkable photographs of life and scenery in their areas. Reproductions of these may be available at low prices. The Empire Marketing Board had made arrangements for the free distribution to schools of reproductions of posters. Here again, railways and shipping companies and travel agencies generally may be able to supply useful collection at a trifling cost. Guides and picture post-cards are also published by museums, and botanical gardens in several countries and also by the important municipal towns of the world. Some pictures may deserve to be kept longer. They should be mounted on heavy paper.

5 Clippings

It would be a good practice for school libraries to supplement the other resources by the use of material, clipped from papers and magazines. Clippings are particularly useful for local history and contemporary biographical sketches. Clippings should be marked with their source and date. They are best mounted on paper of uniform size taking care to restrict the contents of one mount to clippings on one subject only.

6 The Value of Fugitive Materials

The fulness of the fugitive resources of a school library should be a matter of pride to the librarian. They will make class room teaching extremely realistic. Students value them enormously. They love to handle them. They may even volunteer to help the librarian in cutting them, mounting them suitably, and filing them. An enterprising librarian may even extend this voluntary occupation of students by engaging them to make scrap-books illustrating some suitable themes. Such fugitive resources may lack bindings; they may lack presentability of appearance; and yet they will prove to be as valuable as the books in the finest bindings. Indeed it may even be said that the efficiency of a school library is in proportion to the amount of unbound fugitive material temporarily maintained by it.

CHAPTER GG

EXTENSION WORK

1 Three Directions

Any institution giving a specific service, should generally spread its activities beyond that specific service — even to make its own service attractive and efficient. With its specific service as the umbra, there should be a large perumbral area on its either side. This principle cannot be over-looked by a school library. In order to make itself felt within its community it must go beyond the narrow objective of serving the students with reading materials. It will have to go beyond this objective in three directions:

1 Serving the students and the class with educational materials other than printed ones;

2 Rendering service to the teachers themselves; and

3 Extending its services to the local public — particularly to the parents — making them to feel the school library to be a real social centre.

2 Educational Materials other than Printed ones

A school library will do well to take charge of the lantern slides, the cinema reels and the gramaphone records owned or borrowed by the school (*See* Sec HD4). The school librarian should not grudge being in charge of the associated appliances such as the magic lantern, the epidiascope, the cinema apparatus, the gramophone box, and the radio set. In some schools, they are generally left in charge of the science teacher. This leads to the erroneous belief of their being intended to be used only for science teaching. The non-book materials can reinforce class room work in any subject. The school library, being more central than the science department, may be able to push the use of the non-book materials more efficiently. Further the non-book materials will make class room teaching more realistic. In this they really supplement the work of the books and the fugitive materials.

These three resources should be viewed as a whole and selections should be made out of them in a balanced manner in the pursuit of any subject. This aspect of the problem would reinforce the desirability of their being in charge of the school library instead of a single department.

3 Rendering Service to Teachers

The main purpose of a school library is to serve the student. But even to fulfill this obligation, it should also serve the teachers. For, any service to teachers will ultimately, though indirectly, reach the students. The extra materials needed for this purpose, would only be books on the theory and practice of education. Of course, these will not be of interest to the students. This fact should not stand in the way of the allocation of the book fund to books and periodicals on education.

4 Extension Service to the Public

About half a century ago, the school libraries, even of the land of libraries, felt obliged to go outside the school walls and serve the public at large in the locality. It looks as if the school libraries of India will have to render this extension work for a long time in view of the slow development of the Public Library System. This was realised by our far-sighted statesman C Rajagopalachari. At his instance as the Chief Minister of the old composite Province of Madras, the following order was issued by the Government.

> "The Government are of opinion that the usefulness of school libraries may be extended by throwing them open to members of the public, under suitable conditions. The attention of local bodies is invited to this suggestion and they are requested to take steps to adopt it in the case of libraries in schools under their control. The Director of Public Instruction is requested to urge on managements of aided schools also the importance of giving effect to the suggestion in respect of libraries in their schools. The use of school libraries by the public should generally be subject to the conditions set out in the annexure.
>
> 2 Success in this method of spreading knowledge would be in proportion to the amount of public co-operation and support which school authorities are able to enlist. One way of stimulating public

interest would be by securing the services of a suitable honorary worker for each school from among the staff of the school or from among local residents; on days on which the library is open to the public, the honorary worker may act as its caretaker responsible to the headmaster for the safety to the books and other articles and generally be helpful to those who resort to the library. The headmaster may, in consultation with him, fix convenient hours for the use of the library by the public and settle other details of the arrangement.

3 There must be private persons possessing books which they would readily present to school libraries, if approached, and if suitable acknowledgements were written on the books so presented: Headmasters of schools may be requested to do whatever lies in their power to improve the stock of books in their libraries in this manner.

4 It would be an advantage if a certain amount of public relation work could be done to encourage the use of the school libraries by the public. Resident government officials of all departments may take part in such public relation work. Touring officers should, wherever possible, in the course of their visits to places served by libraries, bring home to the public the benefits arising from the use of libraries.

5 The Director of Public Instruction is requested to include in his annual administration report a section on the working of the seheme outlined in this order.

ANNEXURE

"Conditions on school which libraries may be thrown open to the public.

(1) The facilities for the use of the library by teachers and pupils should not be curtailed.

(2) One or two days in a week, preferably Saturdays and Sundays, should be set apart for the issue of books to the public and for their return to the libraries, so that the arrangement may not interfere with the normal working of the school.

(3) Any loss or damage to books should be made good by the person oncerned and should not be debited to the school."

5 Permanent Value of Service to Local Adults by School Library

There is a permanent reason for the School Library paying attention to the adults of the local public. This will make the parents to take interest in the development of the school library. It may also persuade them to make their students use the school library extensively and purposefully. It may even make the parents follow the use of the school libraries by their students and do liaison work between the students on the one side, and the school library and school teachers on the other side.

PART H

WHAT OF SCHOOL LIBRARY HUMAN CONSTITUENT

CHAPTER HA

THREE HUMAN CONSTITUENTS OF A SCHOOL LIBRARY

1 Analogy of Electro-Magnet

What is an electro-magnet? It is a piece of soft iron surrounded by a coil of wire, and through it electricity is passed. The power of the electro-magnet lies neither in the core of soft iron nor in the coil of wire nor in the electric current taken severally. The electro-magnet comes into existence only on the coil surrounding the core and the current passing through the coil.

2 Students: The Human Constituent of a School Library

A School Library is just like an electro-magnet. It is constituted not merely by the bibliographical constituent elaborately described in Part G. A book collection may be a library in a potent tial form. But it manifests itself as a library only at the momen- of its books being used by readers. This necessary condition to enliven a collection of books into a library has been emphasised by poet Rabindranath Tagore in his inimitable way in his essay entitled *What makes a library big* (34). Human Constituent is as necessary as the bibliographical constituent in the making of a school library. The students of the school should contribute largely to the human constituent.

3 Human Agency to Establish Contact between Books and Students

We should not loose sight of the need for a human agency to establish intimate contact between the books and the students. An agent is needed to put the current through the coil. It is to emphasise this that Berwick Sayers wrote (64):

"A wise American librarian once remarked to me that a log of wood with a book at one end and a librarian at another would make a perfect library. That was a picturesque exaggeration, of course, but it is the personal element that the librarian brings into the library which gives it its vitality."

4 Teachers: The Human Constituent of a School Library

In an ordinary library, the readers and the library staff would together exhaust the human constituent. But in a school library, there is a third party playing no insignificant role in enlivening a collection of books and a group of students into the school library. This is the teaching staff. Its members share with the library staff the work of integrating the students and the books. They can make or mar the school library. The influence of the teachers even makes the students to imitate their mannerisms. Hence the use of the school library by the teachers and of their co-operation with the staff of the school library go a long way in bringing about a library in-action. They are like the fuse in a circuit.

CHAPTER HB

HUMAN CONSTITUENT: STUDENTS

1 The Primary Human Constituent

Books — particularly students' books — are after all, artificial entities of comparatively recent origin (*See* Chap PF). We cannot expect students to take to books as ducks take to water. The faculty of reading has not been in constant exercise by the humans for any very long period. Hence, we cannot expect the young ones among them to begin to read as naturally as the young birds beginning to fly. Again, in the early years, the primary senses formed the main channels of the human community for picking up experience. Only after its reaching adulthood economic pressure forced the community to enrich its experience by feasting upon the recorded experiences the earlier generations and of the contemporaries in other parts of the world. This is coming to be experienced during the last one century in some countries and very much later in many other countries. Till then, the community found other means of supplementing its experience as quite adequate. In other words, the students of the school do not feel a natural need to take to books as sources for facts, ideas, and information. Hence, this primary human constituent — the student — has to be coaxed by special methods to contribute to the formation of the school library.

2 Attracting Students to Library

The first step is to attract students to the school library. Every school library should devote its time and thought towards public relation work. For this, the following three principles may be used:

1 Principle of interest;
2 Principle of recency; and
3 Principle of novelty.

With the aid of these principles, the staff of the school library seek to rouse interest in the school library among the students.

3 Principle of Interest

Find out the interests of a student at the moment, and offer him materials germane to his interest. This is the most effective method of attracting each student to the school library. The interest of each student can be found out by

1 Keeping in touch with the progress of work in the class room; and even

2 Keeping in intimate touch with the likely direction of the course of studies, contemplated and planned by the teachers; and

3 Dressing up the library collection so as to light up the local, national, international, and similar events (*See* Chap LF).

4 Principle of Recency

Everything recent attracts attention. Recent arrivals — men or books — do so. This factor should not be lost sight of in attracting students. Recent books should be brought to the notice of students by every possible method. Their list may be put up prominently and promptly on the notice board. They may be orally announced in the class room. Groups of students — the probable users — may be informed personally. These are some of the ways of attracting students not frequently using the library. Another effective method of exploiting the principle of Recency is to have an attractive show case for recent books with a classified list of those book suspended in the top of the show case. In this matter, a school library has much to learn from the business enterprises. This book displayed in the show case will no doubt go a long way in attracting students to the school library. To get the benefit of this for as long a period as possible, it is desirable to release the books in the show case, for loan only, after a period of one fortnight after their arrival. Further, some teacher or a member of the library staff should spend some time during busy hours of the library to stay near the show case of new arrivals and interpret the new books to the students. This will be of some help.

5 Principle of Novelty

Students have a sharp eye for any thing novel. They are not

ordinarily so absorbed and introvert as to be totally oblivious to the changes in their environment. Even any change in the position, of the furniture and in the sequence of the Main Subjects in the stack room will have some chance of attracting the attention of students and thereby adding to their desire too. The school library should exploit this trait in them as much as possible. Arranging talks in the library by well known speakers from other places may be another helpful form of exploiting novelty to attract the students to the school library. Another form of novelty is a special display of an assortment of books in some class room allowing it and in the common rooms. The assortment of books may have relation to some event or other engaging the attention of the students.

CHAPTER HC

RETENTION OF STUDENTS AS CUSTOMERS

1 Sympathetic Reception

Retaining the custom of students using the school library is not less difficult than that of securing it. Unsympathetic, desultory or slow service may scare away students from the school library. To make the student love to go to the library again and again, they must be served sympathetically, exactly, and promptly.

2 Sympathetic Service

The school librarian should love students. His manner should be jovial, his smiles should be bewitching, and his look should be inviting. Apart from this general attitude, there are some ways for creating the atmcsphère of sympathy in a school library. One of the ways is making the students feel their being as much owners of the school library as anybody else and therefore interested in developing its popularity. This feeling may be induced by allowing the students to share some of the routine of the library with the librarian. Another method of manifesting sympathy is to know in advance, the common requirements of the students and anticipate their demand with sympathetic questions and answers. The atmosphere of sympathy can be created in a thousand and one ways by a librarian "living his work with full joy and self satisfaction."

3 Exact Service

The school librarian requires great capacity and preparation to be able to render exact service to students. To do this he must know the books as thoroughly as knowing the students themselves. The highways and byways of the preparation for exact service have been explored in detail in another book of mine (61).
We may mention here a few items of preparation:

1 Size up each new book on its arrival, about its subject coverage, form of exposition — dramatic, story, or narrative form — and standard of exposition.

2 Connect each book with its probable student users, present and prospective, for this purpose,

3 As the eyes rush through the pages of the book, the mind should be divided itself into two parts — one part receiving and assimilating the quality of the book, and the other sweeping the world of students to find out individuals or groups, present or prospective, likely to enjoy reading the book and benefit by it; again,

4 While amidst students, the mind should record associate, and integrate the recent arrivals and spot out and inform the student likely to enjoy their use and benefit by them;

5 Give to the class, a rapid evaluation of the new additions to the school library, from the angle of the students' capacity and interest. If necessary,

6 Some of the recent books may be brought to the "Evaluation Meeting," to read out illustrative passages.

4 Prompt Service

To be prompt in service the librarian must be able to put the reader at ease almost in a trice and help him to enunciate his exact requirements without any reserve or circumwindedness. On the side of books he should have an intimate knowledge of difficult materials such as oblique titles and particularly comprehensive titles. He should also be able to pierce through the form of exposition into the core of the books. He should be familiar with the varying styles and standards of books. He should know in particular all the fooleries such as books within books, and books within periodicals, playing upon readers. He should also be a connoisseur in dis inguishing books with a message, books with a flair, and orientation books from the ordinary dry-as-dust books. This intimate familiarity with books should be reinforced by him by an intimate knowledge of all the help capable of being rendered by the library catalogue, the published bibliographies and the bibliography on slips constantly prepared, in every live library. He should equip himself with intimate knowledge of books on the one side and of the students on the other. The result: A student once attracied into the library by some reason or other will love to come back to it as often as possible.

5 A Never-Ending Process

The methods of attracting the students to the school library and of retaining their patronage permanently should be continued, without stop, all through the life of the school and of the school library. Any slackening of the effort will immediately produce a fall in the number of students using the school library. One example of this from my experience in the Madras University Library is given hereunder.

I started organizing that Library in 1925. The daily attendance of readers was only in the neighbourhood of 10 — a most depressing experience for a librarian. Excellent colleagues, though only raw graduates, but with a full faith in the social value of library service, joined me within a year. After one year of in-training, they began to "live" in full measure in the methods of attracting readers to the library and retaining them. By the time the new library building became fit for occupation (1936), the daily attendance shot up to beyond a 1,000. In the evening hours 4 p m to 8 p m all the 300 seats available in the Library used to be fully occupied. The maximum number of reference staff had to be on duty till 7.30 p m. This level was kept up, even during the deadening period of World War II. I left the Library in 1945. Some of my old colleagues also did so. Thereafter, I had no occasion to visit the Library till 1961. At about 6 p m early that year, Sri C Seshachalam and myself wished to check up the measurements and to find out the defects, if any the Periodicals Display Table, designed and brought into use in 1936. On entering the main Reading Room we felt shocked. There were only two readers in that vast Reading Room. One of them, an old gentleman, came to me and said with some pain, "Look at the present condition of the Library you left behind." I whisphered into his ears, "Do not speak loudly in the library." His prompt reply was, "Who is going to be disturbed by my loud voice in this cremation ground-like reading room? Besides me, there is only one young reader"?

As we went to the Periodicals Room we found it locked up

already. In the earlier years, it used to be the busiest room in the library with hardly any vacant seat. There was only one peon knowing me. He wished to know my requirement. By that time a young librarian came to me. He said, "I used to attend your fortnightly lectures under the joint auspices of the Madras Library Association and of the United States Information Service Library. They used to inspire in me many dreams of what I would like to do in the Library. But after two months, I was asked to do reference service to readers from 5 to 8 p m. I had hardly any reader at that time to help! The only result was my being deprived of listening to your talk. Perhaps, this was intentional." He was kind enough to open the Periodicals Room for us and allow us to make the measurements of the Periodicals Display Table. One of the happiest news to reach me during this year (1972) is, "That young man with faith in real library service has became the Librarian of that University. The following letter I wrote to him on 6 July 1972 was in the fullness of my joy.

"A few visitors have told me that you are reviving in full life the Madras University Library. They told me that the Reading Room is now a days full instead of having only one or two solitary readers, as in the years before you became Librarian. They added that the Stack Room and the Periodicals Room are kept open even after dusk, and that you are also endeavouring to revive reference service in fuller measure...I pray that you succeed in this endeavour."

6 Cause and Effect

All public relation work, genial reception to readers, and sympathetic service to readers are to be continued by a library for ever and even without any break. Then only the library will have the bee-hive hum of the work of readers in its fullness. Slacken or give up any of these methods, the readers drop out, and the library is reduced to a beautiful building with book shelves bursting with closely packed books. But, it ceases to be a library in reality, for want of readers.

CHAPTER HD

TEACHERS: THE HUMAN CONSTITUENT OF A SCHOOL LIBRARY

1 Teacher's Help to the Staff of the School Library

How can the teachers be of help to the library staff? Every teacher in a school should willingly co-operate with the staff of the school library in many matters — beginning with book selection, and right upto making the book work. Details of these have been eleborated in Part G and in the earlier Chapters of this Part.

2 Teachers and Book Selection Work

Book selection is dependent on three factors. It involves the striking of the resultant of supply, demand and finance. A school librarian may be an adept in keeping himself promptly informed of the publications available for purchase first hand or second hand. However enterprising he might be he cannot command as intimate a knowledge of the demands of the world of students as the teachers can. This is one reason for emphasising teachers as one of the constituents of the human factor in a school library. The problem of allocating the available funds among the various subjects is not a task for a farsighted librarian to take care on his unaided shoulders. It is an onerous task. As book funds are notoriously limited in any school, there can be no allocation of them without inducing bitterness in somebody or other. A wise librarian will leave this fight over funds to be faught among the teachers themselves. Not that he would prefer this fight to be carried out in his absence; he should necessarily be present; for often the estimated demand of the several teachers will have to be confirmed or corrected in the light of actual demand. This is best known only to the librarian.

Once the allocation of funds has been made for the year, it would be a good practice for the headmaster and the school librarian to meet the experts in several subjects periodically to make the final book selection from time to time. It would be a good practice to circulate the provisionally prepared book selection cards among the experts, before they meet. The librarian may help them to sort these provisional cards into three groups — selected, rejected and deferred. This method secures the co-operation of the teachers in book selection without the passing on to them of any clerical work.

3 Teachers and Publicity

On completing the classification, cataloguing, and preparation of new books it will be a great advantage to invite the teachers concerned to peruse them; for, they are effective canvassers of student readers for new books. Apart from the teachers mentioning these new arrivals in the class room on their own accord, the librarian should secure the cooperation of the teachers in reading out the lists he furnishes them, with such oral annotations in relation to class room work as the teachers may think appropriate. This can be done not only for new arrivals but also for books ordinarily neglected by the students, always assuming that if they are intrinsically worthless, they are discarded. Otherwise, the teachers can do much to canvass student-readers for them by introducing them in the course of their teaching.

4 Teachers and Class Room Work

The teachers of the school should disclose to the school librarian from time to time the aids they would like to have in their daily teaching. They may ask for an assorted collection of books to be sent over to the class room for demonstration. They may ask for book illustrations to be marked and sent for display in the class or they may ask for any selection of the fugitive materials or for lantern slides, cinema reels, and gramophone records (*See* Sec GG2). All these materials are meant for aiding class room work. The teachers of the school should feel their oneness with the school library and themselves.

As an adjunct to the class room work, the teachers may ask the librarian to assemble select relevant materials and form topical sequences for specified periods to save the time of the students. They form a very effective means of getting the books of a school library to be used on the one hand and of creating a splendid opportunity for inducing the library habit in the students.

CHAPTER HE

LIBRARY STAFF: THE HUMAN CONSTITUENT OF A SCHOOL LIBRARY

1 Supreme Position of School Librarian

Innumerable are the jobs to be done by a librarian in book selection, in the collection, sorting and filing of fugitive materials, in the handling and putting to frequent use of the extension materials, in publicity work, in getting every student his book, and every book its student-reader, and above all, in coordinating the demand for books received from several sections of the teaching staff, and enlivening the class room work, by supply of appropriate materials. Indeed it can be said that the school librarian is the most distinctive and the most responsible human constituent of a school library.

2 How to Secure Supreme Position

This position has to earn for himself by his own identification with the work of the school library — and not by merely propitiating the management and the headmaster of the school or by soliciting the help of the senior librarians of the country. His own personality and his own work in the school library alone should earn him supremacy of position in the school library.

3 Details of Work of School Library

Parts T to Y will discuss in far greater detail, the various items of school library practice needed to be done scientifically and thoroughly, if the school library is to function well. These jobs are, beyond doubt, specialist jobs. They cannot be done by the teachers. Perhaps it is difficult to realise the force of this statement as most of our school libraries are now run unclassified and without a scientifically constructed catalogue.

4 The Spirit of Mahasaraswati

No school librarian, with a knowledge of Mahasaraswati given in the *Mother* of Sri Aurobindo, will regard even the minutest work to be done in a school library as beneath his dignity. Nor will any member of the school staff and of the school managment, with a knowledge of Mahasaraswati, underwrite the status of a school librarian and of his staff on the ground of the enormity of apparently trivial details to be carried out by them. On the other hand they will take the staff of the school library as their equals and partners in a great social enterprise.

5 'Perfect Perfection

In this connection it is worth reproducing here, an extract from the prose poetry of Sri Aurobindo on Mahasaraswati's insistence on attaining "Perfect Perfection" in every piece of work done (3):

"Mahasaraswati presides over their details of organization and execution, relation of parts and effective combination of forces and unfailing exactitude of result and fulfilment. The science and craft and technique of things are Mahasaraswati's province. Always she holds in her nature and can give to those whom she has chosen, the intimate and precise knowledge, the subtlety and patience, the accuracy of intuitive mind and conscious hand and discerning eye of the perfect worker. This Power is the strong, the tireless, the careful and efficient builder, organizer, administrator, technician, artisan and classifier of the worlds. When she takes up the transformation and new building of the nature, her action is laborious and minute and often seems to our impatience slow and interminable, but it is persistent, integral and flawless. For the will in her works is scrupuluous, unsleeping, indefatigable; leaning over us she notes and touches every little detail, finds out every minute defect, gap, twist or incompleteness, considers and weighs accurately all that has been done and all that remains still to be done hereafter. Nothing is too small or apparently trivial for her attention; nothing however impalpable or disguised or latent can escape her. Moulding and remoulding, she labours each part till it has attained its true form, is put in its exact place in the whole and fulfils its precise purpose. In her constant and diligent arrangement and rearrangement of things her eye is on all needs at once and the way to meet them and her intuition knows what is to be chosen and what rejected and successfully determines the right instrument, the right time, the right conditions and the right process. Carelessness and negligence and indolence she abhors; all scamped and hasty and shuffling work, all clumsiness and a *pue pres* and misfire, all false adaptation and misuse of instruments and faculties and leaving of things undone or half done is offensive and foreign to her temper. When her work is finished, nothing has been forgotten, no part has been misplaced or omitted or left in a faulty condition; all is solid, accurate, complete, admirable. Nothing short of a perfect perfection satisfies her and she is ready to face an eternity of toil if that is needed for the fullness of her creation. Therefore of all the Mother's Powers she is the most long-suffering with man and his thousand imperfections. Kind, smiling, close and helpful, not easily turned away or discouraged, insistent even after repeated failure, her hand sustains our every step on condition that we are single in our will and straightforward and sincere; for a double mind she will not tolerate and her revealing irony is merciless to drama and histrionics and self-deceipt and pretence. A mother to our wants, a friend in our difficulties, a persistent and tranquil counsellor and mentor, chasing away with her radiant smile the clouds of gloom and fretfulness and depression, reminding always of the ever-present help, pointing to the eternal sunshine, she is firm, quiet and persevering in the deep and continuous urge that drives us towards the integrality of the higher nature. All the work of the other Powers leans on her for its completeness; for she assures the material foundation, elaborates the stuff of detail and erects and rivets the armour of the structure."

CHAPTER HF

QUALIFICATION FOR A SCHOOL LIBRARIAN

1 General Educational Qualification

To discharge the duties devolving on him in a school library as conceived by us, it will be no longer possible for a semi-literate peon to be in charge of a school library. Nor will it be possible for the drill master or the writer of the school to run it. The general education of a school librarian should be not only such that he can read the books of the library with ease but also evaluate them exactly in relation to standard, style and reliability. Without knowing books how can he establish contact between the right book and the right student? It is conceded that a grain dealer should know about grains of all sorts, a draper should know everything about apprarel, and a teacher should know the subject he has to teach, it must then be equally obvious that a school librarian must have learning and must possess scholarship of a wide range. The general educational qualification of a school librarian cannot be lower than that prescribed for the teacher of the highest classes in the school. The possession of a university degree should be the minimum general qualification. Our schools should remember the saying of Arnold Bennett that if libraries "spent less on books and more on an educated staff far better results would be obtained." It is the attainments of the librarian that will secure these results.

2 Professional Qualification

But mere scholarship cannot make a librarian. The common belief that anything in a library beyond scholarship is manual and clerical is only a measure of the ignorance of the holders of the belief. Not infrequently one comes across a remark such as "What is there in 'Indexing,' (the term 'Indexing' is taken for "Cataloguing"). One only wishes that he were allowed to try his hand in "Indexing" for a couple of months. Then he will discover for himself the mess he is capable of making. The school library to-day is expected to work at such high level and is entrusted with so many tasks that the school librarian requires a balanced professional training with as much grind and as much technique as that required for any other learned profession as Medicine, Engineering, or Law.

3 Pedagogical Qualification

A school librarian differs say, from a public librarian in that he needs to have an additional qualification in the art of education. He must be capable of assessing for his own benefit, the pedagogical technique followed by the several teachers in the several subjects. For, his work with the students within the walls of the school library should be as a preparation for and a follow-up of the work of the teachers in the class room. He must be as much an adept in child psychology and adolescent psychology as the teacher himself. He must be as familiar with the history of education and with the present trend in educational ideas and methods as the members of the teaching faculty. Moreover he cannot make his service to the students register well with their experience in the class room without having had a chance to handle some formal classes. This itself implies that he must have a degree in Education.

CHAPTER HG

STATUS AND SCALE OF SALARY OF SCHOOL LIBRARY STAFF

1 School Library Staff to be on a Par with Teaching Staff

According to the current and developing faith, a school library cannot be maintained as a ritual appendage of a school. On the other hand it must be an integral part of the school. The library staff should be as educated as the teaching staff. Indeed the librarian should have one more University Degree than the teacher — Degree in Library Science. This has been elaborated in Chap HF. These facts emphasise the obligation, if not the necessity, of putting the library staff on a par with the teaching staff in respect of status and scale of salary. Otherwise the library staff would be transformed into a body for grievances and evasion of every kind.

2 Practical Necessity for Equality of Status

The status of a school librarian should be equal to that of a senior teacher of the school. This is necessary to enable him to sit as an equal with the other teachers in the staff meetings. Quite often, the librarian will have to consult the teachers and share their burden. Otherwise, the work of the students in the library cannot be usefully integrated with their work in the class room. A student will be reduced to the condition of a person rowing in two boats at the same time. To avoid this catastrophy, the teacher should be aware of his dealing with a person of equal status. For the words of the poorer status person seldom carry weight.

3 Practical Necessity for Equality of Scale of Salary

Rightly or wrongly, society has built its economics on a money basis. Therefore, the ultimate real value of the service of a person or profession is determined by the salary scale of the profession. Unfortunately teachers as well as students are prepared to benefit by a service only in proportion to the value set on it by money. In the trinity of the library — books, readers and staff — the richness of the staff in worldly goods should be as much as the richness of the other two in number and variety.

4 Slow Response to the Demands of New Education

An important handicap preventing the staff of a school library being put on a par with the teachers of a school in respect of Status and Salary Scale is the unfortunate tradition dogging the problem during the last hundred years. In the earlier years there were very few schools which had libraries. In a school with a library the latter had no organic educational relation with the educational process practiced in the school. The Librarian was therefore put on a clerical scale to accession the books, to safe-guard them from injury by insects or fungi, to prevent any loss of books and to pay the cost of lost books, and to do odds and ends of any clerical work of the school to occupy his free time. Therefore, the status and the scale of salary of the clerk, though carrying the dignified designation "School Librarian," were only on a par with those of the other clerks in the school. But the advent of the "New Education" is totally transforming the relation between the school and its library. As a corallary, it is endeavouring to transform the status and the scale of salary of the staff of the school library. The importance of this transformation to make education of real value and to equalise the teaching staff and the library staff of the school in status and scale of salary, being insisted upon by "New Education" is slow to be realised by the ordinary men in charge of public affairs — particularly educational affairs. How is this handicap to be overcome, and when it will be?

5 Appearance of Statesmen in the Field

In any socio-economical problem, the vision of the common politician is too narrow and self-centered to allow any forward action being taken. Society has to wait for it till the appearance of far-seeing statesmen. But, far-seeing statesmen are not born every year. They appear only once in a generation or two. According to my faith school librarians have suffered and failed to play their legitimate role in vitalising education for quite a number of years, as a result of politicians having been at the head of educational affairs. The true educational statesmen are just coming round the corner. I expect the whole problem of school libraries to be treated properly, during our life time, so as to make them truely serviceable in the lifting up of the educational achievements of our schools.

6 Reform of the Educational Code

About 1930, a brilliant graduate S Parthasarathy, was working with the dignified title "School Librarian," on a monthly salary of Rs 30, in the Hindu High School, Triplicane. He joined the School of Library Science of the University of Madras. He did very well. He took permission to work as a honorary member in the University Library for a few additional weeks in order to get a good grind in reference service and every thing else necessary for it. He then went back and reported himself to the school. The Secretary of the school was a retired judicial officer. He was also a good friend of mine. He put this trained graduate librarian again on the same old salary of Rs 30 in spite of the School having more than 800 students in the secondary classes. One day the Secretary came to the University Library.

S R R.— Your action is not right. He is a brilliant librarian.

Secretary.— If so, I shall garland him on his next coming to the library.

S R R.— Will judges care to work on Rs 30, and derive satisfaction being his garlanded.

Secretary.— What can I do? The School Grant-in-Aid Code does not provide a higher salary for the school librarian.

S R R.— And so, you are guided by precedent. As a judge, were you always guided by precedents only? Or, did you take the changing social conditions into account?

Secretary.— Surely, I follow the latter course.

S R R.— Then convince the educational authorities of the anachronism of the Grant-in-Aid Code of the Victorian period and replace it by an equitable Code worthy of the present day function of the school library, in a school working on the Principle of "New Education."

Then the Madras Library Association took action along these lines. The Director of Education issued Proceedings sanctioning a higher scale of salary to trained graduate librarians in secondary schools. But alas, the inertia of tradition is inexorable. In spite of the Madras Library Association giving the widest publicity to the new Proceedings of the Director of Education, very few schools took advantage of it. The statesmen-educationists had not yet been born at that time.

CHAPTER HH

GROUPING OF SCHOOLS FOR LIBRARY SERVICE: BOTH NECESSARY AND SUFFICIENT

0 Financial and Practical Consideration

The scheme for secondary school libraries outlined so far, is not something capable of being completed in a year. Indeed our financial conditions will perhaps need two or three decades to complete the scheme. Nor is it necessary that we should complete it in one year. It is not wise to cut the coat according to the cloth. It is sufficient if we start the scheme in so many areas as finance would permit. But, the areas should be selected equitably from each of the Constituent States. The further expansion also should be made in a similar equitable way. This Chapter gives an overall picture of the organisation, necessary and sufficient, while putting the scheme into force throughout the country.

1 Assumption

For definiteness, but without loss of generality,

1 A school library is taken to consist of the four final classes of a secondary school;

2 Each class has three divisions each with about 40 students; thus,

3 In each day there are two shifts in the school, in order to meet the building accommodation and other overall changes due to the sudden expansion in secondary education;

4 This expansion is likely to continue for at least three more decades; and

5 The number of students in both the shifts taken together in a secondary school is about 1,000.

2 Grouping of Schools for Library Purposes

Inadequacy of finance and of trained library manpower makes it almost impossible for the library of each school to be an independent one. Even in a rich country such as the USA, this difficulty is felt. The solution is to group together about 20 schools contiguously situated — whether in a city or in a rural area. One of the 20 schools having sufficient space in its building, and if possible centrally situated, will be denoted by the term 'Central Library of the Group of Schools.' This will hereafter be referred to by the term 'Central Library for Schools.' Thus in an average in a group of school libraries we have 20,000 students.

3 Assumptions about School Library Finance

1 The average annual library fee to be payable by a student is Re 1;

2 The annual contribution from management to the book fund is Rs 14,300;

3 The annual salary for library staff, consisting of two professional librarians each at an average salary of Rs 400 per month and two attendants each at an average salary of about Rs 200 per month, is about Rs 14,400;

4 The annual Government Grant to maintain one Central Library for Schools, consisting of one chief librarian at Rs 600 per month, one professional assistant at Rs 400 per month, one library attendant at Rs 200 per month, one peon at Rs 150 per month, and one driver for library van at Rs 150 per month, is about Rs 18,000 — the share for each school being Rs 900;

5 Annual amount to be spent by a school on salary of library staff is about Rs 15,300;

6 The annual salary for other staff of the school, is about Rs 100,000; and

7 The proportion of the salary of the library staff to that of the salary of other staff is 1/6.

4 Advantage of Group System of School Libraries

The group system of libraries, centralises all impersonal work such as purchase, classification, cataloguing, and processing.

These are all done by the chief librarian of the Central Library for schools. Thus, the librarian of a school has only to be in close touch with the work of each class, welcome the students to the library in a genial but assertive way, help the students to satisfy the curiosity roused in the class room by their own reading, organise the students for team study in the library with methods such as dramatisation and so on, and thus play a large part in the method of "Individual Instruction," forming an essential element in New Education. Of course he will have also to supervise the circulation work done by the attendant. The chief librarian of the Central Library for Schools will visit each of the 20 schools at least twice a year, work with the librarian of the school for a few days and push him to a higher level of service to students.

5 Book Selection

Book selection in the 20 schools of the group will be essentially in the hands of the school. The chief librarian of the group will coordinate and administer the purchase and further treatment of books. He should see that 20 copies of each book are not bought to enable each school to have a permanent copy of its own. But, except in the case of reference books, children's periodicals, and educational periodicals for teachers, far less than 20 copies should be bought for the group as a whole. In close collaboration with the librarian of each school the chief librarian will work out a rational system of circulating the books among the 20 schools. This will satisfy Law 2 and also avoid offending Law 3 by allowing books to lie idle on the shelves after they have been read by most of the students.

6 Professional Qualification of the Library Staff

For the qualification of the staff of a school library, see Chap HF. For the chief librarian of the Central library for Schools the possession of a First Class degree in B Lib Sc or a Degree of M Lib Sc is desirable. Apart from this, he should have a powerful personality, dedication to work, organising capacity, and the habit of keeping himself upto date. He should also persuade the Librarians of individual schools to read library science periodicals and books. For this, the Central Library should purchase some important periodicals and books in library science and circulate them among the libraries of the group.

PART J

WHAT OF SCHOOL LIBRARY MATERIAL CONSTITUENT

CHAPTER JA

GENERAL FEATURES OF SCHOOL LIBRARY BUILDING

1 Size of the Stack Room

The following assumptions are made in respect of the school library building:

1 The school works in two shifts a day;

2 In each shift 500 students attend the school;

3 In addition to the reference books kept in a library at any time, the library will have its number of volumes kept at a level of 15,000 supplied in periodical circulation by the Central Library of its group (*See* Sec HH3),

4 Law 5 "A Library is a growing organism" will make the school library follow Adult Growth — that is, old books will be replaced by new books, making the size of the collection more or less the same at all times. There will be no accumulation of outmoded or worn-out books, causing continuous growth in the book collection as in child growth;

5 In respect of the readers of the library also, Law 5 will make the school library to follow Adult Growth. Every year old student-readers will leave giving place to new ones;

6 Nor will there be any appreciable growth in the number of teacher-readers; and

7 Consequently, there will be seldom be need for adding to the library building.

2 Open Access

The following assumptions are made in respect of Open Access System:

1 Except for pamphlets, worn-out books, books of poor physique, and others marked "special" for certain definite reasons, all the books will be kept on open shelves — that is, the book racks will not be provided with doors, locks, and keys;

2 The students will be permitted to walk amidst the book-racks; and

3 The students will be allowed to handle any book.

To provide open access inside the library, the entrance and exit must be under the strictest control and watch. It should not be possible for any one to enter the library or leave it except through prescribed wicket gates. These gates will be controlled by the library staff in the circulation enclosure, with the aid of a mechanical device. Similarly, all the other openings in the external walls of the library, such as doors, windows and ventilators should be fitted with shutters of mesh work, the slits being too small to allow the passage of a book through.

3 Cross Gangways

Groups of students will frequently walk and stay in any cross gangway, between any two consecutive parallel book racks, browsing and handling books. Therefore, the width of a cross gangway should be at least 135 cm.

4 Floor Level

The books will have to be trolleyed from any part of the library to any other without transhipment. For this, the entire floor of the library must be in one level without any obstruction whatever in the form of thresholds, or curbs. This is desirable also from the point of view of the students.

5 Ventilation and Light

The windows should be so placed and so designed in size that the stack room and the reading room should get plenty of natural light. Artificial lights should be avoided except at night. For this, the windows should be designed and placed suitably. This will also automically secure free ventilation. In a tropical country, such as ours, it is unwise to depend on sky-lights. Solar heat also will penetrate into the library along with light and will be directly incident on books and students. This will unfit the students in a short while; this will also dry up and warp the books, thereby shortening their life. To avoid direct sunlight, heat, and even rain water at the sudden beginning of rain, falling on book racks and books, the length of the stack room should run east to west, and all its windows being on its north and south walls. The book racks should be placed across the stack room in parallel lines at right angles to the longer walls. Moreover, to minimise the chances of the books being wetted by sudden break of rain and to prevent sun from directly falling on the books, the free ends of the book racks should not be taken too close to the north and the south walls. On the other hand, on each side there should be a gangway, 90 cm wide, running all down the length of the stack room between the free ends of the book racks and the two lengthwise walls. No doubt there will be saving of some space by having a single central gangway instead of two side gangways. But the temptation to follow this policy should be avoided in view of the need for having one gangway at each end of the line of book racks for avoiding damage due to climatic causes. Avoidance of direct sun is more imperative than the saving of space in this case.

6 Windows in the Stack Room

In times of sudden or heavy rain, side-hung shutters in the windows of the stack room will not give sufficient protection. Therefore, each such window should be fitted with three members of centre-hung shutters with glass panes. These centre-hung shutters will be so fixed as to avoid their projecting into the gang way on opening to a near horizontal position. The expanded metal shutter should be fixed on the outside of the wall so as to allow this.

7 Aesthetics

The school library should have a good aesthetic finish and everything possible should be done to produce an atmosphere of serenity, composure, and loveliness. There should be wall space for portraits, and floor space for flower vases; there should be provision for hangings like curtains; the wall should be distemper-washed — the walls of the stack room in pearl-gray and those of the reading room in a soothing colour such as green. The floor must be smooth, noiseless and without holes and crevices for preventing the accumulation of dirt and insects.

CHAPTER JB

SPECIFICATION FOR LIBRARY BUILDING, FITTINGS AND FURNITURE

1 Stack Room

It is best to begin the data for the stack room with the unit book rack. A detailed specification for it and other elements is given elsewhere (29, 30). It is sufficient here to summarise it as follows: It consists of four bays — two on each face, the two faces being separated by a partition of expanded metal or weldmesh material. The bays are formed by three verticals. Each bay can normally take five movable shelf planks and two fixed ones — one near the bottom and the other near the top. Thus each of the four bays have ordinarily seven shelf planks and the unit rack has twenty-eight planks. This can house one thousand volumes in round figures. The overall dimensions of the unit rack 210×45×190 cm. Making allowance for tolerance we shall have 16 book racks. We shall put two book racks in a line. This will make the length of the cross gangway from wall to wall 6 metres. The width of a cross gangway in front of a unit rack plus the width of the unit rack will be 180 cm. Each volume will require a floor area of about 55 square cm. Further, the length of the stack room will be about 16 metres. Thus the internal area of the stack room will be 16×6 metres — that is 96 sq metres.

2 Reading Room

Each student should have about 3 sq metres of floor area including table space, space for chair, and gangway behind the chair. The reading room should provide seat for about 55 students. The length of the reading room shall be taken to be equal to that of the stack room — 16 metres. Thus the width of the reading room would be about 10 metres. Thus the internal area of the reading room will be 16×10 metres — that is, 160 sq metres. The reading room tables may be fitted with short vertical racks for the display of current issues of periodicals. Thus, the provision of a separate periodicals room can be avoided in a school library.

3 Seminar *cum* Group Study Room

On the side of the stack room, opposite to that of the Reading Room, a room with equal dimensions as the Reading Room may be provided. This can be used for holding Seminars and conducting group studies.

4 Counter Enclosure

The enclosure of the control region — having the counter — should have an area of about 9 sq metres. This is secured by making it run 3 metres east to west and 3 metres north to south. This enclosure may be had inside the entrance lobby. It should be projecting out from about the centre of one of the east to west walls of the reading room. There should be about 90 cm width of passage for exit and entrance on either side of the counter. It may be an advantage from the point of view of supervision to make the counter project 1 metre inside the reading room with the result that some free space will be available in the entrance lobby for showcases and free movement.

5 Plan of School Library Building

See page 168.

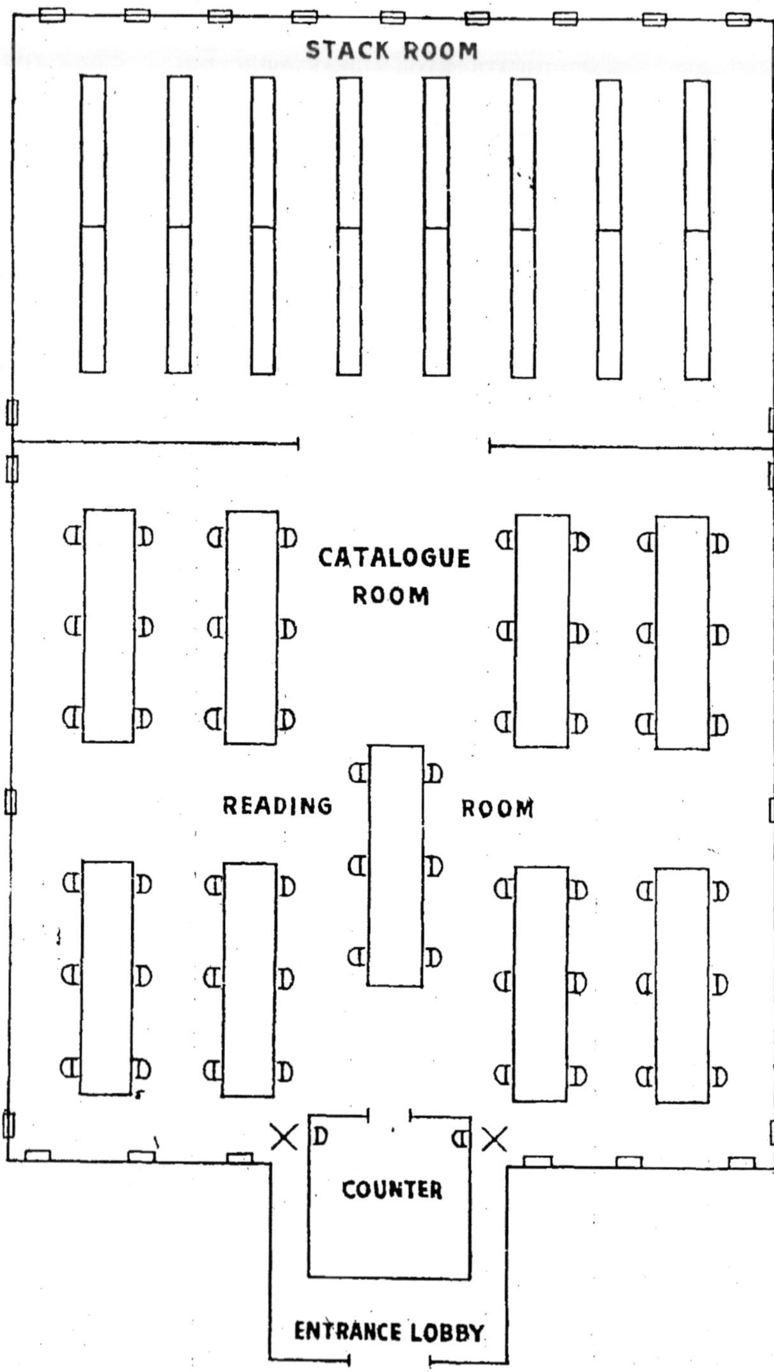
STACK ROOM
CATALOGUE ROOM
READING ROOM
COUNTER
ENTRANCE LOBBY

PART K/N

HOW OF SCHOOL LIBRARY

PART K

HOW OF SCHOOL LIBRARY

OBJECTIVES OF SCHOOL LIBRARY WORK

CHAPTER KA

SCHOOL LIBRARY TO CREATE LIBRARY HABIT IN STUDENTS

1 Familiarising the Student with the Library

The formation of library habit in students requires some detailed examination. On a student coming to the library, the librarian should familiarise him with the varieties of the reading materials in the library, the ways of using them, and the working of the library apparatus.

2 Care of Book

The student must be initiated in the care of a book. He must be made to realise the fragile nature of its physique. His attention must be directed to the internal parts of an ordinary book — title page, back of title page, contents page, list of illustration, preface, bibliography, and index. This is apart from his attention being invited to the arrangement of the text of the book in parts, chapters, sections, and paragraphs.

3 Linguistic Dictionary

Initiation of the use of a linguistic dictionary requires special attention:

1 The use of the dictionary should normally be taught by the teacher. But usually this does not happen. Therefore the librarian has to do it.

2 All the points should not be brought to the notice of a student in one sitting. They should be staggered among the different cycles of the Concentric System in the method of teaching (*See* Chap TF).

3 As often as possible the student should be told about the necessity, throughout life, for looking up a dictionary quite often to pick up the correct meaning of a word and of the correct word for an idea.

4 His attention should be drawn to the following:

41 A dictionary often gives two or more meanings for a word; the student should be trained to select the word with the meaning needed by him; and

42 In the same block, a dictionary gives associated phrases and idioms.

4 Open Access

The student must be shown the different part of the library and the distinctive service expected from each part. He must be made to realise the extraordinary freedom allowed to him in the library — he can go directly to the shelves and pull out and examine any book he likes, unhampered by shyness or fear.

5 Library Classification

To benefit by open access the student must be helped to appreciate the shelf arrangement. It is not necessary, however, to tell him straightaway all about classification.

6 Library Catalogue

The library catalogue, no longer a "one book, one entry" affair, needs considerable initiation. In the case of a card catalogue, the student will have to be told about the cards in a tray progressing from the front to back. He should be made to appreciate the use of guide cards. He should be enabled to evaluate the significance of the colour scheme of the cards. By slow degrees he must be accustomed to the kinds of entries and their respective functions. Eventually he must be helped to observe and appreciate the different parts of an entry and the different kinds of headings. Even graduates tumble over the inversion of surnames and forenames. Books are themselves artificial entities requiring initiation; and in the library catalogue of books we reach an artificiality of a still higher order. They are full of conventions; these can never be known fully without prolonged and proper initiation and practice.

7 Notes-Taking

The student has also to be taught the art of taking notes while reading. The upper quartiles among the students in the intellectual scale may themselves arrive at a suitable method by trial and error. But most of the students may not be able either to realise the need for notes-taking or to evolve a correct technique by their own effort. They stand in need of the school librarian's individual attention for a long while.

8 Bibliography

No doubt, bibliographies of various kinds covering vast subjects exist in a published form. They belong to the class of reference books and as such the student should be taught their structure and their use. But each reader, be he old or young, should have his own bibliography prepared to suit his intimate needs. In the first place it need not be exhaustive. The intension of its subject and the time possible to spare for it, will decide the degree of its selectiveness. Secondly the purpose will limit the scope of the bibliography.

The student has therefore to be taught the elements of the art of bibliography-making. He must be given practice under guidance. No doubt he will be ripe for preparing a full blown bibliography only at the college stage. But even at school he will be in need of constructing miniature bibliographies. At any rate the habit should be started even while young; for a bibliography is vital for an intelligent and exhaustive use of the resources of a library.

CHAPTER KB

SCHOOL LIBRARY TO CREATE LIBRARY CIVICS IN STUDENTS

1 Library: A Public Institution

A library is one of the public projects shared by everybody without direct payment, in all civilised communities of today. Hence it suffers from two handicaps. It is public property for the use of every member of the present generation as well as of the future ones. It will take a long time to make the students understand this. It will take even a longer time for the realisation of the full implications of this fact.

2 Fate of Books in a Library

Many communities have introduced a public library system only during recent years. The fate of the books in these libraries makes one sad. They suffer at every stage:

1 The tops of their backs are broken while being pulled out of the shelf.

2 The stitches are broken by careless and forced opening of the book.

3 Many of the leaves have their top corners folded to serve as book marks; eventually these corners break away.

4 Margins are taken as free spaces to write upon.

5 Line after line in the text is underlined as if it had only one reader to serve. In 1932, the Madras University Library found each line of some medical books underlined in ink. This created a problem for us. On the addition of a new medical book of that kind, it was, as usual, put on the Recent Additions Shelf. A member of the staff was asked to observe the persons using the book. After finishing his reading for the day, in accordance with the Rules, the reader would leave the book on the table and go away. Then the member of the staff, watching this book for the underlining of the lines, would examine it. In the case of some readers this did not happen. But lines were found marked after a parti-

cular reader — let us call him "Med" — left the book on the table and went away. This was followed up till about half of the lines in the book were underlined. The book was then brought to me. I found the underlining of all the lines had been done with ink of a peculiar colour. During the next visit of "Med" to the Library, as usual, he took that book to his seat. Within a couple of minutes thereafter, I went round and took "Med" to my room. In the meantime, that book also reached my table.

S R R.— Do you particularly like this book?

Med.— It is a very good book on the subject.

S R R.— How did you locate it?

Med.— I always go to your Recent Additions Shelf on every Sunday, the day of putting new books on it. I found this new book on one Sunday. I found it absorbingly interesting. Therefore I came to the Library for an hour or two each day and read through the book, line by line with great care.

S R R.— Are you in the habit of underlining each line while reading?

Med.— I am not aware of it.

S R R.— Here is the new book you have been reading. How much of it have you read already?

Med.— About a half of it.

S R R.— Look here, all the lines in the first half of the book have been underlined.

Med.— Could I have done it?

S R R.— You have to decide it. Compare the colour of the ink used for underlining with the colour of the ink in your Fountain Pen.

Med.— I now realise that I myself would have done all these underlinings unconsciously. I feel guilty. I feel extremely sad. I shall buy a new copy of the book for the library.

S R R.— It is very good of you to have said so.

Med.— I shall also replace all the other books spoiled by me in this way.

S R R.— Doctor, you are really generous to this public institution.

Med.— On account of this unconscious despicable habit of mine, I shall not hereafter come to the Library. This habit has evidently become inexorable.

S R R.— This statement of yours pains me. That resolution of yours would make me lose a "reader." There is no greater sin for a librarian than to lose a "reader."

Med.— What can I do to escape committing this vandalism?

S R R.— Will you be kind enough to accept a suggestion of mine. That will save me from the sin. It will also allow you to come to the Library as usual and enjoy our books.

Med.— What is it, Sir?

S R R.— On your entering the Library, leave your pen with the Counter Assistant.

Med.— But, evidently, I cannot read without underlining each line.

S R R.— I shall provide for it. I shall leave this pen-like stick with a blunt end, with the man at the counter. As soon as you surrender your pen at the Counter, take this stick with you. While reading draw this stick along each line. Your habit will be satisfied; at the same time there will be no impression left in the book. On your leaving the library give back the stick to the Counter Assistant, and take back your pen.

Med.— I am extremely grateful to you for this suggestion. I shall adopt it.

S R R.— Thank you Doctor. You have been extremely nice to me.

6 Its pictures were deformed beyond recognition by the addition of beards, caste marks and spectacles.

7 Some pictures were lost for ever.

8 The book as a whole had not infrequently to serve not only against the sun but also against the rain.

9 There was no limit to the load of dirt it had to carry silently.

3 Library Civics and Adults

The first generation of librarians tried all methods to teach the adults the elements of library civics. They

1 Distributed leaflets;

2 Gave talks;

3 Made pictorial appeals;

4 Tried personal persuasion;

5 Pressed the theatre into service;

6 Arranged for dramas with books as characters, narrating their woes;

7 Even went to the desperate length of making splashy demonstrations such as conducting a public funeral of a murdered book and in it the orator bemoaned its premature death and the thoughtless ways which deprived them of the long service the murdered book had intended to render them.

4 Children's Department in a Public Library

What were the first generation of librarians to do? Were they to depose the First Law of library science — Books are for Use — and reinstate the Anti-First Law -- Books are for Preservation? Were they to stop the lending of books? Certainly not. They were heroic enough to develop patience and forbearance. They said "Let the present stock of books perish with the present generation of adults. Let us work for the future generation of books by taking the future generation of adults on hand even in their early age." Accordingly Children's Departments were opened in public libraries.

5 Prophylactic Measure

The prophylactic measure appears to have been effective. For instance, a young girl, often coming to read, brought her little brother one day. Suddenly there was a sound of a slap and a roar from the young boy. Above the tumult was his sister's angry voice "Don't do that. You'll break it. This is the way to open a book." The training of children in library civics is most effectively done in school libraries.

CHAPTER KC

OBJECTIVES OF SCHOOL LIBRARY: FROM THE ANGLE OF STUDENTS

1 Class Room Work and Library Hour

In a sense all class room work may have to be looked upon as a means to make the experience of the students in the school library produce lasting benefits to them. In other words all class room work should have a slant to students' work in the library.

2 Holistic View

This may look like over-emphasis for effect. But it will be so only on taking a distinctive atomistic view of the school-life of students. But the proper view to be taken is the holistic one, not merely of the school life of the student but of his whole life --- in the school, in the field, in the home, and indeed in whatever environment he may be from moment to moment. All the experiences of students are concrete and they hang together. From the point of view of the student the experience in the formal class hour cannot be separated from that in the library hour. In his experience in each setting, he is acting and reacting integrally on his experiences in every other setting. Any one setting of his at any moment colours his experience in other setting and reciprocally it also gets coloured by them.

3 Principle of Holism and School Library

The statement, ventured already about all class room work being focussed on the school library, is not an over-emphasis for effect but a reality flowing from the Principle of Holism. The particular enunciation of this general Principle, pertinent to our problem, is:

1 Class room work and school library work influence each other reciprocally;

2 Either should be focussed on the other; and

3 Moreover school library work will have similar reciprocal

relation with the physical and social environment of the student whatever be the extent in which it is taken — from the distant stars to the road surface and from the distant international occurrences to the intimate happenings at home.

For, to the school student his entire environment is a unity and his experience is itself part of that unity. He is like the young Ulysses saying,

"I am a part of all that I have met;
Yet all experience is an arch where thro'
Gleams that untravelled world, whose margin fades
For ever and for ever when I move." (71)

PART L

HOW OF SCHOOL LIBRARY: MEANS

CHAPTER LA

FALLACIES

1 Two Fallacies

Two fallacies usually appear in the way of the adoption of all the available means to get the students linked up effectively with the school library. One of them is typified by an incident of 1935.

2 Fallacy 1

On making the library hour compulsory, the headmasters and the teachers naturally asked for some guidance in the use of the hour. In response to this the University of Madras decided to arrange for a vacation course on school library work for teachers (*See* Sec AD4). Then came in, the choice of the person to give the course of instruction. Fortunately at that time the choice was not vitiated by the usual considerations of patronage-distribution. But according to some the person competent to give a course on the subject should be drawn from the professors of English. This view was at bottom based on the fallacy of equating school library work with reading books in English literature. This in its turn led to the second fallacy about a professor of English literature alone being capable of guiding the students in school library work. Little was it imagined that every lesson in the school can and will have to be so conducted as to establish necessary contacts with the school library. Nor did it occur to many that the use of the school library hour required for its background a proper educational theory. The professors of English had no experience in guiding the library work of students; at any rate they did not have the exclusive monopoly of that qualification. By chance or with deliberate intention, I had been invited to attend the meeting about the choice of the lecturer on school library work. This was a fortunate event. For, after a long discussion the meeting decided upon the librarian to be the correct person to give the course of lectures.

3 Fallacy 2

The second fallacy is typified by the way of mangling the idea behind the library hour within a few months of its creation. The order promulgating the library hour was soon eclipsed by another order saying that each class library should consist, say, of ten copies of four books and that these were the books to be perused by the students in the library hour. There was no doubt an extra-academic reason for such a preposterous order. The library hour had replaced the so-called "non-detailed study hour." With the result, the three or four influential publishers of the area lost their market to sell about twenty thousand copies of a publication of theirs. The forces of vested interests were therefore released and the Head of the Department could not have peace, without providing for the forced sale of at least ten copies of their respective publications in the place of the old forty copies, in every class of every school. Notwithstanding the business world's interested argument in favour of this, there is no denying the fact that this implied either an ignoring of the psychology of interest in linking up students with the school library or, what is worse, a woeful misreading of that psychology so as to believe that enduring and creative interest can be induced in students by official orders. This *ex cathedra* choice of reading material by the headmaster or more often by the lay management at the beginning of the school year ignores the interests of the individual students taking shape from moment to moment; and yet the students are blamed for ignoring the school library; and the library hour is naively pronounced to be a failure. Any deviation from the principle of ten copies of four books was condemned, if not penalised, by the inspecting officers. This not only proves an ignorance on their part of the "business origin" of this uneducational principle but also effectively suppresses every urge of even well-informed and well-intentioned schools to do the right thing by the library hour.

4 Right Mode

The right thing is neither to make the library hour a modified English hour nor to put all the students on the predetermined Procrustean bed of four books. The proper thing is:

1 To recognise the chief varieties of books — the ready reference and other informative books, the recreative books and inspirational books — standing in need of being introduced to the students as a preparation for life;

2 To be on the look-out in every formal class-hour for opportunities to stimulate interest in students to anticipate or to follow up class room experience by work in the school library with its plentiful collection of every variety;

3 To explore the elements in the extra-mural experiences of students, likely to rouse an attitude of curiosity in them, and to link them up with school library work; and

4 To help the students in so organising their work in the school library as to lead to the formation of desirable library habits capable of helping them in after-life.

HANDICAPS

1 Role of Teacher in Making the Student to Think of School Library

Eventually, many students may feel the need for using their school library quite often. But, it is also desirable for the teachers to make the student to think of school library as a place to go to for enlightenment and information.

2 Reasons for Making External Stimulus Essential

There are several reasons for deliberate external stimulus being made essential;

1 Books are artificial aids of comparatively recent origin to draw satisfaction from;

2 The project of offering a common pool of books for the gratuitous use of everybody is too recent to have so impregnated society with the habit of going to it;

3 The sheer force of imitation attracts the young ones to the temples in many of the up-country townships and villages;

4 The attraction of the library has to work mainly through the intellect, unlike that of social institutions such as the temple, the cinema, and the playground, capable of working through the primary senses of seeing, hearing, and of the motor-senses.

Hence, there is need for the young ones to be inducted by the elders into the use of this new intellectual cultural institution — library. Such inductance falls definitely in the sphere of educational institutions.

3 Occasions in Class Room Work

A lesson may offer three kinds of occasions to help a student to think of the School Library. These may be for:

1 Preparing Work;
2 Parallel Reading; and
3 Follow-up work.

CHAPTER LC

STUDENT'S PREPARATORY WORK IN THE LIBRARY

1 Pre-Class Library Work by Students

The preparations of students to enjoy participatively and benefit by class room work may do well by their looking up and collecting relevant data by working in the school library. The student may not be able to anticipate what to look for and what to read. They must be told by the teacher concerned. They may have to be culled out from outside the prescribed textbooks. Therefore, the teacher and the librarian will have to guide them about the books or parts of books to be looked up.

2 Practice in Pre-School-Library Days

In the pre-school-library days, it was naturally impracticable to make the students themselves to do at least part of the search and the collection of data. Therefore, the teacher had himself to give all the information. But, it amounted to passive listening, with all its bad consequences. In particular, a splendid opportunity to make the student to do some independent investigation, with all the pleasure of anticipating a useful result, was lost. Along with it was also lost, the opportunity for the student's getting some quantum of training in self-education.

3 Team-work

The method prescribed in Sec LC1 also gives much opportunity for team-work. The students themselves will soon learn to break up the area of investigation into different sub-areas, each fit for team-work. Then, the plums collected by the different teams can be brought together. At this stage the students will realise the joy of group-life. Incidentally, it will also help each student to find out any defect in his work. The teachers will have to lead them in this kind of pre-class-room background work. After some experience, the students themselves may be able to plan out their pre-class preparatory work and get it whetted and put on sound lines by the teacher.

CHAPTER LD

STUDENT'S PARALLEL READING

1 Starting Parallel Reading

Certain class room work may warrant the prescription of some parallel reading to be done by the students in the school library. The books or parts of books for parallel reading should be suggested by the teacher during the class room work, whenever possible. It should not be made the task of every student to study every book suggested for parallel reading. It is sufficient for each student to do a few of those books, attracting his interests.

2 Informal Follow-up by Teacher

There should be nothing compulsory about parallel reading. Certainly, no examination on it! At the same time each student should be encouraged to include in his Library Diary the results of his parallel study. In a purely informal and friendly mood the teacher may look into the Library Diary, along with the student. This will give him an opportunity to give any informal suggestion to the student about the notes — particularly in relation to the origin of that parallel study — in the Library Diary. Another informal work might be to encourage each student by turn — at least once in a year — to give his class an oral exposition of the best benefit derived by him from the best book he had for parallel reading. It may not be too much to get the best of such expositions written out by tne student concerned and publish it in the school magazine.

3 Librarian's Role in Parallel Reading

As in all other cases, the teacher and the librarian should work hand in hand in the case of parallel reading also. The librarian should assemble the relevant books in a topical sequence bay and fix at its top the purpose of the topical sequence. If necessary, the librarian may also borrow useful books for this purpose from the other libraries in the locality such as public, college, and even specialist. Naturally, this inter-library loan will figure most in the service to the highest classes in the school. These students would step out of the school in a year or two. Then, some of them having had the use of the books of other libraries in the locality may like to go to these libraries. Thus, this practice will be of reciprocal advantage to the library giving and to the library taking. But the habit of follow-up study should be deliberately cultivated by the teacher in the students of the lower intellectual scale. In this he should get the best cooperation from the libraries of the school. Special topical sequences may be formed by him for the follow-up study of each class. The librarian should also intensify his public relation work among the students to coax them to look into the topical sequence appropriate to him. With some students he will have to continue this many times till their getting interested in the matter and showing some evidence of enjoying follow-up work in the library. At the time of book selection the librarian should also bring up the acquisition of books necessary for follow-up work by the students.

CHAPTER LE

STUDENT'S FOLLOW-UP WORK

1 Right Time to Hand Over the Student to Follow-up Work

In good educational technique, everything is not told to the student. The teacher should know where to stop and leave the student to follow-up by his own work in the library, from where he stopped. The follow-up library work of the student may involve,

1 Finding out supplementary facts and data;

2 Reading additional books or parts of books to get a full and satisfactory picture of the subject; and

3 Studying the biographies and a popular version of the achievement of some of the well-known authors in the field.

The last mentioned purpose will humanise the subject and atleast some of the students will be inspired by the examples of the well-known authors.

2 Suggestion *vs* Expression

"Suggestion and suppression are of greater value than full expression" is a truism among men of letters. It is equally so in Methods of Teaching. The potency of carrying "suggestion" upto, but not into, everything to be taught is a technique of much value in the art of teaching — in organising and developing work in the class room. As a student, I had enjoyed the greatest satisfaction from the work of the teachers practising this art. Surely many others also would have had that experience.

3 Special Care of the Average Students

Some in the upper quartiles in the intellectual scale may do follow-up work of their own accord. For, curiosity is at its best in them. But, the habit of follow-up study should be deliberately cultivated by the teacher in the students of the lower intellectual scale. In this, he should get the best cooperation from the librarian of the school. Special topical sequences may be formed by him for the follow-up study of each class. The librarian should also intensify his public relation work among the students to coax them to look into the topical sequences appropriate to him. With some students he will have to continue this many times till their getting interested in the matter and showing some evidence of enjoying follow-up work in the library. At the time of book selection the librarian should also bring up the acquisition of books necessary for follow-up work by the students.

CHAPTER LF

EXTRA-MURAL STIMULUS

1 Kinds of Extra-Mural Stimuli

Stimulus other than from formal lessons can also make a student to use the school library. Let us call them "Extra-mural stimuli." An Extra-mural stimulus generally centres round recurring or isolated events and festivals of local, national, and international interest. The student should be encouraged and welcomed to come to the school library to collect information about any such extra-mural stimulus.

2 Methods of Exploiting the Extra-Mural Stimulus

All students may not be sensitive to such extra-mural stimulus. But the school library is interested in attracting all students to itself on the basis of every possible stimulus. For this, the librarian should be a person of wide interest. Books and other reading material of the library bearing on any extra-mural stimulus should be brought to the notice of the students by all the possible methods of public relation work such as,

1 Formation of topical sequence;

2 Making list of the books in the topical sequence, with an attractive inviting heading, for distribution among the students directly, and through the headmasters and other teachers, and through the students' associations;

3 Arranging, wherever warranted, special talks by persons generally known to attract students;

4 Wherever wanted, putting up a special exhibition to be opened in a splashy manner and kept on view for some days— the exhibits including illustrations from books; and

5 Whenever warranted, making the students express and discuss the significance of the event in the meetings of their associations.

3 Cooperative Effort in a Locality

Some of the extra-mural stimuli may admit of being celebrated not merely by each school individually, but collectively by all the schools in the locality. There should be at least one such collective endeavour among the schools in each year. This larger celebration may carry greater weight than the celebration in an individual school. Incidentally, it will help the students of each school of the locality to get an idea of the collections of books and other reading material in the other school libraries of the locality. In the case of the system of having a central library for a group of about 20 libraries, the chief librarian of the central library may distribute the celebrations among the various schools of the group on different days (*See* Chap HH). In such places, he may put on view as many as possible of the relevant books and other reading materials owned by the group as a whole.

CHAPTER LG

STORY-HOUR FOR THE YOUNG STUDENTS

1 Story-Telling: A Folk Method

On every possible occasion, and at least once in a week, there should be a story-hour organised by the librarian for the young students. This would amount to adapting one of the ancient folk institutions. These form a heritage from the simple folk without ability to read or write. They have unusual charm. Even the adults of today would like to hear stories. They have even been institutionalised, with the name "Story telling with music" (*Katha, Katha Katha, Kālakshepam, Kathā Kālakshepam,* and so on), for the benefit of the adults. It is no wonder that students are enthusiastic about the story hours in library.

2 Introduction in Croydon

In November 1924, I was working as a probationer in the Croydon Public Library, UK. There the Chief Librarian, W C Berwick Sayers, was having weekly story-hours. After attending his story-telling for two weeks, I told him about our combining music with story-telling. At his request, I showed him the various stages in the story for the next week, admitting of appropriate songs. He carried it out. It was a splendid success. The children asked him, "Mr Sayers, why did you not tell us stories in this way till now? Please continue this method hereafter."

3 Library Use of the Story Hour

In the school library, the story-hour is a means to establish contact between the students and the books. For this purpose, the story-telling should be interpolated at appropriate places, with the reading out of titles of books relevant to the theme expounded. By the time the story-hour is over, the titles mentioned during the story-hour should be exhibited at the end of the hall, along with a sufficient number of copies of the list of them to enable each student to have a copy of it. By the next morning, the books exhibited should have been put up in the stack room in the special story topical sequence.

CHAPTER LH

FACT FINDING

1 Promotion by Questionnaire

Students should be trained in finding out facts from reference books and also from other books. Initiative can be taken by the school librarian himself in this work. It may take the form of distributing to the students lists of "Find me out" questions. The lists on all the subjects should not be given at the same time. Only a few subjects should be covered at each distribution.

2 Samples of "Find me out" Questionnaire

2B MATHEMATICS

B1 What do the following words signify: Stocks, Shares, Consuls, and Discount.

B2 Anecdotes about mathematicians and on the mathematical subjects taught (Source.— *Memorabilia mathematica*; the end pages of the *Mathematical gazette*).

B3 Short biographies of mathematicians, such as Euclid, Bhaskara, Aryabhatta, Newton, and Ramanujan (Source. — Encyclopaedias; Histories of Mathematics; Biographical Dictionaries).

2C PHYSICS

C1 Definitions of technical terms (Source.— Encyclopaedias; Dictionaries).

C2 Inventions using principles of physics (Source.— Physics dictionaries; Books on inventions).

C3 Short biographies of physicists, such as Archimedes, Watt, and Raman (Source.— Encyclopaedias; Histories of physics; Biographical dictionaries).

2E CHEMISTRY

E1 Name of the inventor of each substance (Source.— History of chemistry).

E2 Properties, such as atomic weight, specific heat, density, conductivity, and solubility of substances (Source.— Table of physical and chemical constants).

E3 Short biographies of chemists such as Dalton, Priestley, and P C Ray (Source.— Encyclopaedias; Histories of chemistry; Biographical dictionaries).

2G Biology

G1 Pictures of plants and animals.

G2 Short biography of biologists such as Darwin, Malthus, and Huxley. (Source.— Encyclopaedias; Histories of biology; Biographical dictionaries).

2O Literature

A class on literatures usually centres round a prescribed text. Hence the concreteness of the situation gets even more individualised than in other lessons. Hence, general illustrations become impossible; and so the illustrations given here relate to certain texts.

O1 Text: Toru Dutt's *The lotus*

1 Where was Toru Dutt born and educated?

2 The titles of the other poems of Toru Dutt

3 The names and years of some other Indian poets who have written English poems.

O2 Text: Rudyard Kipling's *Children's song*

1 The years and the titles of other works of Rudyard Kipling.

2 Rudyard Kipling's connection with India.

O3 Text: Alfred Tennyson's *Morte D'Arthur*

1 What is meant by Poet Laureate?

2 When was Tennyson Poet Laureate?

3 Two other Poets Laureate of the past.

4 The present Poet Laureate.

O4 Text: *Speech of Antony,* selected from Shakespeare's *Julius Caesar*

1 When did Julius Caesar live?

2 The parts of Brutus and Antony in *Julius Caesar*. (To make the student look up the entire drama).

3 The circumstances of Caesar's death.

O5 Text: Selection from Shakespeare's *King Henry V*

1 The allusions to Phoebus, Elysium and Hyperion.

2 The dates of King Henry V.

3 Who was Erpingham?

O6 Text: Selection from Shakespeare's *King John*

1 What position did Hubert occupy in King John's court?

2 What happened to Arthur ultimately?

O7 Text: Rabindranath Tagore's *Cabuliwallah*

1 The titles of some other stories written by Rabindranath Tagore.

2 Year of birth and death of Tagore.

3 When did Tagore get the Nobel Prize?

4 The value of the Nobel Prize.

5 Who awards the Nobel Prize?

6 The terms of the award of the Nobel Prize.

7 Who else in India have won the prize?

O8 Text: Baldwin's *On England*

1 When was Baldwin Prime Minister?

2 What was he before becoming Prime Minister?

3 Who succeeded Baldwin as Prime Minister?

4 How was Baldwin related to Kipling?

O9 Text: Selection from Thomas Hughes's *Tom Brown's School days*

1 When was Thomas Arnold headmaster of Rugby?

2 What is prefecture system?

3 What is fagging?

2U Geography

U1 Population and capitals of different countries (Source.— Directories; Atlases).

U2 Disposition of mountains, lakes, rivers, seas, and deserts in different countries (Source.— Geographical Atlases).

2V History

V1 The important years in the history of different countries (Source.— Dictionary of dates).

V2 The names of the members of the British Cabinet.

3 Questions Brought Up by Students

31 Perhaps a student has had a controversy with his sister at home as to whether gold was heavier or silver. He may be encouraged to bring up this problem to the school library and find out the correct information from a table of physical constants.

32 In the playground a discussion about the changes in the rules of a game might have arisen. The students may be allowed to settle the issue by looking up the appropriate reference book or any book on the game in question, in the school library.

33 It is not unusual to take the students of a school on excursions to museums and galleries. The students wander into the birds room. There birds are posed in life-like attitudes and arranged in cases following the seasons. Perhaps next to such exhibits, they see exhibits arranged to illustrate evolution from microscopic creatures to whales and elephants. In the mineral room they are attracted by sparkling crystals, precious stones and nuggets of gold. Volcanic products and photographs of volcanoes such as Vesuvius and Etna are seen in another room. An excursion like this sets the students in the pursuit of various facts, ideas, and information. The school librarian should, so to speak, capture the students in that mood of inquisitiveness and literally display all the reference treasures of his library.

In an article entitled *The machine age, the child and the book* (19) Flora Delgorza rightly emphasises that the present machine age has made radical changes in our daily life and with these outward changes the inner thoughts and interest of the boys and girls have also changed. The sight of the royal mail van may induce a student to find out details of postal organisation. In one of his visits to the cinema a student may suddenly wish to know the "How" of the Cinema. There is no end to the number of facts a student is made to look up while moving about on business or as a pastime. The same writer records that a boy wanted to use Miss Edith Ackley's book on *Marionettes*. He came in several times to copy patterns for the new marionettes he was making. He knew a great deal about his hobby and offered to give a lecture on marionettes to one library club. That is how extra-mural experience should bring students to the library for fact-finding.

CHAPTER LJ

READING FOR INFORMATION AND PLEASURE: A SAMPLE

B Mathematics

B1 Ball (RS). Mathematical recreations.

BX Astronomy

BX1 Lewis (Isabel M). Astronomy for young people.

BX2 Noyes (Alfred). The watchers of the sky. (A verse story of the passing on of the torch from one astronomer to another).

C Physics

C1 Chambers (Mary D). Nature secrets.

D Engineering

D1 Collins (A Frederick). The boys' airplane book.

D2 Collins (A Frederick). The boys' book of submarines.

D3 Hawks (Ellison). Engineering for boys.

D4 Mills (John). Letters of a radio engineer to his son.

D5 Van Metre (T W). Trains, tracts, and travel.

D6 Williams (Archibald). Engineering facts: Great achievements simply described.

E Chemistry

E1 Collins (A Frederick). Wonders of chemistry.

E2 Rush (Charles Everett) and Winslow (Amy). Modern Alladdins and their magic: The science of things about us.

E3 Slosson (Edwin). Creative chemistry.

E4 Yates (Raymond Francis). The boys' play book of Chemistry.

F Technology

F1 Eliot (Ethel Cook). The little black coal.

G Biology

G1 Blanchan (Neltje). Nature's garden.

H Geology

H1 Arnold (Augusta F). The sea beach at ebb tide.

H2 Mills (Enos A). The romance of geology.

J Agriculture

J1 Verill (AH). Harper's book for young gardners.

J2 Hudson (William Henry). Far away and long ago.

K Zoology

K1 Hudson (William Henry). Adventures among birds.

K2 Cheesman (Evelyn). Everyday doings of insects. McBride. Life history of insects.

K3 Clark (G Glenwood). Tiny toilers and their work.

K4 Maeterlinck (Maurice). Children's life of the bee.

K5 Patterson (Alic Jean). The spinner family.

KX Animal Husbandry

KX1 Fabre (Jean Henri). Our humble helpers.

KX2 Johnson (Constance). When mother lets us keep pets.

KX3 Macself (A J). Pets for boys and girls.

KX4 Mukerji (Dhan Gopal). Gay-neck: the story of a pigeon. Winner of the Newbery medal in 1928.

KX5 Mukerji (Dhan Gopal). Jungle beasts and men.

KX6 Mukerji (Dhan Gopal). Kari the elephant. Dutton.

L Medicine

L1 Grenfell (Wilfred T). Yourself and your body.

L2 Haviland (Mary S). The most wonderful house in the world.

O Literature

O1 Text: Toru Dutt's *The lotus*

1 Dutt (Toru). Ancient ballads and legends of Hinduism.
2 Das (H). Life and letters of Toru Dutt.

O2 Text: Rudyard Kipling. *The children's song*

1 Kipling (Rudyard). Select poems.
2 Kipling (Rudyard). Puck of Pook's Hill.
3 Tagore (Rabindranath). Gitanjali (Songs 35 and 36).
4 Palgrave (F T). Golden treasury.
5 Lincoln (A). Speeches and letters.

O3 Text: Rabindranath Tagore's *Cabuliwalah*

1 Tagore (R). Hungry stones and other stories.
2 Tagore (R). Broken ties and other stories.

O4 Text: Selection from Baldwin's *On England*

1 Gardiner (A G). On certain people of importance.
2 Baldwin (S). On England.
3 Emerson (R W). English traits and representative men.

O5 Text: Selection from Thomas Hughes's *Tom Brown's School days*

1 Thackeray (W M). Vanity fair.
2 Darwin (B). English public school.
3 Arnold (Matthew). Rugby chapel.

U Geography

U1 Biographies of travellers, aviators and mountaineers.

U2 Histories of explorations like Mount Everest expedition, Arctic expedition, and Antartic expedition.

U3 Travel books of all sorts and descriptive books like those in the "Peeps at many lands series"

V History

V1 Biographical stories of historical personages.

CHAPTER LK

INSPIRATIONAL BOOK

1 Necessity for Special Efforts

A spiritual mood is necessary to enjoy inspirational books and benefit by them. It is seldom however that such a mood sets in at school age. Nor, as a rule can it be induced by deliberate effort: it usually comes upon one casually and unexpectedly. A high emotional pitch inducing a mood for the enjoyment of the beautiful or a mood of love and devotion is the next best preparation for the understanding and enjoyment of inspirational books. As the sense of beauty or the motion of love or devotion is universalised, the mood approximates to the critical point of its being sublimated into a spiritual one; so it is that inspirational books can be approached by heightened emotion. Such an enhancement of sensibility and imagination may very well be induced in students by deliberate effort.

2 Quality of School Librarian

For this, the teacher or the school librarian concerned should himself first attain that pitch; then his talk will be so spirited and his personality will, so to speak, vibrate so effectively in harmony with the work he expounds that his audience will be thrown into a state of sympathy with it. A few of the students at least will derive a lasting benefit on their having this experience at least once a term and so acquire a genuine taste for the inspirational books in the school library.

3 Importance of Inspirational Book

There is nothing in the recorded heritage of man that is of greater value than the inspired sayings of souls speaking from the very centre of their personality at moments of identification with the Centre of the Universe. Whatever be the apparent theme of such expressions — not necessarily religion or philosophy, but also physics or biology or even dry-as-dust mathematics — they constitute poetry; they translate the inner meanings of nature and life into language of distinction and charm; they touch the primordial and are capable of enriching, ennobling, and elevating all reading or hearing, and sharing them. However difficult the task may be, the school library should therefore try its very best to see that students get to know and enjoy inspirational books. It should at least occasionally invite outsiders with the necessary qualities to inspire the students in this way.

4 Occasions for Introducing Inspirational Book

Such books are to be used for parallel reading or follow-up work. The occasion for introducing them may arise in any lesson — perhaps more often in lessons on Literature and even sometimes in History lessons, here an approach may be made through admiration of nobility or heroism. And the occasion for introducing such books may be created by the school librarian himself on getting an opportunity. He should always regard such an opportunity as the prize of his life. For, by settling upon a student this magic gift of enjoying inspirational books he has given him a sure means of delight. It may not be easy to find such an opportunity or when it has been found to turn it to the best account. This requires effort and preparation as well as a sincere longing. In the midst of his routine work the school librarian should be gathering the necessary mood and the necessary setting for this most important effort all through the term. On their reaching the proper pitch, he should act. The moment for him to act successively is, as Blake might say, the moment containing "Eternity." The greatest service he can do for students is to find that moment and share it with them. The library talk is one obvious means of charming students to an appreciation of inspirational books.

5 Illustration: Introductory Words

"On your way home from school you may see just what you will. You may choose to hasten along thinking how hot the sun is and how glad you will be to lay down the huge pile of books and note books when you reach home. You may be thinking of the savoury which your mother will have ready for you. You may be thinking of the new ball that will be put in the play field. Any one of a dozen things may fill your mind as you hurry along regardless of the way.

"On the other hand, you may walk the very same way and see a cloud drifting along the blue sky and a group of birds fluttering along with the cloud in the background. You may notice one person relieve another of a load and catch sight of the smile on the face of the weary relieved of his load. Any one of these things may stir you; but unless you look for it, it is not there for you.

"And wherever you go in this world there is something waiting to stir you if only you try to find it. Try!

"Some people find it easily and are able to express it for people who do not find it readily. Sometimes they express it in a picture, sometimes in music, but often they put it in words. Such words enable you to be stirred by some of the things you see. Once you are stirred you feel that these words voice your own feelings and you are glad to re-live your experience by reading these exquisitely expressed words again and again."

Punctuate the introduction with examples of gifted children having been stirred. For example, Sri Ramakrishna Paramahamsa was thrown into ecstasy by the flight of the birds with a black cloud in the background. Shelley was stirred by a skylark, Tennyson by a brook, and Blake by a school boy. They have recorded their emotions. Through those records, their emotions can be shared by others.

6 Demonstration

After the introduction, read specimens of inspirational writings. Ask the students, to scatter themselves among the tables having such writings spread out in display. Move about among the students giving help and interpretation according to needs. Find out by conversation what situation appeals to the several students and help them to find writings suited to their respective moods and temperaments.

CHAPTER LL

LEARNING OF LIBRARY HABIT

1 Learning by Experience

The library habits are to be formed by actually living them in the library.

2 Formal Lessons

Occasionally formal lessons may be given to clinch those learned by experience and imitation. Thus, formal library lessons may be made a means of teaching the students proper use of the resources of the library and the library apparatus. The school librarian is the proper person to give such lessons. Some of the formal lessons may be conducted in the traditional way with the librarian as the active centre of the picture and the students as passive listeners: some may follow the laboratory method.

3 Supervised Study

Supervised or directed study is another form. Under this a student is given a carefully prepared, detailed assignment to be worked out by him under the supervision of the school librarian. The advantage is that each student works at his own speed and receives the necessary help individually. Zaidee Brown's *Library key* is a book of such assignments suited to American students. Assignments suited to Indian students await to be prepared. It is a virgin field affording opportunity to the enterprising school librarians of each Constituent State of India. Organs of the State Teachers' Association such as the *South Indian teacher* must be ready to offer the hospitality of their pages for the experimental assignments. After they are well thrashed out in those pages and get crystallized, it will be time to publish model assignments for each State.

4 Project Method

Project method is another modern form of conducting a lesson.

It is called Problem Project Methods. In this method subject-matter is not organised into logical sequences and taught to students before they have met the problem needing solution. But the material is so arranged that the student experiences the problem first and then masters the subject-matter necessary for the solution. In this method the student has a series of problems, challenges or contracts so arranged that in solving them desirable attitudes, habits, skills, and ideas are acquired along with information. The contract provides for individual differences by minimum and maximum assignments. The project may be assigned to individuals or to groups according to the nature of the problem. *Find it yourself : a brief course in the use of book and libraries under the contract system* by Elizabeth Scripture and Margaret R Greer gives many typical contracts suited to American students. Here again, as in supervised study, the enterprising ones among school librarians and organs like the *South Indian teacher* have a splendid opportunity to do the primary work.

PART M

HOW OF SCHOOL LIBRARY STUDENT'S WORK

CHAPTER MA

NEED FOR KEEPING DIARY

1 Secondary Work of Student in School Library

The primary work of a student in the school library is making use of its books. The library should provide all facilities to promote this primary work. Apart from this primary work, there is a secondary work for the student to learn from a school library. It is the formation of the habit of keeping a systematic diary of library work.

2 Hazards of Not Keeping Diary

The absence of the habit of keeping a diary for library work, often lands adults in embarrassing situations. Inner memory unaided by records, often proves treacherous especially as one advances in years. There are moments of our having a vague recollection of some books we read at some time on a particular topic. But we may not be able to recollect exactly either the name of the author or the size and colour of the book or the approximate year of our reading it, or even the library having that book. What is worse, memory sometimes plays a trick on us and makes us assert wrong things about all these factors. One comes across many humorous incidents of this nature in the day-to-day work in a library.

3 Illustration 1

In 1930, a middle aged Professor of Physics came to the Madras University Library with a feeling of great disappointment.

Prof.— What has happened to that fat red book?

Ref Lib.— Which book?

Prof.— Once I did take that book from such and such shelf of this library. But today it is not there.

Ref Lib.— In a growing library books will have to be constantly shifted from shelf to shelf.

Prof.— That is really confounding us readers — particularly busy persons.

Ref Lib.— Please quietly sit down for a moment and try to recollect the name of its author.

Prof (After a few minutes).— I have got it now. It is "Rewett."

Ref Lib.— Thank you. Let us locate it now with the aid of the catalogue.

Prof.— Oh! It is all waste of time to wade through the catalogue.

Ref Lib.— I shall do it for you.

Prof.— All right.

Ref Lib (After some time).— That name is not in the catalogue.

Prof.— That is extraordinary! What is happening to this Library? I knew that this card system would lead to all kinds of abuses.

Ref Lib.— Why do you generalise and jump to conclusions like that? Perhaps your memory has played you false.

Prof.— Surely not. I am quite certain that some of you have played false with the catalogue.

. . . .

Chief Lib.— What can I do for you, Professor?

Prof.— I wish you had asked "What you can do for yourself."

Chief Lib.— Why, what is the matter?

Prof.— All is not well in your Library.

Chief Lib.— I am concerned to hear that. Perhaps I can help you.

Prof.— I am afraid you must give up this open access system and the card catalogue system. Books are being lost hopelessly.

The librarian and the professor changed their subject of conversation. Some time was spent on enquiries about personal matters, about families, and so on.

Prof.— The trouble is, I have to preside over a meeting this evening. The subject is "Service of science to industries and human progress" in general. Two years ago, I remember having read a fat red book here in this library. So far as I could remember, the author of the book is Rewett. The book is not now in that place. The catalogue has not got even the entry of the book and your reference librarian begins to give me advice on good conduct!

Chief Lib.—Never mind the reference librarian. Why don't you examine the classified part of the catalogue. You may get something to serve your purpose at the meeting. Shall I come and help you?

Prof.— No. Thank you. I shall do it.

Chief Lib.— Just one more tip. Perhaps you will find more material in the pamphlet collection. It is very likely that a pamphlet will serve your purpose better than a regular volume.

After some time, the professor came back to the Librarian, with a thin green pamphlet, in an apologetic manner.

Prof.— I have after all found out that book. Here it is.

Chief Lib.— I am glad. But surely it is not a fat red book!

Prof.— I have really come to apologise. My memory played me false. It played me false even about the author of the book. The correct name of the author is "Jewett" and not "Rewett".

Chief Lib.— Oh! It does not matter. Memory is often treacherous. Let me look into that pamphlet...You say you took it on loan on the last occasion.

Prof.— Yes. I took it.

Chief Lib.— That was two years ago?

Prof.— Yes. However, now I know where I am with my memory. I won't assert that it was exactly two years ago. It was about 1936 or so.

Chief Lib.— Look? This date label of the book tells a different tale! It has never gone out since 1928.

Prof.— Oh dear, dear! What has happened to me today! I am getting old, I suppose!

4 Illustration 2

Here is another experience with a young man not yet passed the thirtieth year. He was the head of a department of studies.

He asked for Faucett's *Provinces of England*. It could not be found in the Library. He searched the catalogue. It was not there either. He felt so cock-sure about his conclusion that there was something rotten in the library. Being inexperienced and accustomed to pride himself over his bluntness, he paraded before the librarian his proof that the Library was rotten. In spite of repeated requests by the librarian, he asserted that he had borrowed it from that very Library on more than one occasion. The librarian suggested that he might have borrowed it from some other library in the city. But he would not accept that theory. Then the librarian found out from the reference catalogue details about the book and told the young head of department that it was a small pubication of 1919 costing only 2s 6d and that it was very unlikely that in the absence of a department of geography in those days, a book like that would have been acquired for the Library. But still, he asserted that it was in that Library and that he had used the book. Anyhow, the librarian assured the head that in case of his being really in need of the book, he would immediately take steps to buy a copy. Accordingly a book selection card was prepared. After checking the library catalogue for it, the book selection assistant checked the outstanding order cards as part of his routine. To his surprise this title was found among outstanding orders. With this clue the connected file was perused and it was discovered that that very head of department had sent an indent for the acquisition of the book and in the indent, he had added the note that a copy of it was not available in the locality but that he knew that the book was worth having as he had read it in a library in London!

5 Maintenance of Three Diaries by Students

One can multiply such instances of false memory in the matter of books once read. The school should certainly endeavour to train the student in methods for saving them from such difficulties in after-life. For this purpose, the students should be encouraged to maintain three diaries:

1 Fact finding diary;

2 Diary for recreative books; and

3 Diary for inspirational passages.

CHAPTER MB

FACT FINDING DIARY

1 Physical Form of the Diary

Use "Find me out" type diary for fact finding work. This diary may be a bound, ruled, octavo note book with alphabetical finger tabs pasted at the edges of the leaves. As an alternative, it may have class numbers, instead of the letters of alphabet.

2 Entry in the Diary

On finding out a fact, the student should turn the page in his diary belonging to the alphabet or the class number of the fact, as the case may be. Then write the following:

1 The fact obtained;

2 The name of author, title, and the exact page in the source document;

3 The various documents consulted before getting at the correct one; and

4 The total time taken for finding out the fact.

3 Diary: Externalised Memory

A find-me-out diary will be of life-long use to the student. He need not carry all kinds of facts in his memory. He can externalise the memory, so to speak. A person accustomed to maintain and use such a find-me-out diary will always have an advantage over others in all business transactions.

4 Advantages of a Find-me-out Diary

A personal diary of this nature is not a mere copy of the reference books available in print. It is not only briefer but also exactly articulated to one's personal needs. In the particular form suggested, it is easy to put one's fingers at the correct page without unnecessary fumbling about or wasting of time on anybody challenging the fact furnished, the details in the entry helps the tracing of the fact to the original source. Moreover the date in the entry acts as a necessary warning. A change might come over the fact by efflux of time. Then there would be no point in resisting the challenge merely on the basis of that entry. The proper thing would be to look up the latest edition of the reference book concerned.

5 Need for Training the Students in the Habit of Maintaining Diary

The diary should not be crammed with all kinds of sundry entries. Surely very common facts need not crowd its pages. One need not, for example, enter in the diary about the sun rising in the east in spite of its being a fact! Apart from such a common fact, each man's profession and daily life will make certain facts as familiar to him as that of the sun rising in the east though they may be new to others. The find-me-out diary is a purely personal one. Hence the recording of specialised facts, but familiar to the owner of the diary, can be ruled out. It is only by practice that one will develop the correct flair to select the worthwhile entries for the diary. The earlier the practice is begun, the more unerring the flair will become. Therefore, there is need for training the students to maintain this diary even from their school days.

CHAPTER MC

RECREATIVE READING DIARY

1 Physical Form of the Diary

Maintenance of an appropriate diary may also be prescribed in connection with the recreative reading, done by a student during the library hour. This diary may be a ruled, bound note book of the quarto size. A page may be devoted to each book read.

2 Entry in the Diary

The following information may be written about a book in the relevant page:

1 Date of commencing the reading;

2 Date of completing the reading;

3 An estimate of the number of hours taken for completing the reading;

4 Name of the author;

5 Title;

6 Year of publication;

7 Number of pages;

8 Name of publisher;

9 New words, phrases, and turns of expression learnt from the book. (In the school age, the learning of language goes on incessantly and simultaneously, whatever be the main objective of the work being done by the student);

10 Gist of the book — in not more than three sentences;

11 A short account of striking illustration, if any; and

12 The book being a drama or a novel, the best character in it.

CHAPTER MD

INSPIRATIONAL READING DIARY

1 Spiritual Urge in Students

It is not frequently that students of school age can go in for inspirational books such as religious poetry, or first-rate literature of any form. No doubt, the exceptional few having an unusually premature spiritual urge may do so. History shows that they are indeed very exceptional. We rarely come across boy saints like Ramalingaswami of Chidambaram, or Sai Baba of Shiridi, or Sri Ramakrishna of Calcutta, or Sri Ramana Maharishi of Thiruvannamalai, or Tirujnanasambandar of Shiyali. They are, again, already saints and they are in need of hardly any external discipline to facilitate the unfoldment of their personality. They express themselves spontaneously. Rules and methods are not for them, and yet their life is far more productive and fuller than that of the average student faithfully following all the rules.

2 Entry in the Diary

The students should be introduced, while they are still young, to inspirational books of all kinds. On reading an inspirational book the student should write the following in his diary:

1 The most appealing passage

2 The reason for his being attracted by the passage; and

3 The necessary references to that book, as given in Sec MC2, for later verification and re-enjoyment.

3 Value of the Diary

This diary will not be filled up as rapidly as the other two diaries, as far as ordinary students are concerned. But, the other two diaries will get choked up or their use will be outgrown by the student, as his age advances. On the other hand, the diary for inspirational reading, having had its thin beginnings at the school age, will slowly gain in value and in volume. And ultimately, it may prove to be the only diary to be of frequent and much help, even long after leaving school.

CHAPTER ME

FACT FINDING: HOW TO MAKE IT PLEASURABLE

1 Bibliographical Game

Fact-finding can be converted into a game to make it pleasurable. Students welcome the familiar game of setting puzzles in reference questions and bibliographies, to their mutual enjoyment and edification. The arrival of new reference books or new editions of old reference books, would form the occasion for setting the students in such bibliographical games. A resourceful school librarian can work the curiosity and enthusiam of the student to a high pitch indeed in the pursuit of such games. Incidentally, this would make the students familiar with all the new features of the new arrivals, without having to learn them as a task. The puzzles may be enunciated by the students themselves. Not merely the solution of the puzzles but their enunciation also involves familiarising oneself with the reference books. Such of the findings in these games as deserve to go into the find-me-out diary may be recorded in it. The others may either be absorbed by the students in a general way, or special notes may be taken of them for temporary use, if warranted.

2 Essay Writing With Books

Another way to systematise the fact-finding urge in students is to let the students into the school library, for collecting data on any topic, and, to ask the students to weave them into an essay. The notion about essay writing as a ceremony performed under strict supervision in the examination hall should be given up. A good deal of the boredom experienced by the students in the essay hours can be avoided. On the other hand, the process of essay-writing should be made a means of enriching the awareness and the alertness of the students. To secure this, a student should be allowed to write his essay in the library. He must be given the freedom either to refresh his memory or to pick up new relevant facts, ideas, and information in any book in the library. Examination with books are allowed in our country only for middle-aged folk — in penal code, account code, and so on. Surely, it is time that the educational world examine the potentialities of essay-writing with books and adopt it on a much larger scale. In the meantime library hour should be made more purposive.

3 Annual Thesis

A generalised form of essay-writing with books is the writing of one annual thesis by each student. The subject of the thesis may be decided with due reference to the interest of the student and the resources available in the libraries within his access. It is not necessary and it is not proper even for the same subject to be prescribed to all the students. The essay-writing engages the students in the purposive use of the school library for just about one hour. But the annual thesis would engage him in purposive reading throughout the year. Moreover, this attempt will enable the student to view the help of the library in proper perspective and not to form a distorted notion of it. The student may be permitted and encouraged too to embody in this annual thesis all kinds of factors — those gathered from not merely books but also by observation, experience, and enquiry. The annual thesis will also give an opportunity to get intimate familiarity with the parts of a book and their relative values. For, each student should be asked to produce his annual thesis in the form of a regular book with a title page, contents page, preface, acknowledgment, index, and bibliography. The text should also be divided into Parts, Chapters, Sections, and Paragraphs. It should be illustrated appropriately with pictures drawn by himself or by any friend of his. In the latter case, he may be adopted as a collaborator for this purpose. The student should also be asked to maintain a diary of all the work he did in relation to his annual thesis — reading, observing, consulting and taking help from others. The purpose should be mentioned in each case.

4 Reading Habit Competition Conducted by the Madras Library Association

The Madras Library Association launched an experiment on the annual thesis under the caption "Reading Habit Competition," to encourage purposive reading. It has collected more than one hundred manuscript books written by students of the fifth and the sixth forms. They demonstrate how freely they draw out the entire personality of the student in due proportion. They disclose many of their potentialities going undetected for want of an opportunity, to do at least one piece of sustained creative work of the kind, in their school career. No doubt, this particular form of work appeals most only to the upper quartiles. Let us encourage it in them; and let us not force it on others. Occasionally, I meet some of these competitors, later in their life. They always recall this experience with some joy and satisfaction.

CHAPTER MF

RECREATIONAL READING: HOW TO MAKE IT PROFITABLE

1 Epitomising

One way of combining recreative reading with improvement of linguistic capacity is to ask the student occasionally to write an epitome of the book read by him. The school librarian and the teacher should be careful in the choice of the book for this exercise:

1 The book should be capable of being easily epitomised;

2 The student should like the subject of the book; and

3 To make the exercise profitable, the book should be intimately connected with some part of his formal course in the school.

2 Debate

Another way for making recreative reading profitable is to arrange for occasional debates round the book read. Naturally, only books read by several students can form the basis for debate. The following organisation may be adopted:

1 Prescribe a theme for debate;

2 Choose the participants from among the students — either as speakers or as observers;

3 Allow a certain time to collect pleadings on both sides of the question from the books in the school library; and

4 At the end of the prescribed time, hold the debate.

During the debate, allow the students to make use of the notes taken by them. They may be asked to cite authority for their statements; Wherever warranted they be asked to read relevant extracts from the books used by them.

3 Dramatisation

A third way for enlivening the school library work is to arrange occasionally for the dramatisation of the theme of some suitable recreative books read by a group of students. Such recreative books need not be novels or dramas of the ordinary kind. Books expounding positive sciences in the form of fiction or drama will also lend themselves to this treatment. In this way, students with histrionic quality may be encouraged to reinforce their school library work. Further, it will also have considerable public relation work value, in making other students interested in the books of the school library. This value will be considerably enhanced by using music along with dramatisation (*See* Chap LG).

CHAPTER MG

INSPIRATIONAL READING: HOW TO MAKE IT PLEASURABLE

1 Recitation

Some inspirational passages are worth memorising. They are most fitted to develop the memory. Memory is very much amenable to development in the school age. In that age we even memorise without difficulty, nonsensical passages. Rote memory is then at its best. Some use can be made of it, at least in later life, by filling it with the words of master minds. The urge to learn by-heart — very much like the urge of the infant to bite something during the teething period — should be satisfied and turned to good account. The passages for memorising may be marked by the teachers or in the case of the students belonging to the upper quartile of intellectual level, they may be asked to find them out for themselves. They must then copy them out in the appropriate diary. For this purpose, a school library should be particularly rich in anthologies of all kinds; for, students of school age will find collected works too cumbersome and baffling. The passages transferred to their diary should be memorised. Indeed an incentive to memorisation and to transcribing passages for it from inspirational books, is the desire to participate in recitation exercises. The recitation may be even in the form of a chorus. One may be shy to recite by oneself, but may gladly join a chorus. A resourceful school librarian will know the proper time for arranging such recitation.

2 Selection

A student may be deeply interested in some particular theme. He may be encouraged to explore the library and find out for himself the utterances of great minds on that theme. An occasional library hour, may be spent in this way in hunting for exquisite passages on a pet theme. Transcription of these passages in the diary would eventually build up a tiny anthology.

3 Anthology

For the exceptional student, the work of selecting passages on a pet theme in occasional library hours, may be expanded into a sustained building up of a fairly full anthology. This work may be spread over the whole year. The student may make them into a book with a title page, contents page, an index of authors, an index of titles, and a first-line index. He may also add bibliographical and biographical notes on the authors of the passages in the anthology. This piece of work, only very few can do at the school stage. But let not the exceptional student be denied the opportunity to fulfil himself in this way by putting the school library to this particular use. A suggestion may help such students to discover their aptitude for this kind of work; and then it will be a joy for them to walk into the library, and pluck the plums of their liking.

CHAPTER MH

SCHOOL LIBRARY: THE TRAINING GROUND FOR RESPONSIBLE CITIZENSHIP

1 Civics-in-Action

Civics-in-action is the development of the procedure and process of making for the greatest good of the greatest number. It promotes:

1 Public mindedness;
2 Consideration for others;
  21 Right attitudes towards obligation to public life;
  22 Avoidance of difficulties to the other members of the community;
3 Respect for the rule of queue;
4 Formation of correct habits of public and private hygiene;
5 Fire prevention; and
6 Personal manners.

2 Emphasis on Behaviour

Civics-in-action places emphasis upon behaviour rather than upon theory. All affecting the well-being of social life is considered a part of civics-in-action.

3 Role of School Library in Developing Responsible Citizenship

As the library is a social institution, guided by the most democratic principles, life in a library itself implies a civics of its own. It presents all the important factors of citizenship. Hence, the library forms a very effective laboratory for practical training in citizenship. Librarians running large and busy libraries and the clientele having not had in their boyhood the advantages of a well-organised school library, will have occasionally a very amusing time but more often a most troublesome time. Perhaps the best way for one to demonstrate the modern library being a field for civic training, is to follow the reader from the moment of his entering the library to the moment of his getting out of it, and indicating the opportunities turning up, at different points, for civic training.

CHAPTER MJ

PROMOTION OF PUBLIC-MINDEDNESS

1 Opportunity in the School Library

Public-mindedness in adults will make their life successful and useful to the community. This habit cannot be got all of a sudden. It has to be practised from the very childhood. The practice of this can be profitably started in the school days. Perhaps, the school library is one of the places to give training in this quality. The librarian should make use of this opportunity in creating public-mindedness in students.

2 School Library: Public Property

Any student is entitled to use his school library with full freedom, in spite of its being a public property. The librarian should train the students in the way of using public property profitably to himself without any handicap to the other members of the public. He will get many opportunities for demonstrating this.

3 Examples

The following are some examples of the opportunities for the school librarian to demonstrate the promotion of public-mindedness among students:

1 Careful handling of the books;

2 Keeping the library and its premises neat and tidy; and

3 Observing silence within the library.

CHAPTER MK

CONSIDERATION FOR OTHERS

1 Casual Misplacement of Book

One of the unintended difficulties brought about by readers in an open access library is the misplacement of books. A misplacement within the same shelf-plank may be unavoidable. But the placing of a book into a wrong shelf plank or bay or tier should be avoided. A book misplaced is virtually a book lost — not only for others, but also to the person doing it. On realising this, a reader will certainly respect the request of the library. A reader should be told not to replace any book taken out from the shelves. Several readers pick up a quarrel with the library staff on this point. To avoid this, the habit of not replacing books on the shelves should be created in childhood. The school librarian should demonstrate to the students the havocs created by misplacing books, denying their use to readers.

2 Deliberate Misplacement

A serious anti-social quality is found in a few readers. This is hiding a book in unexpected parts of the stack room with the sole object of depriving its use by anybody else, except by himself. Unfortunately, this criminal quality is often found among students appearing for competitive examinations — our probable future "rulers." This is a social danger. No theoretical instruction can perhaps purge our bright young readers of this unfortunate selfishness. But a healthy life in a free open access library at school may be able to prevent the setting in of such a quality. The important civic rule of the greatest good for the greatest numbers can get woven into the texture of the moral personality of our students by making them begin to live that principle even from the very first occasion of their use of the school library. The school librarian has an important role to play in this.

3 Restriction on the Number of Volumes for Home-Reading

The rule about the maximum number of volumes allowed

for home-reading at any one time, often creates resentment in readers. Every reader should realise that this Rule is intended not to inconvenience an individual, but to benefit the public in general. A library book at the house of one reader denies its use by others in that period. The Rule about the maximum number of volumes, minimises this denial. The school librarian should make the student realise this.

4 Period of Loan

41 OVER-DUE CHARGE

The Rule on the restriction of the period of loan of a book, causes much vexation in readers. Experience has shown the difficulty, if not impossibility, in enforcing this Rule without an overdue charge for its infringement. The favourite penalty is a monetary charge of so much per day for the retention of a borrowed book beyond the date allowed by Rule. The idea here is, not to make this over-due charge a source of revenue. But, it is the minimisation of the denial of that book to other readers. Further, the library tries to help the reader in every possible way to avoid paying over-due charge. The school librarian should make clear to the students the implications of the Rule, and help them in developing the habit of returning each book borrowed by them before the due date.

42 DIFFICULTY IN EDUCATING AN ADULT JUST BEGINNING TO USE A LIBRARY

The Madras University Library was thrown open to the graduates of the University in about 1925. They never had used a library before that. As a result, the restrictive clauses in the Rules irritated many of the strong-willed readers. One reader was thrown into a temper on receiving a Reminder Card. He was a good friend of mine, and yet he wrote to me, "Your methods are like that of an income tax officer. Nobody will care to use your library." I simply replied, "I cannot help doing my duty, particularly when it is for your advantage. Without this Reminder Card you might have forgotten about the book for even six months.

By then, the overedu charge might have mounted up to about Rs 12." Then he called on me and apologised for his rude letter.

5 Mutilation

Mutilation of books and other reading materials is another criminal tendency in many readers. They may do it by:

1 Tearing away some important pages for their personal use without the patience to copy them and without realising other readers being deprived of the use of these pages by the vandalism of theirs;

2 Disfiguring by writings, drawings, etc; and

3 Using as a protection from rain and sun, and even as a pillow.

These anti-social qualities are best prevented at the stage of school library.

CHAPTER ML

QUEUE SYSTEM

1 An Experience

Perhaps, the best way to begin the Rule of Queue is to narrate an actual experience. It happened on the day the Madras University Library began to function in its new buildings. The curiosity about the new arrangements made in the new building caused an unprecedented rush of readers. Our schools had not done anything in the past to familiarise our people with the Rule of Queue. The result was a most unsightly crush at the entrance. It was due to good luck that nobody sustained any injury. Within a minute, I saw this, and I posted myself at the spot. I had the unpleasant job of asking the highly educated adults and students to form a queue. The queue however was such an unknown entity that a knighted graduate of the University began to ask for the meaning of the word and later for its spelling! The queue was nearly 300 feet long. A most serious situation arose. An elderly gentleman was irritated beyond control by my request to stand in a line and await his turn to enter. "I refuse to obey you. I refuse to stand in a line." So saying, he stood aside. He had to be told on his not falling into line, his turn might not come at all till the end of the day. However mildly and however distantly this was hinted to him, he got exasperated and balled out "We are not school children to stand in a line." What a commentary on his school days! His shouting continued, "No civilised institution will make educated people like us march in a line as if we are prisoners." He yelled, "Once the Police Commissioner passed a similar stupid order and I fought it out till it was withdrawn. I am not going to allow you to treat us in this manner!" The whole queue stood aghast at this outburst of his. My heart was breaking. The queue was lengthening. I begged him to come into my room and discuss it with me privately. But, he cried out, "I am not going to enter this Library so long as we are asked to stand in a line like labourers and sepoys"; so saying he went away. Fortunately for the library he seems to have cooled down at home.

For, he turned up two days later and showed no signs of bitterness.

2 Mechanical Formation of Queue

The school library provides a good opportunity to train the student in following the Rule of Queue. On the dispersion of a class, its students come to the library in large numbers. To suggest the idea of queue the entrance to the library is made narrow. This mechanical arrangement gently makes the students to form a queue while entering the library.

3 Human Intervention

It is not possible, nor is it wise to make the entrance lane sufficiently narrow to make it impossible for anybody going ahead of the other. For there may be justifiable reasons to allow precedence to a late-comer. However, this carries with it, the risk of everybody asking for precedence. Then this will be the very negation of queue. Here the tact of the librarian alone can persuade the students to respect the rule of queue and not seek precedence for insufficient trivial reason.

4 An Automatic Help

At the end of the entrance lane is the Charged Tray. Many of the students will have to stop there for a minute to get their books discharged. This will automatically make the students respect the rule of queue.

5 Learning by Experience

This practical experience will gradually induce the students to respect the Rule of Queue both while within the school and also outside the school. In this subject theory can be of little use.

CHAPTER MM

PUBLIC AND PRIVATE HYGIENE

1 Catalogue Room

The catalogue in a modern library would be in cards. These cards would be filed in cabinets. Their handling should be such that they can last longest. This implies:

1 The readers should make their hand clean and dry before touching the cards;

2 They should on no account wet their fingers with the tips of their tongue, in order to turn the cards;

3 They should turn the cards by their side edges; and

4 They should not turn the cards by their top edges. For in due course this would make the easily visible top edges dirty.

These habits are easily formed while using a school library. They are difficult to form in later life. Some libraries have grown desperate and protected the top edges of the cards with glass-cover. Even here, it is most amusing to see the adult readers sticking their fingers against the glass and then with mild curse in their lips beginning to operate the cards by the side edge.

2 Scrap of Paper

Generally, readers stay longer in the general reading room. Hence, the hygienic and sanitary responsibilities of the readers are high while in that room. But the woeful neglect of this responsibility is visible in our big libraries today. It should be largely due not to their unwillingness but to their not having been habituated, while young, to the right mode of life in a public institution, such as a library. Any amount of telling has little effect. Therefore I adopted an extreme measure. The very moment of a reader throwing a scrap of paper on the floor of the reading room, I would go and pick it up and put it into the waste paper basket. The reader would apologise. But one such apology has seldom been found sufficient to reform himself. There are cases of my having to do so with an individual reader about 20 times. Then he had the goodness to come to my room and promise that he would never do so in future. The students should be educated, while using school library, in the use of the waste paper basket provided in the library.

3 Spitting Across the Window

Some readers in the Madras University Library, habituated to chewing tobacco, would go to the window of the reading room and spit out their red saliva, dirtying the window frames and the floor of the quadrangle outside the reading room. It was found very difficult to reclaim such people to a sense of public hygiene. The only way is to educate one while he is in his school days.

4 Excreta

A much more disgusting habit is for a reader to blow his nose on the floor of the reading room. This bad habit can be avoided only by a long process of training in civic hygiene being given to students in their school libraries.

CHAPTER MN

FIRE PREVENTION

1 Hazards of Fire Inside the Library

Fire should be kept away from explosives; like this it should be kept away from books also. Any kind of fire should not be allowed inside the library. Hence, smoking should be prohibited. The students should be told about the risk involved in smoking inside the library. Similarly at home also, books should be kept away from fire.

2 How To Control Fire

In spite of all preventive steps, there are known cases of libraries having had caught fire. Hence, a library should have fire extinguishers of some kind or other. The students should be trained in the use of fire extinguishers.

CHAPTER MP

PERSONAL MANNERS

1 Sitting on the Floor of Stack Room

One extra-ordinary anti-social conduct appearing now and then, among our readers, is in the stack room. By its very look and construction, the stack room is not a place to settle down for study. It is only a place for browsing and selecting books. The place for study is the adjoining reading room. But, now and then readers squat on the floor of the stack room and begin to read. Using the wrong place instead of using the right place is due to lack of manners. A manifestation of an extreme form of lack of manners occurred in 1940. The reader in question was a senior Professor of a College. He had been engaged by an unscrupulous publisher to do some hack-work — in fact, to prepare notes for one of the prescribed texts. One morning this reader was found actually lying on his back in one of the gangways in the stack room with a number of annotated editions littered about him. He was dictating notes to a young chap sitting on the floor by his side.

S R R.— Sir, you should not squat on the floor of the stack room with so many books spread about you.

Reader.— Why not? Where is the Rule against it?

S R R.— Where is the Rule for the reader to lie down in the stack room? Thes library Rules need not provide Rules against such wrong ways of using the stack room. It is intended for the readers to walk through and browse.

Reader.— I am not convinced about that argument.

I had ultimately to tell him that force will have to be used against him, or as an alternative to call the police for help, unless he goes to the right place to read. Then only he left.

Such bad manners can be minimised, if not eliminated if the school library trains the students in such matters.

2 Noise

Quite often many readers walk round within the library, making much noise with their feet. Gossiping within the library is also not uncommon. The sound produced by such undesirable action will disturb the serious readers very much. These kinds of unmannerly habits should be eliminated from a library. They can be eliminated most effectively at the student stage by the school library.

3 Placing a Book

Some readers place their books on the reading room tables producing much sound. This trivial bad manner among readers should be corrected while at school stage.

4 Disgusting Actions in the Reading Room

Many kinds of disguisting actions by readers may happen in the reading room. Oft occurring ones are:

1 Sleeping;

2 Sitting with feet shot up high in the air, the table acting as a prop; and

3 Dressing long hair, now and then dropping down tiny rolls of black stuff.

Any such disgusting action is due to lack of training in childhood. The school library can play an important role in educating the student-reader against any such disgusting action.

CHAPTER MQ

STUDENT'S WORK WHILE ATTENDING LIBRARY LESSONS

1 Formal Lessons

On familiarising the students with the library techniques and library habits, they should be reviewed, corrected, and clinched by occasional formal lessons. The student's work in such a lesson, conducted along traditional lines, would be to:

1 Listen with interest;
2 Follow the demonstration;
3 Take the exercises given;
4 Answer orally any questions; and
5 Write essays as and when assigned.

2 Supervised Study

21 HELP FROM LIBRARIAN

On the lesson being conducted on the plan of supervised study, the student's work is no doubt to work out the assignments honestly and at his speed. He has the liberty to take help from the school librarian, whenever needed.

22 ASSIGNMENT

A specimen of two assignments on the use of the library catalogue — one for Cycle 1 or for junior students and another for Cycle 2 or Senior students — is given hereunder.

211 *Cycle* 1

1 Name two books in the school library by Jadunath Sarkar.

2 Who wrote the *Post office*?

3 Give the call number, author and title of one book in the school library on aeroplanes.

(*Note:* In each case pick out the copy from the school library and bring it to the librarian).

212 *Cycle* 2

1 Name any two books in the school library edited by H A L Fischer.

2 Name any two books in the school library belonging to the Heritage of India Series.

3 Find out the latest book in the school library on Radio.

(*Note:* In each case, bring the book from the school library; if it is not there, bring the neighbouring book on the same subject).

3 Project Method

As in the case of supervised study, the student's work in the project method is to work out his assignment by himself on its being an individual contract or his share of it, on its being group contract. He has the freedom to take help from the teacher or from others; but according to the conditions of the contract, he must record the help so taken with the name of the helper and the stage of his taking help. A specimen project relating to the use of reference book is given in the succeeding sections.

4 Specimen Project

The student's work begins with receiving the work sheet. This briefly gives:

1 The aim of the lesson;

2 Information about the library apparatus and techniques involved to make it possible for the student to work intelligently; and

3 Groups of problems (contracts) to be solved.

The contracts run from easy to difficult. Each student undertakes as many contracts as he can manage with his ability. He first listens to the explanations given by the librarian; then he reads the instructions in the work sheet, gets his doubts cleared by the librarian; then he goes into the school library to work on his contracts. Help of the librarian can be sought at any stage in difficult situations. While the slow covers the minimum contract, the superior student keeps himself busy with additional contracts. In planning the lesson, the librarian has to pay careful attention with regard to:

1 Aim;

2 Subject matter;

3 Method of using the reference book;

4 Problems and drill work; and

5 Verification of the result.

5 Aim

The aim of the project is to learn the use of the *Essay and general literature index* — popularly known as *Essay index.*

6 What is Essay Index?

To make the resources of the library readily accessible, it is necessary to have various indexes. We have the index to each book, and the index to the whole library — namely the library catalogue. In the lesson today we study the index to one group of publications — papers in a particular group of periodicals. It is called the *Essay and general literature index.* It indexes articles and essays in several volumes of collections and miscellaneous works.

It is issued semi-annually and annually. It is also cumulated at intervals of a few years. The foundation volume covered the period 1900–1933 and indexed about 40,000 essays and articles, found in 2.144 volumes of collections and essays and miscellaneous works. The next cumulation covered 1934–1940 and indexed 23,090 essays and articles found in 1,241 volumes.

7 How to use Essay Index?

71 General Instructions

(Read the Introduction to the Foundation Volume). The titles of periodicals indexed are given at the beginning and the books indexed are given at the end.

72 ARRANGEMENT OF ENTRIES

The Index arranges in one alphabetical sequence, all author entries, subject entries, and such title entries as are likely to be remembered in correct form. They usually begin with a proper name or the whole title may form a proper name. The same information including pages, is given for all entries — that is, under author, subject, and title. Entries under the same author are arranged as follows:

1 Author's works;

2 Works about the author under the subheading "About"; and

3 Criticism of an individual work by the author under the subheading "About individual works."

(Then the work sheet gives a description of each type of entry and gives examples).

8 Problems and Drill Work

81 SEARCH BY SUBJECT TERM

Select a subject of your interest. Find out five references and write out the details in the following form.

Subject

S N	Title of Paper	Author	Title of Host Document	Vol N	Year	Page
1						
2						
3						
4						
5						

82 SEARCH BY NAME OF AUTHOR

Select an author of your interest. Find out references to three of his recent papers and write out the details in the following form:

Name of the Author

S N	Subject	Title of Paper	Title of the Host Document	Vol N	Year	Page
1						
2						
3						

83 Search by Title

Ask the school librarian for a title. Then find out its exact reference and write out the details in the following form:

Title

Subject	Author	Title of the Host Document	Vol N	Year	Page

84 Indexing

Index an essay in a recent issue of a periodical taken by the school library just as it would appear in the *Essay index*. Make such author, subject, and other entries as you consider necessary. Feature your entries as they would be in the *Essay index* Use the back of the work sheet for this.

85 Abbreviation

What do the following abbreviations stand for:

Am M	No Am
Book m	R of Rs
Cur hist	VA QR

86 BIBLIOGRAPHICAL GAME: DRILL

Two of you should work in co-operation and play a bibliographical game. Set problems mutually and compete with each other. Each has freedom to explore the book in his own way and set really baffling problems to the other. Keep a record of the score and report the scores finally to the librarian.

87 EXPOSITION

Prepare a note on the use of the *Essay index*. Describe the *Essay index* as for the use of a junior of yours.

9 Verification

On completion of the project, the student submits the result to the librarian for such correction, guidance, and help as may be found necessary.

CHAPTER MR

NOTES TAKING WORK

1 Physical form of Note-Book

Notes-taking must be practised by the student on any continuous reading. In the school stage, it may be sufficient to have a bound, ruled, quarto note-book for the purpose; later he will have to change over to the slip-method of taking notes.

2 Instructions to be Followed

The following are some simple instructions to be followed in notes-taking:

1 Read a comfortable unit through.

2 Make short notes on the main ideas in your own words, in the sequence of their occurrence in the book.

3 In case of there being minor ideas belonging to a major idea, their subordination should be shown by indention.

4 While writing down the notes, use abbreviations — standard ones whenever available or otherwise your own consistent ones.

5 Omit articles and other auxiliary words, if practical, without affecting intelligibility; use "telegraphic language."

6 Put the words of the author within quotation marks; but they should be copied only in exceptional cases — say on account of their charm or effect.

7 Repeat the above processes for each instalment of reading, till the completion of the book.

8 In the case of a book of many pages, give the page reference for each instalment noted and give the date also. The book being a short one, say a pamphlet, or a paper in a periodical, it may be sufficient to give the date only.

9 Write the call number, name of author, title, and the library.

CHAPTER MS

BIBLIOGRAPHY BUILDING WORK

1 Elementary Level Work

In the case of the younger students work connected with bibliography can only consist of observing, and appreciating and practising the use of the short bibliographies at the end of articles in encyclopaedias, at the ends of chapters of books, or at the end of the books themselves. Bibliography building can be practised only by the senior students of the school. Even they can do this work only at a very elemenatary level. At college level alone full-blown bibliographies can be attempted.

2 Instructions with regard to Bibliography Building

For school purposes, it will be sufficient to follow the simple instructions given below in building a bibliography:

1 *Sources:*

11 Library catalogue.

12 Encyclopaedias and their supplements.

13 Reader's guide to periodical literature.

14 Bibliographies included in standard books dealing with the theme.

15 Published bibliographies.

2 *Selection:*

21 See that the item selected is relevant to the theme on hand.

22 See that all aspects of the theme are covered by the selection.

23 Do not try to swell the bibliography; but evaluate the materials by reading the annotations given, if any, and include only the really helpful ones from the point of view of the language, standard, and authoritativeness.

3 *Recording*

31 Record each item selected on two separate slips using carbon paper as indicated below:

311 For a whole book:

Call Number, Name of author.
Title, in brief form.
Date, Publisher. Number of pages.

312 For part of a book:

Same as above, and in addition, a new section showing the title and pages of part dealing with the topic chosen.

313 For a periodical:

Class Number.
Name of periodical, volume, year, pages.
Author of the paper.
Title of the paper.

314 For Clippings:

Same as for books, and in addition, name of the periodical from which it is taken.

Its volume number, year, and pages.

4 *Classification*

For books and periodicals not in the school library, the call number should be constructed with the help of the school librarian, if necessary.

5 *Arrangement*

51 Arrange one set of the slips by the call numbers. This is the classified part of the Bibliography.

52 Arrange the second set of the slips by the names of authors. This is the alphabetical index to the names of authors.

53 In the alphabetical part of the bibliography, insert also the name of each class used in the classified part, followed by its class number.

PART N

HOW OF SCHOOL LIBRARY ACHIEVEMENT TEST

CHAPTER NA

FACT FINDING

1 Fact Finding Diary

11 Omission and Mistakes

The find-me-out diary maintained by each student should be scrutinised at intervals. This test is best done by the school librarian. In the first place, it must be verified whether the student has given information under all the prescribed heads under each of the facts found out by him. Rigid conformity to form, in such matters, is not easily forthcoming, one reason for it being the student not visualising now the benefits expected to accrue at some distant date from such conformity. Hence he has not got a compelling interest to maintain conformity. Partly on account of this and partly because of the impatience usually setting in, while turning through huge tomes for stray facts, the student may omit one or other detail unconsciously. He may, for example, fail to note the page number. Sometimes, boredom may set in and disturb conformity. Mistakes may also occur out of ignorance, say in the rendering of the a name of an author or in transcribing a title. The last mentioned type of mistake is likely to occur more in the earlier years.

12 Accuracy of Fact

It is also necessary to make a random test of recorded facts. The recorded fact may be faulty on its being taken out of its context or overlooking some general instructions in the reference book concerned. For example, the population column may be headed "in millions." A young student may miss it. The budget figures of governments are given usually in thousands. A beginner may overlook the instruction and copy down 200 instead of 200,000. Some systematic error may run throughout reference book and the correction to be made may be given in preface, introduction or an errata slip. Such things may occur rarely, and so the student may overlook them.

13 Route Followed

The library should also scrutinise the route followed by the student in getting at his facts and the total time taken by him. Gentle suggestions will develop in him, flair for the shortest route in quickest time.

14 Dishonesty

A small percentage of students may be found to have a tendency to dishonesty. They may cook up the diary by copying from others. There is nothing more damaging to the personality of the student than allowing such aberrations to go undetected and unchecked. A careful scrutiny coupled with some little cross examination is advisable at the time of terminal tests. Whatever faulty tendencies are detected the student must be told about them personally, and about the need to avoid them.

2 Terminal Test

The capacity of the student to find out fact quickly and accurately from ready reference books should be tested by the school librarian. In this work, the school librarian may take the help of senior student. It will not be possible for him to test all the students of the class at the same time. A more practicable plan will be to take them in small convenient groups. Each student may be given half a dozen facts to find. The questions prescribed should have relation to his diary. It is not fair to make him search for unfamiliar facts in books. These conditions will rule out giving the same questions to all students. The student may be asked to make entries as per his diary and his script may be examined in relation with his diary. The findings may be used along with the result of the scrutiny of his diary to formulate suggestions for his improvement.

3 Terminal Essay

The capacity acquired by the student in exploring the resources of the library for information on all the facets of a topic may be tested once in a term by asking him to write an essay with books in a library. The subject of the essay need not be the same for all the students. It may be chosen in relation to the field of specialisation of the student. This terminal essay is best set and examined by the specialist teacher concerned. A report of the result may be communicated to the school librarian.

4 Annual Thesis

The thesis is a free performance of the student done at home. So, special care must be taken to detect in the annual thesis, the help, if any, given by fond parents. It is not merely the student's desire to bluff, affecting the genuineness of the thesis as in the case of the student's diary, but even the parents' ambition to see their children attain high positions may vitiate the genuineness of this thesis. Internal evidence proving to be insufficient, the student may be subjected to viva voce. The honest student will stand to gain by it and he can have no grievance. But the dishonest student should not have the fraudulent element in his thesis go undetected.

This annual thesis is best scrutinised by the specialist teacher concerned. It is remembered that it is only the upper quartiles that will be enthused to write it. But, the teacher need not look upon this wcrk as an overwhelming burden. His function is to help the natural unfoldment of the student and his prize is to enjoy the fruition of that process. Any teacher should welcome the opportunity that the annual thesis offers to win that prize.

CHAPTER ND

RECREATIVE READING

1 Recreative Reading Diary

One obvious method of testing of recreative reading is to test the diary maintained by the student for the purpose. The number of books read and the time taken for a book will give a measure. The trustworthiness of this measure can be tested by a scrutiny of the linguistic and other parts of the entries under the various books read.

In scrutinising the linguistic part, it may be worth while to test the new words, phrases, and turns of expression recorded by him. He may be asked to construct sentences using them. With regard to entries relating to fiction he may be asked to expand the reasons he has recorded for singling out particular characters for noting down in his diary. The scrutiny of this diary may be done by the school librarian or the class teacher.

2 Terminal Test

Occasionally, a student may be asked to write a reproductive essay, the subject matter being chosen from the books enjoyed by him. An essay like, this, will disclose to the student, any faults of his in his reading the book. The prospect of his having to write such an essay, sometime in the term, will also make him read even the recreative books with some seriousness. The essay should be set from the book enjoyed most by the students. This means that it is not obligatory for the student to read every book thoroughly. It gives him freedom to skip over those books not gripping him. But in young men, this tendency to skip over may grow to a fault. They must develop the will to come to terms at least with some books and read them with respect and earnestness. Without some such pressure, as the terminal essay, the reading habit may degenerate into the eyes pouring through a printed page without the co-operation of the brain. In such cases reading may develop into a pathological form of relaxation. Reading of newspapers has taken such a form in the case of many. The productive essay is best set and valued by the class teacher of the student.

3 Directed Reading

The habit of purposive participative reading is not easily formed. It requires careful nursing. To this end it may be worth while to set for each student one or two books to be studied with care. The book may be selected jointly by the student and the librarian, or the teacher. Once it is selected the librarian or the teacher should himself peruse the book and set a few questions in advance for the student to write at the end of the term of the year. The questions must be so framed as to cover the entire field of the book and compel the student to read the book for writing upon it. Perhaps, this form of test will not be necessary for students already having the habit of participative reading. But it must be enforced on all students who evade responsible reading.

CHAPTER NC

INSPIRATIONAL READING

1 Inspirational Reading Diary

The inspirational reading diary of each student should be scrutinised at intervals. Verify, in particular, the remarks about his appreciation and the stimulus having had led him to each passage recorded. It will take much time for the majority of students to size up these qualities and express them. Hence, each student must be slowly accustomed in this by personal discussion while scrutinising his diary.

2 Terminal Recitation

Once in a term each student should single out from his diary, the passage appealing to him most and recite it. He needs special attention, till he recites it with fervour and understanding and is able to bring out the spirit of the passage, by the style of his rendering it. It is not rote memory that is tested here. What is tested is whether—

1 In the course of the term the student has had an intimate appreciation of at least one inspirational passage; and

2 It has become part of his bone and marrow, as it were.

3 Annual Anthology

There will be, ordinarily, very few annual anthologies in a school library. On any exceptional student producing one, it must be gone through with him. His pleasure should be shared by the school librarian. Such a step blesseth both the librarian and the student. This will be a great encouragement to the student; for, such students are very sensitive to sympathetic, participative appreciation. Reciprocally, the school librarian will himself feel considerably encouraged at the thought of his being associated with the happy unfoldment of the personality of such exceptional students.

CHAPTER ND

LIBRARY HABIT

1 Daily Conduct and Condition of the Library

An obvious and automatic test of the formation of correct library habit in a student can be found in his daily conduct:

1 Orderly ingress and exit with due respect to the queue system;

2 Inspiring silence filling the library;

3 Clean condition of the library catalogue;

4 Orderly way of handling books while browsing in the stack-room;

5 Clean state of the floor and table tops;

6 Friendly relation with the school librarian; and

7 General look of joy, alertness and satisfaction while working in the library.

In short the geniality and the charm marking the atmosphere of the library form one supreme general test of the success of the library in the formation of correct library habits.

2 Traditional Test

The traditional written and oral examinations are possible in testing the formation of certain habits. The questions in such examinations may cover:

1 The uses of the library;

2 Description of the library;

3 The benefits of the shelf-arrangement obtaining in the library;

4 The parts of the library catalogue and its functions;

5 Annotations on some of the rules of the library; and

6 The enumeration of the books most enjoyed by the student during the year with annotations.

3 Modern Test

Achievement tests fall into three broad categories:

1 True-False test;

2 Completion test; and

3 Multiple choice test.

Such tests are now being evolved for several school subjects. The school librarian must fall in line with this movement. Some sample tests are given in the succeeding sections, covering the problems relating to library habit, including the use of ready reference books.

4 True-False Test

Some of the following statements are true and some are false. For a true statement put a tick (√) mark at the left of the serial number, and for a false statement a cross (×) mark.

1 A new book must be opened more carefully than an old one.

2 A book should be pulled out of the shelf by its head band.

3 The index of a book is usually at the end.

4 The date at the bottom of the title page, always tells about the oldness of the material in the book.

5 The printer's name is given at the bottom of the title page of the book.

6 The quickest way to find information in a book is to look through the table of contents.

7 The preface explains the purpose of a book.

8 The table of contents is usually an alphabetical list of the topics treated in the book.

9 It is not important to know the name of the publisher of a book.

10 The date is of particular importance in the copy of the Ramayana.

11 Books are arranged on the shelves from left to right by their call numbers.

12 Library books are arranged on the shelf from the bottom shelf plank on to the top shelf plank.

13 The Call Number in the top of the main card is different from the index number at the end of the author card.

14 Geography books will be found in the Main Subject V of the Colon Classification.

15 The book number differentiates various books having the same class number.

16 Algebra books will be found in the Main Subject B of the Colon Classification.

17 Books on soap making will be found in the Main Subject E of the Colon Classification.

18 Unless the name of the author is known, a book cannot be found in a library catalogue.

19 Any article in the Encyclopaedia Britannica can be found from the library catalogue.

20 The library catalogue of a library is like a combination of the contents and the index of a library.

21 No book contains more than one entry in a library catalogue.

22 The initial definite and the indefinite articles are disregarded in a library catalogue.

23 All the cards of the library catalogue are arranged by call numbers.

24 A library catalogue contains cards for parts of some books.

25 Knowing the subject of a book one can find the book from the library catalogue.

26 The library catalogue has cards for the articles in periodicals.

27 The library catalogue has no cards for each poem.

28 A dictionary gives a longer account of "Aeroplane" than an encyclopaedia.

29 The Encyclopaedia Britannica has a separate volume for index and atlas.

30 The Imperial gazetteer of India gives the names of the Viceroys of India.

31 Who's who gives the life of Gopala Krishna Gokhale.

32 The Indian year book gives the names of headmasters.

33 The Dictionary of national biography does not give the names of living persons.

5 Completion Test

Fill up the blanks in the following by proper words to make the statements correct:

1 In rainy weather books should not be taken out ——

2 To find the page of a book having the name of a particular person, look up ——

3 Books are arranged in a library by their ——

4 Call Number of a book is made up of two parts, namely ——

5 Books on Indian constitution will be found in the main subject —— of the Colon Classification.

6 To find the Call Number of a book by Rabindranath Tagore, look in the library catalogue under——

7 To find the books containing some chapters on Shakespeare, look up the —— cards.

8 For lives of eminent British contemporaries look up ——

9 For areas of several countries of the world look up ——

10 For the normal exchange rate of the money of different countries look up ——

11 For the distance between two cities of India use ——

12 For the names of the chief printers in India look up ——

6 Multiple Choice Test

Underline the best completion of the following statements:

1 Pens make

(a) safe bookmarks
(b) injurious bookmarks.

2 The preface of a book is of value, because

(a) it saves the trouble of reading the book through
(b) it indicates the purpose of the book
(c) It tells us about the qualification of the author.

3 Books in the library are arranged by

(a) their subjects;
(b) their thicknesses;
(c) their weights;
(d) their years of publication.

4 A book on the history of Biology will be found in the Main Subject.

(a) G Biology
(b) V History

of the Colon Classification.

5 Shakespeare's Henry VI will be found in the Class

(a) History
(b) Poetry
(c) Drama

6 In the space before the name of the subject write its class number taking it from among the class numbers given in the second column.

Subject		*Class numbers to be matched*
Analytical Chemistry	..	T,2
Evolution	..	C-4;2
Kalidasa	..	E-3
Tamil Phonetics	..	P,31;1
Thermometry	..	..
Travels in India	..	U-8;2
Secondary Education	..	..

7 To find out quickly if Rabindranath Tagore's *Post office* is in the library, look up the catalogue under

(a) Rabindranath
(b) Tagore

(c) Post
(d) Office

8 To find out all the books of the library wholly or partly dealing with the *Merchant of Venice*, I shall

(a) Ask the Librarian;
(b) Ask the teacher in English;
(c) Look up the library catalogue under 'Merchant';
(d) Look up the library catalogue under the Class number for *Merchant of Venice*.

9 For the life of Mahatma Gandhi consult

(a) Imperial gazetteer of India;
(b) Dictionary of national biography·
(c) Who's who.

10 For the value of the imports and exports of India in 1942, consult

(a) The Encyclopaedia Britannica;
(b) The Statesman's yearbook;
(c) An atlas of India.

11 For the names of the Vice-Chancellors of the Universities of India look up

(a) The Encyclopaedia Britannica
(b) Who's who in India
(c) The Industrial year book of India
(d) The Indian year book.

12 For the festivals of the chief South Indian temples look up

(a) Imperial gazetteer of India
(b) The Indian year book
(c) The Tamil almanac for the year.

CHAPTER NE

NOTES-TAKING

1 Information to be Tested

The capacity in notes-taking may be measured by a scrutiny of the notes taken during term-time. While doing this, the following should be examined:

1 Quality;

2 Relevance;

3 Consistent use of abbreviations;

4 Proportion of author's words used; and

5 Details of bibliographic information.

2 Use of the Notes by the Student

The note-book should be tallied with the recreative reading diary. This will disclose the proportion and the nature of the books being included in the notes. Ask the student about the notes having been actually used by him while writing. Examine the concerned essay with the notes. Wherever necessary give advice to the student.

3 Test Paper

A practical test paper may be givent o each class once in a term. The answer paper should be corrected with the student.

CHAPTER NF

BIBLIOGRAPHY BUILDING

1 Subject for Bibliography

Once in a term, a theme may be set for the compilation of a bibliography. The student should be asked to work it out in a specified period — say within a week. To prevent the students influencing one another, different themes will have to be given to several students. This will also satisfy the desirable condition of the theme for each student lying within the field of his interests.

2 Opportunity for Improvement

After the performance, each student should be given an oral test. This will give an opportunity to know the way of the working of the mind of the student. Another profitable method will be to ask the students to scrutinise each other's performance and offer suggestions for improvement. An intimate discussion like this between equals will give them more freedom to see the possible variations in the building of a bibliography.

PART P/R

PRESENT DIFFICULTIES

PART P

PRESENT DIFFICULTY: BOOK FAMINE

CHAPTER PA

MEDIUM OF EXPRESSION

1 A Wrong Belief

There are some not conceding to the absence of children's books. They usually have in mind, the plentiful existence of children's books in English. But they forget the inability of children to take with any avidity to books in a foreign medium. Even some Indians, as adults, being able to read in English with ease, forget the experience and handicaps of their childhood and fondly believe about books in English being capable of satisfying all the needs of Indian children. But, "The toad beneath the harrow knows Exactly where each pin point goes."

2 Need for Examining the Problem of Medium of Expression

All except the few in the uppermost centiles — the gifted few capable of triumphing over obstacles of any kind — refuse to have anything to do with books in English. A book in the foreign medium, forcedly lent to a student, will be returned on the due date, without having been thumbed. This leads some teachers to blame the student as "ne'er-do-well." But they ought to probe deeper before making such pronouncements. The educational officers too should go beyond passing laconic remarks against the heading "school library work" and trace the root-cause of the unpopularity of library work. On their being so they cannot miss this stumbling block of the medium of expression.

3 Havoc of Foreign Medium and the Upper Centiles in the Intellectual Scale

The havoc of foreign medium is far-reaching. Here is a common remark: "There has been very little creative work in India during the last one hundred years." How far this remark is traceable to the upper centiles of the people of India having begun to learn and think through and in a foreign tongue. It has been said: "Men who can speak a number of different tongues are notorious for having little to say in any of them" (28)

Ballard agrees with this view. For he writes:

"How fares the child who is bilingual from the first? An investigation carried out in Wales a few years ago caused much perturbation because it seemed to indicate that to learn two languages concurrently in early childhood retards mental development (8).

"Thought and inner speech are so closely interwoven that they grow and decay together. Hence we cannot cultivate the one without cultivating the other. And training in the use of the mother-tongue—the tongue in which a child thinks and dreams — becomes the first essential of schooling and the first instrument of culture."

4 Mother-Tongue

The havoc of a foreign medium has not only contributed to the stifling of creative thinking of the upper centiles but it has also acted as a barrier to the flow of worthwhile current thought from the upper centiles to the lower quartiles of the community. For "There is no path to the heart save through the mother-tongue. The mother-tongue! that in which mother croons lullabies over the cradle, that in which the infant learns to lisp, that in which he first learns to play at his mother's knee, that in which he jokes and plays with his fellows, that in which the youth whispers words of love into his sweetheart's ears, that which enters into all the most sacred memories of a man's life, the mother-tongue — the music of the heart and home...it is the key which unlocks the door of a people's heart" (36).

Surely our teachers and educational officers should realise the full force of this observation of Macleod. It is unfair to turn our school student into a library of books largely in foreign languages. The overlooking of this fact by those having power, makes the progress and popularity of school library work so doubtful today in our land.

5 The Saddest Tragedy

Macleod paints the problem of foreign medium and the suppression of the mother-tongue even in a more lurid light as follows: "The last tragedy for broken nations is not the loss of power and distinction, nor even the loss of that independence which is so vital to the commonweal. It is not perhaps even the loss of the country, though there is no harder thing than to see the smoke of the stranger, or to hear upon the wind the forlorn business of the going of those who are dispossessed and the coming of those new in possession. The last tragedy, and the saddest, is when the treasured language dies slowly" (37).

We should not blame our students for their reacting unsatisfactorily to our school libraries filled mostly with books in an alien tongue.

Macleod goes further and almost frames a charge: "The whole tendency in our modern days is for the stronger nations, such as Britain, France and the United States, to overwhelm the weaker, to annihilate their culture, to swamp their language. This makes not for the enrichment but for the impoverishment of humanity. Losing its native speech, a people loses its continuity with the past and sinks to intellectual helotry" (38).

6 India's Responsibility

In fairness to the students, the handicap of language must be removed without any hesitation or delay whatever. Neither the Department of Education, nor the world of teachers nor the community at large, should rest on its oars until the students of Indian schools get their birthright in the matter of books in mother-tongue, and are put on a par with their American, European and Japanese contemporaries. They should have, in their mother-tongue, plenty of books of all kinds — inspirational, recreative, and informative books including reference books on all subjects.

7 Renascence and the Ray of Hope

The political independence, of the setting in of modern renascence have brought a ray of hope, into the field of children's books in India. My family and myself had been living in Zurich from June 1954 to February 1957. Before we left India there was no sign of anybody thinking of producing children's books in Indian languages. But on our return home in 1957, we found an agreeable change under the leadership of Ala Valliappa and Tambi Srinivasan. The former had voluntarily begun to write children's books in Tamil even early as 1945, when he was only 23 years old. In 1957, he called on me with a complete collection of about 250 children's books in Tamil. I had not known him before. But he seems to have become *persona grata* among the children. As he was coming up the stairs, the children in the house rushed to him announcing "Valliappa is coming with a bundle of books." They referred to him as "their author." At the request of Valliappa, I analysed the bundle of books he had brought according to subjects and according to standards. Fiction carried the first place, with 70 books. Current thought had 27 books for its share. The remaining 25 positive subjects shared among themselves about 36 books. These were not rehashes of adult books as it used to be earlier. They were all specially written for children. Today the number of children's books produced in a year has been steadily increasing. As many as 40,000 copies of such books are said to be sold out. This is indeed a good sign. This is not a forced production or sale. This is naturally the result of the great social changes occurring in India today.

CHAPTER PB

CHOICE OF WORDS

Mono-Syllabic Words

Next to the imperative need for the mother-tongue to be the medium o children's books, comes the choice of words — the very bricks out of which the narrative structure of books is built A few generations ago, an opinion was in vogue: "students" books should be built largely, if not wholly, of monosyllabic words. Refractory words, without monosyllabic equivalents, were even camouflaged monosyllabic with a profusion of hyphenations. Many masterpieces such as Robinson Crusoe and Aesop's Fables, so dear to a student's heart, were mercilessly mangled and beaten so as to fit into the monosyllabic dress, even though the charm of the originals fled away in the process. I still remember the painful surprise met by me on a young cousin of mine fleeing away from my home, on my beginning to read with him and enforce on him the monosyllabic Robinson Crusoe, with all the faith, the enthusiasm of one having had just emerged from the Teachers' College fully possessed of the mania for monosyllables. The children are scared away not by the length, but by the unfamiliarity of the word and the idea behind it. They handle the polysyllabic word 'aeroplane' with greater ease and willingness than they would the monosyllabic word 'axe.' They brave the polysyllabic word 'elephant' with greater cheer and boldness than they would the monosyllabic word 'nag.' "Children are best started on books with words of one syllable and then taken in succession through books having words of two three etc, syllables" is a wrong belief. The authors of students' books should avoid the pitfall of such an imagination.

2 Basic Words

The new cult of "Basic Words" is another danger to be avoided by the authors of students' books. Restriction to a few basic words is in its proper place in books written in the mother-tongue for students. The authors o students' books need not be influenced by the fear of the load of vocabulary. They have to be guided only by the Canon of Currency. Students have already learnt half their vocabulary before they are ten. They would have acquired before leaving school, nearly three-fourths of the words they would ever learn. All this, they learn by association and sheer imitation. Books usually add only a small percentage to their vocabulary. According to Ballard, "Between the ages of eight and fourteen, he increases his store of understood words at the rate of 900 words per annum. That is to say, the ordinary child learns the meanings of two or three new words every day" (6).

3 Vocabulary at Different Mental Levels

Here is a detailed analysis on the vocabulary at different mental levels (72):

Years		No. of words
8	..	3,600
10	..	5,400
12	..	7,200
14	..	9,000
Average Adult	..	11,700
Superior Adult	..	13,500

Ballard presents the subject from another angle in the passage:

"Here's an interesting question: How many words pass through a man's head during the day? How many words does he speak, hear, read and think of during the fifteen hours, when he is presumed to be awake? Mr. Gustav Spiller gives, 50,000 as the probable answer. This figure brings home to us the amazing amount of practice a person gets in acquiring and maintaining the mother-tongue. Its staple words and forms and phrases are beaten into the brain by countless repetitions. It is easier for the right hand to forget its cunning than for the tongue to forget the habits it has formed in early childhood and has been deepening and hardening ever since" (7).

CHAPTER PC

SENTENCE AND STYLE

1 Style and Rhythm in Students' Books

No doubt, words form the basis of the structure of a book. But, its attractiveness depends upon the way of getting—

1 Words linked up to form Sentences;

2 Sentences linked up to form Paragraphs;

3 Paragraphs linked up to form Sections;

4 Sections linked up to form Chapters;

5 Chapters linked up to form Parts; and

6 Parts linked up to form the Whole Book.

This linking up depends upon something tangible — the style, the rhythm, and the different levels of the Principle of Unity of Idea (42).

2 Aesthetics in Students' Books

There is necessity for the play of aesthetics in students' books. Its play must be subtle. It must be achieved through short, simple sentences. Further, it must have the quality of striking to memory.

3 Born Author

The author of a student's book should be a specially gifted person. Though there is room for improvement by practice and training, he is really born and not made. Perhaps, every linguistic community has within it the necessary number of born authors of students' books. But, they go undetected and unused at present. The reasons for this may be:

1 We have very few childrens' librarians in India; and

2 Our school libraries have not realised the imperative need for feeding our students with proper books in the mother-tongue.

The moment the school libraries press their demand, the now dormant natural-born-authors will come forward.

CHAPTER PD

FUTILITY OF TRANSLATION AND ADAPTATION

1 Student's Book: True to the Environment

There are some people conceding about the language of student's books being the mother-tongue. But, according to them, the present book famine could be removed, by translating books written for the students in other latitudes. Perhaps, famine in adult's books could be met by translations. For, adults have already learnt to replace the use of primary senses largely by intellect. But, in students, abstract thinking and intellectual pursuit are still in the formative stage. Students can enjoy only a book starting with and keeping close to the experiences verifiable by primary senses and, now and again, adding a dash of alien stuff so as to accustom them to intellectual pursuits by slow degrees. The result: The experiential background be true to their environment.

Remember Jasperson's boy

"On hearing that his father had seen the king, enquired 'Has he a head at both ends?' His king came from the realms of playing cards!" (5).

The Italian pictured by Samuel Butler in the following words is an exception rather than the rule: "I once asked a young Italian, who professed to have a considerable knowledge of English literature, which of all our poems pleased him best. He replied without a moment's hesitation:

> 'Hey diddle diddle, the cat and the fiddle;
> The cow jumped over the moon.
> The little dog laughed to see such sport,
> And the dish ran away with the spoon.'

He said, this was better than anything Italian. They had Dante and Tasso, and ever so many more great poets; but they had nothing comparable to 'Hey diddle diddle' nor had he been able to conceive how any one could have written it. Did I know the author's name, and had we given him a statue? On this I told him of—

The young lade of Harrow

Who would go to church in a barrow

and whatever rhyming nonsense I could call to mind, but it was no use; all of these things had an element of reality that robbed them of half their charm, whereas 'Hey diddle diddle' had nothing in it that could conceivably concern him" (15).

Mrs. Mitchel has pointed out that children are interested in those stories which make contacts with their own experience (41).

2 Impact of Change in Environment

It is well-known that latitude makes a world of difference in the environment. How can Indian students read with interest, books having for their background:

1 Totally unequal days and nights;

2 The feast of spring flowers closely following the black winter of leafless trees;

3 Skating, snow balls and snow men;

4 Birds, insects, fruits and vegetables quite unfamiliar in their latitudes; and

5 Cultural, social and national festivals quite alien to them. It is within the province of recreative and informative books to smuggle carefully distributed doses of alien stuff amidst heaps of familiar ones to widen the field of interest of the students. But, it would be futile to fill the entire background of the book with things alien and novel. Salt is good, but too much salt makes the porridge uneatable. Translations of books, written for the students in other climes and latitudes, are likely to be ignored by Indian students.

3 Futility of Adaptations

Another faulty way of producing students' books is to abbreviate and adapt adults' books. Adult psychology is different from child psychology, and adult experience is different from child expersence. Several generations of students have been wronged by thrusting down their mind mangled versions of adults' books. Countries such as UK and USA have learnt the futility of this. Our country is still to realise this.

CHAPTER PE

NEED FOR INDIGENOUS BOOKS FOR STUDENTS

1 Right Person to Write Student's Book

Normally, only persons born and bred up on the soil of India, can write, for the use of Indian students, books charged with the right kind of experiential background. Only they can make our students' books register well, so to speak, with the expe Ince of the students, with the aid of their primary and other apperception of thesis. Only they will have the flair to determine the correct proportion of information about other latitudes, cultures, and nations to be included in our students' books. This holds good in the case of all classes of books, be they inspirational, recreative or informative.

2 Qualities Needed for an Author of Student's Book

Learning the writing of students' books in the hands of the narrow, bigoted, traditionalist type of persons, is injurious. The author of our students' book should be an Indian. He should be a widely read and widely travelled person. He should be capable of describing worthwhile foreign things with sympathy and colour, rather than in the manner of Miss Mayo's *Mother India.* His writings should be capable of enriching our cultural heritage rather than decrying it or in-breeding it.

CHAPTER PF

HISTORY OF STUDENTS' BOOKS IN ENGLISH

1 Age of Dry-as-Dust Didacticism (1475–1760)

While Caxton was printing Aesop's Fables and stories of Troy for the adults, he was bringing out solemn treatise, on conduct for students. The earliest known students' book is Babee's book or a little report of how young people should behave (1475). On the other side of the Atlantic the famous New England primer, published in 1691, introduced the alphabet in couplets and triplets such as:

In Adam's fall
We sinned all.
** ** **
Zaccheus he
Did clim a tree
His Lord to see.

It included also the Lord's Prayer, the Creed and the catechism and ended with a dialogue between Christ, a Youth, and the Devil.

2 Age of Sugar-coated Didacticism (1760–1800)

According to John Locke (35) students were entitled to have interest of their own, they should be treated as rational creatures, and they should be taught how to think and not what to think. One result of its influence was to dilute the dedactic stuff of the previous age with an element of fable and attempt to reach students through that imagination. During this age the first outstanding publisher of students' books appeared in England. He was John Newbery (1713–1767), a bookseller of St. Paul's Church Yard. He employed men of eminence of his time like Oliver Goldsmith and Samuel Johnson in writing books for students. His Goddy two shows, published in 1765, is commonly ascribed to Goldsmith. Its introduction was said to contain an exact picture of the Deserted Village. An earlier book of Newbery, Mother

Goose's melody published in 1760, was collection of nonsense verses. In this also it is likely that Goldsmith had some part. Newbery was the first to publish books to give joy to students. He should have put up the sign board 'Juvenile Library' in the place of honour over his door. Issac Watts, Ann and Jane Taylor, Darton and Harvey followed with their own didactic books for students. The latter's original poems for infant minds strove through poems like Meddlesome Matty, Heedless, Eliza, and Lucy the Chatterbox to emphasise by contrast the virtues to be cultivated by students. Maria Edgeworth is perhaps an outstanding writer of this age. Her Parent's assistant and Moral tales were the first to give students' stories with plots having both adults and children characterised.

William Blake's Songs of Innocence and Charles and Mary Lamb's Mrs Leicester's school, though they fall towards the end of this period, really belong in spirit to the next period.

3 Age of Imagination (1800–1900)

In this period the didactic import was definitely dropped and pure joy was the aim. Some old stories like Robinson Crusoe (1714) and Gulliver's travels (1726) originally written for the enjoyment of adults were now republished for students. So also Fairy tales such as Anderson's tales, Arabian nights and Aesop's Fables published in the first epoch for adults — now came to be republished for students. Charles Kingsley retold the beautiful Greek stories for students. Dickens, Scott, and Thackeray wrote special stories for students. John Ruskin contributed his King of the golden river. E H Mortineau struck new ground by giving a picture of a foreign culture — Facts on the flord. Her Crafton Boys and Thomas Hughes' Tom Brown's Schooldays pictured school life. Alice in Wonderland is another masterpiece of the period.

4 Age of Experience

Only during the turn of the present century students' books came to be written on a realistic basis occupying the whole spectrum of their interest. Anatole France pleaded: "Little things though they be, they are already possessed by their hunger for knowledge which makes the student and the poet. They long for someone to lay bear the secrets of the Universe, the hidden mystic Universe" (23).

Mitchel is even more emphatic: "It is the blind eye of the adult that finds the familiar uninteresting. The attempt to amuse children by presenting them with the strange and the unreal is the unhappy result of the adult blindness. Children do not find the unusual piquant until they are firmly acquainted with the usual; they do not find the preposterous humorous until they have intimate knowledge of ordinary behaviour. They do not get the point of alien environments until they are securely oriented in their own. Too often we take excitement for genuine interest and give the children stimulus instead of food. The fairy stories delight the sophisticated adult. They excite and confuse the child."

The present age has therefore ignored the didacticism of the earlier ages and pierced through the boundaries set by the nineteenth century to the field of students' books. Today there is no limit to the range covered by students' books except that purely intellectual stuff is naturally excluded. Realism is the keynote of the students' books of today. Subject to this limitation, every subject is covered; the sky, the sea, the earth and its wonders, flowers, ferns and fungi, animal world, birds, butterflies and insects, invention, engineering, aviation, travel and adventure, mountaineering, exploration, history, myths, legends and folk tales, customs and manners, games and amusements, fine arts, occupation and handicrafts, health and character, and so on.

This wave of realism has reached its most forward form today in the USSR. According to Klaus Mehnert's *Youth in Soviet Russia,* the young Russians are furnished with books in which they find themselves. By providing books directly concerned with the students' interests, Russian authors are giving a stimulus to the student's intellectual life to express itself in action instead of encouraging it to waste its creative abilities in unpractical day-dreams. At first these books erred by being too materialistic and by a lack of humour and yet they point a finger towards a closer association of students' interests and students' books and they aim at a type dealing intellegently with the world around the students.

5 A New Profession

Today authorship of students' books is regarded as a profession — a specialist profession. Every effort is being made to encourage the stabilising of this profession. In 1922 the USA founded a medal to be awarded each year to the best students' book written in the year. It is rightly called after Newbery, the first to publish books designed to give joy to students.

CHAPTER PG

BOOK INDUSTRY IN INDIA

1 Publishing

For a long number of years publishing in India had been largely concentrating its attention on school textbooks so far as books for students go. There is hardly any publisher specialising in students' books of a general nature. The shyness of the publisher in entering the field of students' books is largely traceable to the operation of the law of supply and demand having not yet reached dimensions attracting enterprising publishers. A situation like this calls for State action. A similar situation prevailed with regard to school textbooks about a century ago. Thus, the State entered the field, cut the vicious circle of supply and demand and withdrew, in favour of the publishing trade, on the latter finding it paying to enter the field. Something similar should now be done by the State in regard to students' books other than textbooks.

2 Marketing

There is a great difficulty in marketing the few indegenous books for students. Marketing of books in Indian school is too much vitiated by the control of laymen forming the management. Their criterion in book selection is, not infrequently, expressible only in terms of the political influence of the bookseller. The intrinsic value of the books concerned is thrown into the background. The needs of the students seldom reach decisive status. This is illustrated by the following experience.

Some years ago the Director of Public Instruction of a State found that the so-called non-detailed textbooks set for the Secondary School Leaving Certificate course usually degenerated into textbooks done with negligence. Hence he decided that the reading habit, the objective of the non-detailed textbooks, could be better fostered by converting the "non-detailed hours" into "library hours." Orders were passed accordingly. But the very next moment a dark cloud came over the sky. It was created by the influential publishers of the State. One publication of each of them had been all along prescribed for non-detailed study. This ensured for them a sale of about 20,000 copies. Little did the Director imagine what a hornets' nest he was disturbing. The clouds of protest hemmed him in on all sides. He had no alternative but to surrender. The surrender took the form of a compromise. For the library hours, the school should get ten copies of four different books for each class! The library work of the student should be largely centred on these volumes! It goes without saying that this influence by the business world made the library hour something painful and forced rather than something pleasurable. No wonder if the fate of non-detailed books threatens to follow the library hour in schools.

3 Children's Authors Association

In 1950, a children's authors association was formed in Tamil Nadu, at the residence of Sri Palaniappa Chettiar. It has got the patronage of Sri Vaithanna and of the Government. Several publishers have begun to specialise in the stimulation and publication of attractive books for children in Tamil. All these spontaneous developments fill our heart with hope.

CHAPTER PH

A TENTATIVE SOLUTION

1 A Proposal to State Teachers' Association

In the absence of State effort to set on foot the normal play of the law of supply and demand in the matter of students' books and in the face of the indifference, if not of the positive antagonism of the book trade, one is forced to think of other agencies to ward off the book famine. In this connection the potentiality of the State Teachers' Unions such as the South India Teachers' Union comes to one's mind. To such a body I want to put a concrete proposal — a proposal likely to ward off the present book famine in five years. No doubt such efficient work will entail sacrifice. Without sacrifice, in some form or another, no good is ever done. Without sacrifice of some form of another nos ubstantial change can ever be effected. But in the scheme I propose, the sacrifice will not become incident on one or two individuals but it will be spread over the entire teaching profession in a manner that the share of sacrifice falling to each teacher, would be something bearable.

2 A Teachers' Association to Write out One Book

Let us take that on an average, there are about 600 schools in a Constituent State, with about 600 Teachers' Associations. Each Teachers' Association should give annually to the State Association, the manuscript of one book written by its members. For this, the State Association should provide 600 topics each year, covering the entire field of subjects.

It should also set the necessary bibliographical standard to be observed, such as, the number of pages, the number of illustrations, and the kind of index. The State Association should print these manuscripts in attractive style, in bold types, in large thick paper, and bind them in an attractive way, each volume being a sumptuous and inviting one.

3 Finance

An edition of five hundred copies will easily pay its own cost. On each of the 500 schools guaranteeing the purchase of one copy of each of the books produced by the State Association each year, the problems of finance will be solved by itself. The teaching profession and the managements, should discipline themselves to carry out this programme for five years. Then the market will have 3,000 books written specially for the students of the State in question. Then the book famine will disappear and the creation of the reading habit will become quite an easy matter.

4 Organisation of the Work

The book may be written by the Association on a co-operative basis. The Headmaster may plan the whole thing carefully so that each teacher contributes his best to the book. One teacher may be capable of giving illustrations. A few others can supply the matter for the different chapters. Somebody having the power of expression might revise the manuscript and clothe it in a uniform style suited to the students' level. Some teachers might merely collect the data necessary for these writing out the matter. Some others may read the proof. At least some of the monthly meetings of the Teachers' Association might be converted into business meetings; instead of merely listening to some vague talk, they might appraise the work done over the manuscript and, by a careful discussion and if necessary by experimenting with students, try to improve the manuscript and make it as effective as possible.

5 Wish

The enterprising secretaries of each of the State Teachers' Associations should take up the suggestion as early as possible. Then, within a few years, each of our Constituent States will be self-sufficient in students' books. This is my wish.

PART Q

PRESENT DIFFICULTY: MANAGERIAL APATHY

CHAPTER QA

TECHNICAL STAFF

1 Strength and Status

Library staff forms a necessary important constituent of a school library (*See* Chap HE). The management of our schools have yet to be educated on this point; nay, even the Departments of Education have to revise their ideas in the matter. So long as the grant-in-aid code and the associated prescription of qualification, pay and status continue to be what they are even the few managements intellectually satisfying themselves with the case for a technical staff of the right kind, plead inability to act and give effect to their intellectual convictions. Educational matters are rigidly centralised practically in each Constituent State of India. So the first step in the solution of difficulties about the employment of technical staff in school libraries should be taken up by the Government. The grant-in-aid code and the associated orders should be so amended as to make it compulsory for every school to employ as full-timed librarians graduates holding Degrees in Library Science and in Education. Their scale of salary should be similar to that of the graduate teachers holding a Degree in Education. They should be given the same status and privileges as any other teacher of similar standing. They should not be given any work other than the administration of the school library, the conducting of library classes, and the technical and reference service germane to library work.

2 Training

Is there adequate provision in India for training libraries to the necessary number? The first library school in India was founded by the Madras Library Association in 1929. The school is now being conducted by the University of Madras, by a full-timed staff of four, with the Sarada Ranganathan Professor in Library Science as its Head. This Professorship was founded in 1957 at the suggestion of Mrs Ranganathan. During the last ten years there has been a great increase in the number of such schools.

At present in India, there are about 30 library schools at University level, conducting Diploma or Degree Courses in Library Science. So there will not be any scarcity of trained personnel.

3 Documents on Library Techniques

The next problem connected with the technical staff is the provision for feeding them with up-to-date technical documents. Each school should vote an adequate sum for books and periodicals on library science. There is plenty of American and English staff available. Thanks to the far-sighted policy of the Madras Library Association, India has now its own literature on practically almost all aspects of library science. The number of books alone exceeds 100; and the number of papers exceeds 1,000. The Sarada Ranganathan Endowment for Library Science founded in 1961, also has been promoting the publication of advanced books on Library Science. Further, there are about 40 periodicals on Library Science being published from India (58). So, there is no scarcity of documents on Library Science and Service.

CHAPTER QB

SPACE AND EQUIPMENT

1 Library and Old School Buildings

In Chap JB, the details of the space and equipment required for a school library have been given. But it is difficult to provide for them in an ideal way in most of the older school buildings. For, those buildings had been designed after a model not contemplating the Library functioning as the heart of the school. In such a case, it is best to build the library as an annexe designed as a library rather than adapt any existing class room for library purpose.

2 Library and New School Building

A more important thing is to prevent the difficulty being perpetuated in the new school buildings. To this end, the Department of Education should amend the standard specifications for schools by revising the dimension, the position, the orientation, the distribution of windows and doors, and other details in conformity with the modern requirements of school libraries. So also fresh specifications should be put on the approved list for readers' tables, chairs, and other library furniture and equipment. Lastly, managements should set their heart to the work of providing the school library with the latest equipment.

CHAPTER QC

FINANCE

1 Financial Problems

Lastly we come to finance — many a pious hope gets shattered here. Most of the difficulties obstructing the development and functioning of school libraries along right lines ultimately cluster round finance. To fit up the library we want money; to maintain an adequate technical staff we want money; and to buy books we want money.

2 Source of Finance

The management should therefore be prepared to spend money on the school library. The government also should give help. The suggestion of forming 20 schools in mutual neighbourhood into a coordinating and cooperating unit will go a long way in giving relief (*See* Chap HH).

PART R

PRESENT DIFFICULTY: PEDAGOGICAL INERTIA

CHAPTER RA

ROLE OF STATE GOVERNMENT

1 Help Through Various Ways

The State Government of each Constituent State should help the Department of Education, or the University and the Training Colleges. The Department of Education should make or cause to be made periodical surveys of the library provision in the schools — the building, the furniture, the books, the periodicals, the adequacy and the variety of the service rendered and the extent of their use. It should be part of the duty of its inspecting officers to report on these from year to year.

2 Quinquennial Survey

At least once in five years, the services of the Department of Libraries, if there be one, or otherwise of librarians of repute and experience, should be requisitioned to make a quinquennial survey and report on matters calling for improvement/rectification. *Libraries in secondary school, a report to the Trust* (1936) by a Committee appointed by the Carnegie United Kingdom Trust is an example. The *School library yearbook* by the Education Committee of the American Library Association first brought out in 1927 is an annual functioning in that way.

3 Refresher Course to Teachers

The Universities of each Constitutent State should arrange for refresher courses for the benefit of school teachers — to have their reorientation in the methods of teaching standard-centred and library-centred instead of the old curriculum-centred textbook-centred way. Such refresher courses were given under the auspices of the Madras Library Association (*See* Chap AD3). The training colleges should include in their curriculum — and here they will require the sanction of universities in the form of additions to the regulations prescribing the course of study — a stimulating course on school library work extending at least over twenty hours. The aim of this course is not to teach the teachers under training library science. It is only to establish the teachers in a viewpoint showing the intimate correlation existing between their period-to-period work in the class room and their methods of teaching on the one hand and the school library hour and the inevitable dependence of the students on the use of libraries on their growing into adulthood. This theoretical course must be followed up by instruction by their several professors of education in using the library in various types of teaching and in relation to various kinds of subject-matter. This in its turn should be lived actually by the students under training in their practice-teaching. A very feeble attempt had been repeatedly made in Madras along these lines by the Teachers' College inviting me to give the theoretical course in four consecutive years. With change of Principal this was lost sight of. In a later year the Training College for Women arranged for a similar course. But the other two items — incorporation in the lectures of the professors of education of the methods of implementing the ideas and of giving practice in conducting classes on these lines — do not seem to have been attempted.

CHAPTER RB

ROLE OF MANAGEMENT

1 Participation in Quinquennial Survey

In their turn the managements should act in a participative manner. They should take an intelligent interest in the quinquennial surveys and reports by expert visitors and come forward to implement the finally approved recommendations.

2 Encouragement of Participation in Refresher Courses

The inertia of the teaching profession should not cling to managerial coldness, indifference or discouragement as its last pillar. The management should also encourage the staff to benefit by the refresher courses by giving special study leave and financial facilities for the purpose.

3 No Interference with the Changes Made in Teaching Method

To integrate the school library as an organic part of the life of the school, the teachers will have the necessity of making some modifications in the methods of teaching. The Management should abstain from interfering with such modifications. The teacher and the librarian should be given the necessary freedom to modify the methods of teaching in mutual consultation in the light of the "New Education."

CHAPTER RC

ROLE OF TEACHERS' ASSOCIATION

1 Inner Change in Teachers' Outlook

The help coming from the Government and managements though necessary is by no means sufficient. Its effect needs completion by an inner change in the teachers' outlook. The Teachers' Associations should try to bring out such an inner change. Their periodical conference should provide a platform to discuss the intimate relation between school library work and class room work.

2 School Libraries' Section of the American Library Association

In America, the School Libraries' Section of the annual conference of the Americal Library Association provides such a platform in certain years. The following are some of the topics brought up for discussion in one such year (1):

1 The importance of the teacher inthe school library situation;

2 The teacher and the library;

3 Co-operation between the class in "Methods of teaching the use of the library" and other methods—classes in the Teachers' College;

4 Recognising obstacles in the teacher-library co-operation in the secondary school; and

5 Tendencies and trends in teacher-librarian co-operation.

3 Melting away the Pedagogical Inertia

The periodicals of the Teachers' Associations, should set apart some pages for exchange of views and for the record of creative ideas on this topic. The teaching profession in UK has a special organ — *The school library review*, the first number appeared in the spring of 1936. *The Wilson library bulletin* of the USA is usually rich in articles calculated to give a library-orientation to the teaching profession. *The South Indian teacher* and the *Educational review* of Madras have had occasional articles on the subject. But, such articles should form a regular feature of such a periodical. Perhaps it is too early in our country today to have an independent periodical for the purpose.

PART S/Y

LIBRARY TECHNIQUES

PART S

FIVE LAWS OF LIBRARY SCIENCE

CHAPTER SA

FIVE LAWS OF LIBRARY SCIENCE: THE FOUNDATION OF LIBRARY WORK

1 Schematic Representation

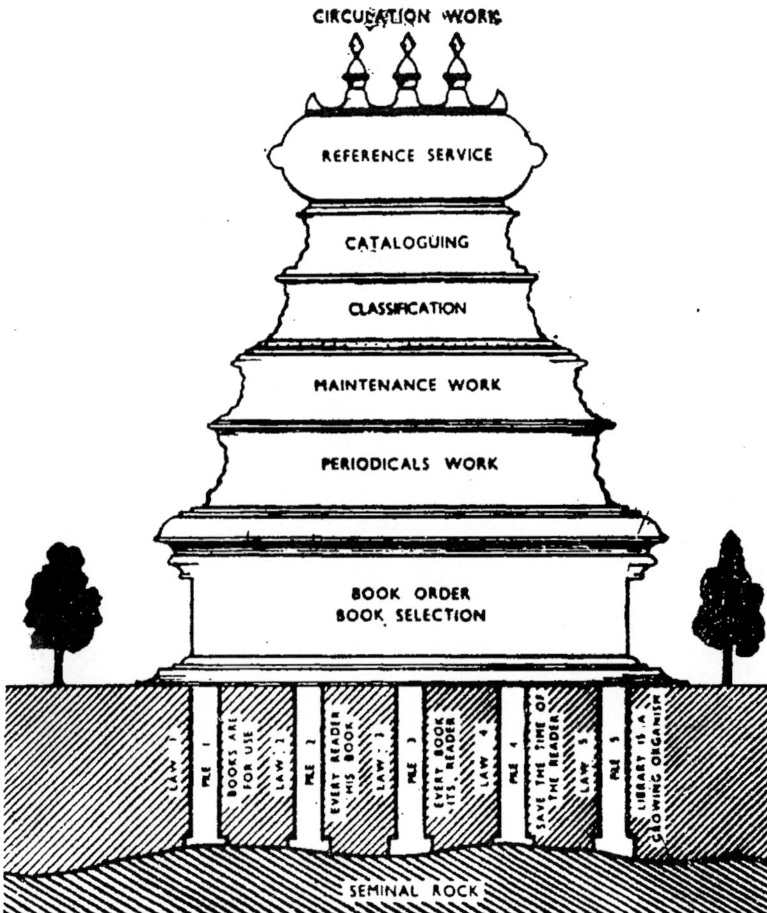

CHAPTER SB

ROLE OF THE FIVE LAWS OF LIBRARY SCIENCE

1 The Five Laws

The normative principles known as the Five Laws of Library Science (52) form the foundation of Library Science and of all kinds of library work. These normative principles are:

1 Books (Documents) are for use;

2 Every Reader his Book (Document);

3 Every Book (Document) its Reader;

4 Save the time of the Reader; and

5 A Library is a Growing Organism.

PART T

REFERENCE SERVICE

CHAPTER TA

DEFINITION OF REFERENCE SERVICE

1 Reference Service and the Five Laws of Library Science

The ultimate aim of library service is the satisfaction of the Five Laws of Library Science. In this, Reference Service plays an important role. Reference Service is the process of establishing contact between a reader and the books by personal service, thereby bringing the right reader and the right book together to the satisfaction of the Laws of Library Science.

2 Equality of Opportunity and Reference Service

In the case of intuitive or hereditary knowledge, reference service may not be necessary. But with our present insistence on equality of opportunity reference service becomes essential.

3 Reference Service in School Library

We have a real library, only at the moments of intimate and integrated relation between the reader and the book being established by the reference staff. Apart from service to teachers three distinctive types of reference service can be recognised in a school library:

1 Initiation of students;

2 Service to individual students; and

3 Service to the class.

CHAPTER TB

QUALITIES NECESSARY FOR INITIATION WORK

1 Requisites to Initiate Students

The requisites to initiate students are,

1 Geniality in receiving and working with students;
2 A clear grasp of all items needing initiation;
3 A good knowledge of youth psychology-in-action;
4 Some knowledge of the methods of teaching.

2 Human Quality of Initiation

The librarian must know to make the initiation free from boredom; nay, he must make it pleasurable. He should know to charge it with mirth and laughter by narration of anecdotes; and indeed the anecdotal aroma of the initiation should be strong and enduring enough, for the students to recall it at the instance of even the feeblest association. For, children learn and remember the use of aids, apparatus, and rules of conduct far more effectively in a concrete setting than in an abstract one. These are the essential human qualities in initiation. What they should be initiated in, what should be the student's work in that process, and how the effectiveness of the initiation should be tested have been described in Parts K to N. Here we have only to consider the methods of initiation. Three methods may be recognised; and they supplement one another:

1 Apprenticeship;
2 Practical guidance as and when need arises; and
3 Formal lesson.

3 Items to be Covered in Initiation

Initiation of student into the use of Library should include:

1 What he should be initiated in;
2 What the student's work should be in that process; and
3 Achievement test in respect of Initiation.

CHAPTER TC

APPRENTICESHIP METHOD OF INITIATION

1 Inherent Urge in Students to Imitate

Students like to imitate. They love to do what is often done as a task by adults. Do not their elders scare them away from such imitative work by ridiculing them? In due course, such ridicules cause a sense of shame in doing such things.

2 Encouraging Students to Imitate Library Routine

On the other hand a student wishing to do library tasks may be profitably admitted as a newcomer-apprentice. Most of the items needing initiation are best learned by a student by

1 Observing the librarian's work;

2 Imitating the librarian's routine in such matters; and

3 Helping the librarian by relieving him from some of the items of routine, in the manner of an apprentice.

3 Items of Library Routine Admitting of Apprenticeship

The following are some of the items of library routine fit for apprenticeship by a student:

1 Opening, with care, of new and newly bound books, to ease the stiffness in binding;

2 Arranging books on the shelves in the stack room, and rectifying the same from time to time;

3 Writing of the Call Number in the different places of a book;

4 Revising the Call Number written in each book by comparing it with the Call Number in its Main Entry;

5 Insertion of catalogue cards in the catalogue cabinet;

6 Doing the routine involved in charging and in discharging books;

7 Tidyng up and rectifying the arrangement in the display table for periodicals; and

8 Maintenance of the different rooms of the library in a clean and presentable form.

CHAPTER TD

PRACTICAL GUIDANCE AS A METHOD FOR INITIATION

1 Freedom for a Student to Go on His Own Way

A supplement to the Apprentice Method is to guide a student out of his difficulty in imitating a particular routine. To have the best educational effect, the guidance must be given at the late stage. The student should have already exhausted his initiative and resources. And he should have reached the point of giving up the task in despair.

2 Psychological Moment for Giving Practical Guidance

Such a psychological moment is always late in coming. Generally, a student wishes to fight his battle by himself. Any premature correction or help will take away the student's innate urge for self-learning.

3 Difference in Sense of Time between a Student and an Adult

Further, time does not count for a student as it does for an adult. Thank God, there are no hustlers among students at least! They go about their business in perfect ease, leisure, and geniality, in the knowledge of the eternity of time. Adults, invariably becoming hustlers sooner or later, should control themselves from offering help prematurely.

4 Items for Practical Work

Effective practical help will be called for in accustoming a student to the:

1 Internal parts of a book and their use;

2 Structure of entries in and use of reference books;

3 Purpose and use of the different kinds of entries in the library catalogue;

4 Writing of notes while reading; and

5 Preparation of reading list—that is, bibliography for personal use.

CHAPTER TE

FORMAL LESSON AS A METHOD OF INITIATION

1 Spacing and Subject of Formal Lessons

Periodical spirited formal lessons should clinch the experiences gained by the students in apprenticeship under guidance. Sometimes, a formal lesson may even lead to the opening up of new areas of initiation. Therefore, formal lessons should be distributed throughout the school course in accordance with the Principle of Emergent Evolution. Therefore the spacing and the subject of each formal lesson will have to be sensed jointly by the students and the librarian.

2 Concentric Method

The formal lessons are best done by the concentric method. In this method, the same problems are repeatedly tackled more and more intimately and in detailed ways, as determined by the experience gained from time to time.

3 Formal Lesson Should Not be a One-Way Lecture

Formal lessons should not be mistaken for "lectures from the platform." The conduct of each formal lesson must be a participative one. It should be rich in mutual give and take — questions and answers. Then only the pupils will be kept in a state of alertness, and interest. Otherwise they will fall into a mood of passive listening, often staring at the teacher with their minds vacant or switched on to something else. The lessons of the first cycle should be interspersed with anecdotes, songs, and stories. There should be plenty of demonstrations. There should also be ample opportunity for the pupils to experience and thereby verify the points clinched in the lessons.

CHAPTER TF

A SAMPLE OF TWO CONCENTRIC CYCLES

0 Plan of the Chapter

As an illustration, here is a scheme of lessons to cover the whole field of initiation in two concentric cycles. Each cycle is planned to be completed in nine lessons. Under each lesson, the matter to be covered is shown in two blocks — one for each cycle.

1 Lesson 1

11 CYCLE 1: CARE OF BOOKS

Clean hand; opening of new books; turning pages carefully by upper right hand corner; use of book-marks; taking a book from the shelf without injuring its back — particularly its top; shelving books right-side up and back out; putting books in safe place at home; wrapping books in rainy days.

12 CYCLE 2: PHYSIQUE OF BOOKS

Demonstration with a partially bound book; back of cover sides; outside hinges; body-sections; end paper; inside hinges.

2 Lesson 2

21 CYCLE 1: LIBRARY RULES

Maximum number of volumes allowed on loan at one time; period of loan; due date stamp; over-due charge.

22 CYCLE 2: LIBRARY BEHAVIOUR

Queue system; soft steps; silence; library, property of all — of the present as well as of the future; live and let live; civic responsibility.

3 Lesson 3

31 CYCLE 1: MAKE-UP OF A BOOK

Title-page and the information contained in it; distinguishing name of auther, collaborator and publisher; surname or the last word in the name: table of contents; index.

32 CYCLE 2: MAKE-UP OF THE BOOK

Title-page; imprint; year of publication; preface; dedication; maps and illustrations; glossary; notes; bibliographies — that is lists — of other books on the same or related topics.

4 Lesson 4

41 CYCLE 1: DICTIONARY

Guide words at the top; spelling; pronunciation; syllabification; accent.

42 CYCLE 2: DICTIONARY

Physical make-up; comparison of different dictionaries; foreign words and phrases; names of the places and persons; abbreviations; derivation of the word; different meanings; phrases commonly going with a word; proof readers' signs; flags of nations; and other unexpected extraneous information.

5 Lesson 5

51 CYCLE 1

511 *Encyclopaedia*

Encyclopaedia; inclusive letters at the back and the title-page of each volume; index.

512 *Who's Who*

Year of issue, only living people; brief biography.

52 CYCLE 2: REFERENCE BOOKS

Encyclopaedia: date; exhaustiveness; illustrations; maps; index; bibliographies; index volume; map volume. Year books: current information; recent statistics; world events; sports. Who was who: only dead people; frequency of publication. Biographical dictionary: only dead people; supplements. Atlas: scope: information in addition to maps; population; location of places, with the aid of index.

6 Lesson 6

61 Cycle 1: Classification and Catalogue

Familiarising with the classified arrangement of the books in the stack room; guide cards in the classified part of the catalogue; class number; book number; collection number; card cabinet; arrangement of trays; arrangement of cards; arrangement of entries in a card.

62 Cycle 2: Classification and Catalogue

Need for classification; main subjects; filiatory sequence; divisions of a main subject; class number; plan of the stack room; types of catalogue entries; main and added entries; questions answered by different types of entries.

7 Lesson 7

71 Cycle 1: Periodical Publications

Current events; newspaper; periodical; issues or numbers; continuous pagination in the successive issues of a volume; title-page; index.

72 Cycle 2

721 *Periodical*

Periodicity of the issues of a volume; weekly, fortnightly, monthly, bimonthly, quarterly, and half-yearly; periodicity of volume; specialisation in subject matter; standard; cumulative index; collective index.

713 *Serial*

Annual; Government report; and other serials.

8 Lesson 8

81 Cycle 1: Notes-Taking

Purpose; how to take notes in one's own words; extracts and use of quotation marks; source — call number, heading, title, page reference; samples of notes.

82 Cycle 2: Notes-Taking

Personal short-land; abbreviation of commonly recurring words; omission of connecting auxiliary words; comparative study and analysis of the actual notes of several pupils.

9 Lesson 9

91 Cycle 1: Bibliography

Meaning; use; samples; in the middle of the text; at the foot of pages; at the ends of chapters; at the ends of books; at the ends of articles in encyclopaedias; bibliographies forming a volume by itself; readers' guide; library catalogue; guide to historical fiction.

92 Cycle 2

921 *Compilation of Bibliography*

Sources; reference books; treatises; books on related subjects; periodical indexes; pamphlets and clippings filed by the librarian.

922 *Mechanics of Compilation*

"One entry one slip"; 125 × 75 mm slips; each entry to give call number, heading, title, pages of chapters, volume number and date, and author and title of a paper in a periodical; filing of slips; receptacles for slips; demonstration and drill work.

CHAPTER TG

SERVICE TO INDIVIDUAL STUDENTS

0 Kinds of Reference Service

Reference service is essentially personal in its nature (*See* Sec TB1). Hence we reach its ideal in the school library only in the service to individual students. Such individual service is of two kinds:

1 Ready Reference Service; and

2 Long Range Reference Service.

1 Ready Reference Service

Ready Reference Service is service finished in a very short time — in a moment if possible. In other words, time is of the very essence in this service. It usually takes the form of helping an enquirer to find out a specific fact from reference books, and occasionally even from ordinary books. In a school library this service should not go to the full length of finding the fact for the student. For, stimulation of self-help is of the very essence of a school library. Nor should the service shrink up to the other extreme limit of providing the books and keeping absolutely out of the way of the student. The via media should be pursued. The librarian should take an active interest in the student's pursuit of facts. He should give him a helping hand whenever caught up in difficulties. The librarian should divert him from an utterly wrong course by gentle and suggestive questions, not amounting to formal instruction. He should suggest to him the need for looking up supplementary sources. Further the librarian should finally satisfy himself about the correctness of the fact got by the student. Why such help is necessary and how exactly it should be rendered are discussed in detail along with a number of case studies in my *Reference service* (60). A perusal of the relevant pages of that book will repay amply. It would take the size of this book beyond economic limits to reproduce all such matter.

2 Long Range Reference Service

Long Range Reference Service differs from Ready Reference Service in the longer time permitted to complete it. It will also go beyond the use of reference books -- into all kinds of published and even unpublished materials. This is necessary to locate facts, ideas, and information quite out of the way and are either too new or too old to find a place in ordinary reference books. It may also help in furnishing the student with opinions and points of view of different shades. Long Range Reference Service will therefore involve much time in the getting of materials and even in pursuing correspondence with outsiders. In all these processes, the student must be taken as a partner and he must be told and shown the way of pursuing his problem. Here again it is impossible to go into further details. *Reference Service* gives a full discussion, develops the necessary technique, and gives several illuminating case studies (62).

CHAPTER TH

SERVICE TO THE CLASS

1 Peculiar to School Library

A teacher may notify the librarian about a particular topic being pursued by him in the class. He may ask the librarian to have the relevant books and other kindred reading materials assembled for the benefit of his class. Then the librarian should

1 Carefully picks out all the books, the whole of which or part of which is relevant to the topic, atlases, maps, and charts, etc;

2 Delves into the cabinet of clippings and combs out helpful ones; and

3 Selects from the photographic, lantern slides and cinema collections — all with a slant upon the topic pursued by the class. From this point of view he should have given cross reference entries to illustrations in books, He should also insert book-marks at the proper pages.

2 Service on Demand: Topical Sequence

The librarian should make a temporary special sequence of all the materials collected. He should put up a suitable tell-tale bay guide at the top of the bay containing the sequence. This will enable him to send to the class room at a moment's notice the materials needed by the teacher. It will also helps the students to look through the books and the other kindred materials in the topical sequence, without wasting time in searching for them all through the stack room. On hearing from the teacher and the pupils "We have done with this, we do not want this any longer" the librarian should redistribute the material to their respective proper places. Before doing so he should make a list of them. This will enable him to form a similar topical sequence on the same or related subjects more expeditiously on a future occasion.

3 Service in Anticipation

An enterprising librarian may form similar temporary special sequences on topics likely to be pursued either for a particular class or by the school as a whole. The librarian should make the necessary topical sequences from time to time, in consultation with the headmaster and the members of the faculty. Once the topic is chosen, the routine of the service is similar to that described in the preceding sections.

CHAPTER TJ

SOCIAL ROLE OF REFERENCE SERVICE

1 Cultivation of Human Resources

According to the ancient Tamil poem *Thirukkural* of Thiruvalluvar, "its people form 'the wealth of all the wealth' of a community" (73). The development of the natural and industrial resources forming the material wealth depends on the prior cultivation of its human resources.

2 Cultivation of Mind

What does cultivation of human resources amount to? It is essentially the cultivation of the mental resources. For, according to a vedic passage, "Man" is essentially "Mind." We can recognise five elements in mind — Memory, Emotion, Absorbing Intellect, Creative Intellect, and Sublimated Emotion. In its variety of books, the library provides manure, so to speak, needed in the cultivation of each of these five elements. The variety of books comprehends:

1 Reference Books or Externalised Memory;

2 Entertaining but Elevating books — such as biography, fiction, and travel;

3 Ordinary books suited to the needs of the generalist readers;

4 Treatises and advanced books and periodicals suited to the needs of the specialist readers; and

5 Seminal books in literature and religion capable of sublimating the emotions.

3 Reference Service: The Means of Cultivating the Mind

All such "manure" needed for the cultivation of the mental resources of a community is to be ploughed in by the various items of library work. The resultant of this ploughing is to be sorted out by Reference Service in such a way as to make it compatible with the mental make-up of each respective member of the community. Thus, Reference Service forms the penultimate stage in the library's achievement of its ultimate end of cultivating the mental resources of the community. The cultivation of the mind of a person should begin in his very infancy and get reinforced from the school stage onwards.

CHAPTER TK

CULTIVATION OF MENTAL RESOURCES OF A COMMUNITY: SCHEMATIC REPRESENTATION

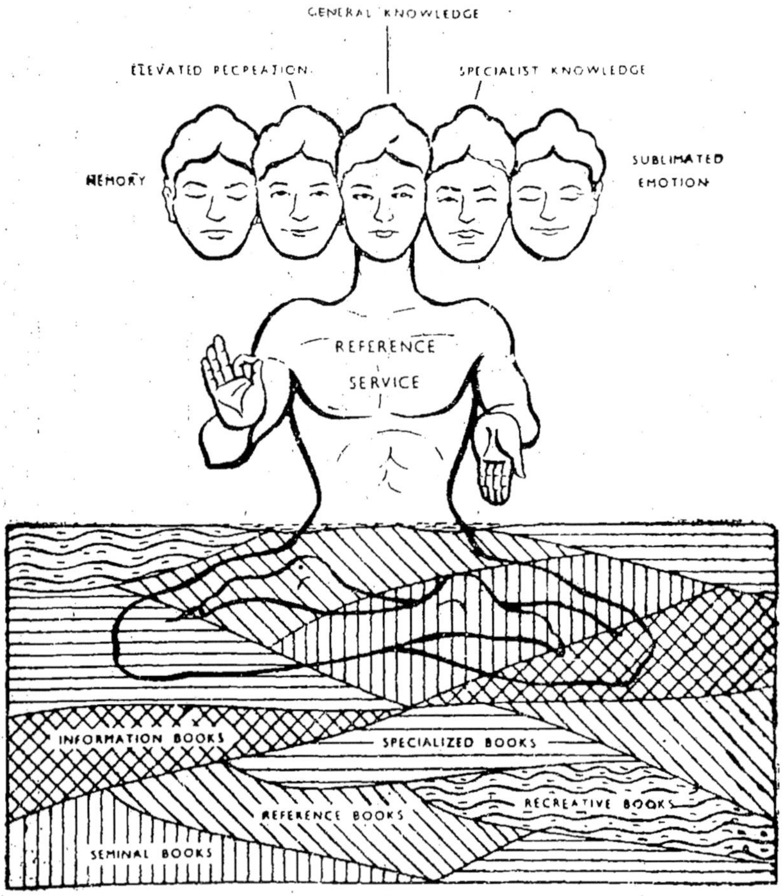

CHAPTER TL

REFERENCE SERVICE: THE HUB OF LIBRARY WORK

1 Schematic Representation

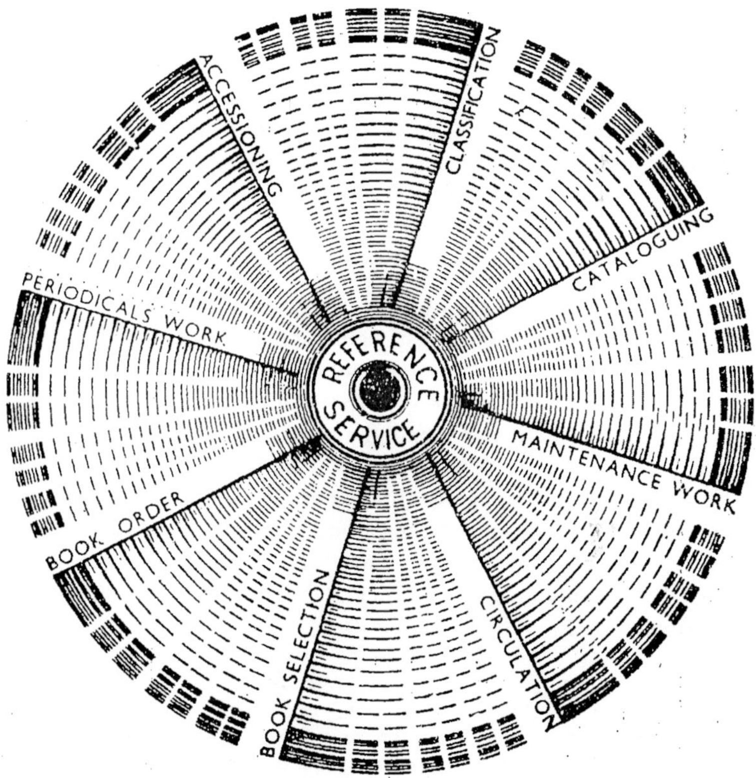

2 Reference Service

Reference Service gives a stimulus to every item of work in a Library.

3 Book Section and Reference Service

An important document is not in the library. But the Reference Librarian finds the need for it sufficiently often. Then, he requests the Book Section to procure a copy of it. Since the selection and the procurement of a copy of it are in response to an actual demand from readers, the Books Section feels true zest in its procurement.

4 Cataloguing and Classification Sections and Reference Service

The Reference Section may locate in a few pages of a book the material needed by a reader but not found entered in the library catalogue. It passes on this information to the Classification and Cataloguing Sections. These Sections prepare the necessary Cross Reference Cards and the associated Added Entry Cards, and insert them in the library catalogue.

5 Maintenance Section and Reference Service

Occasionally, the Maintenance Section also may get stimulus from Reference Service. A specialist reader may require for immediate reference, the current volume of a periodical lying in the Bindery. It then either gets the volume from the Bindery for temporary use, or it may send the specialist reader to the Bindery with a letter of request that he might be given facilities to consult the volume. Further, the Maintenance Section can learn from the Reference Librarian about the periodicals having frequent demand on account of some special work in progress by some readers. Then the Maintenance Section asks the Bindery to give line-clear-treatment to the volume in question.

6 Other Sections

The Reference Section may ask for line-clear-treatment to be given to certain books by all the other Sections to fulfil the human purpose of meeting the urgent needs of readers. This fact can humanise the outlook of each of the Sections doing routine work and make them realise the importance of their routine in the over-all purpose of the Library.

All the items of library work are related to Reference Service and they turn round Reference Service as the Hub.

The picture in Sec TL1 is a schematic diagram showing this.

PART U

CIRCULATION WORK

CHAPTER UA

RULES OF A SCHOOL LIBRARY

0 What After Reference Service

According to Chap TA Reference Service is the penultimate item of work in a library; and Circulation work is the last item of work. Circulation work is governed by the rules of the library. They are given in the succeeding sections of this chapter.

1 Hours of Work

11 Definition

The term 'Hours of Work' denotes the working days in the year and the working hours in a day. The term 'Working hours' denotes, the hours of access to the library to its users — consultants and members.

12 Fixing of the Hours of the Library

The headmaster will fix the hours of the library from time to time.

13 Sample Rule About Hours of the Library

For the time being the headmaster has fixed the working hours of the library as follows:

1 On all days from 7 a m to 9 p m; however

2 The loan counter will be closed at 8 30 p m.

2 Admission to the Library

21 Library Identity Card

Each student of the School will be given by the headmaster a Library Identity Card. A small size photo of the bust of the student will be affixed to the Library Identity Card.

22 Production of the Library Identity Card

Each student should show, to the circulation assistant at the entrance gate of the library, his Library Identity Card to enter the library.

23 Teachers and Outside Members

No Library Identity Card is necessary for a teacher of the School or for a specially admitted outside member.

3 Library Civics

31 Prohibited Categories

No reader will be allowed to take into the library:

1 A stick, an umbrella, a box, a bag, or any similar receptacle; or

2 Any book of his or of the library, without special permission of the circulation assistant;

3 Dog or any other animal; and

4 Any person accompanying the reader, except with the special permission of the circulation assistant.

32 Prohibited Action Inside the Library

While inside the library no reader will be allowed to:

1 Break the silence in the reading room by talking to others or by action of any kind, such as humming a tune, putting something on the table with a bang or dropping anything down to the floor;

2 Spit or smoke in any part of the library;

3 Sleep in the reading room or in any other part of the library; and

4 Stay in the library after the closing hour.

4 Respect to Library Property

No reader shall:

1 Do any damage to any fitting or furniture or the floor or the wall of the library;

2 Do any damage to any book or other kindred reading material of the library;

3 Write or make any mark on any page of any book or other kindred reading material of the library;

4 Trace or mechanically reproduce anything from any book or other kindred reading material of the library, without written sanction of the circulation assistant;

5 Replace on the shelf any book or other kindred reading material taken for use; in particular,

6 Deliberately misplace any book or other kindred reading material and thus lead to difficulty in its being located by anybody else.

5 Responsibility for Damage Done

The reader concerned shall:

1 Deposit with the circulation assistant the cost of the damaged book or other kindred reading material, as fixed by the circulation assistant;

2 Replace the damaged book or other kindred reading material by a fresh copy, and then get back the deposit made by him in this behalf; or

3 Authorise the library to buy a fresh copy, and to adjust his deposit amount thereafter; and

4 Do similarly with regard to any other property of the library.

Note.— In the case of one volume or some volumes of a multi-volumed book or other kindred reading material being damaged, the reader is liable to replace a complete set of the volumes of the multi-volumed book or other kindred reading material.

6 Loan Privilege

61 PERSON ENTITLED TO LOAN PRIVILEGE

The following are entitled to borrow books from the library

for use outside its premises:

1 Each student of the school;

2 Each teacher of the school; and

3 Any specially admitted outside person.

62 MEMBER OF THE LIBRARY

The term 'Member of the Library' denotes any person entitled to the loan privilege of the library.

63 MEMBER'S TICKET

Each member will be given Members Tickets as shown below:

1 Each student.— Two tickets with their backs reinforced by green calico;

2 Each teacher.— Six tickets with their backs reinforced by red calico; and

3 Each outside-member.— Two tickets with their backs reinforced by yellow calico.

64 ISSUE OF A BOOK

A book will be issued to a member only in exchange for one of his member's tickets to be kept in the Charged Tray of the counter.

65 RETURN OF BOOK

In returning a book to the library, on or before the due date, the member should get back from the circulation assistant one of his charged tickets.

66 RETURN OF OVER-DUE BOOK

On returning an over-due book to the library, the member should pay to the circulation assistant, against a receipt to be granted by him, the over-due charge, before claiming his Member's ticket.

7 Lost Ticket of a Member

71 REPORT OF LOSS OF TICKET

On loosing any of his tickets a Member should make a written report about it to the headmaster stating the Number of the Ticket Lost.

72 PERIOD OF TIME FOR SEARCH

Three months' time will be allowed for a Member to trace out his lost ticket. If traced out he should inform the headmaster about it. If not, at the end of the three months, he should give to the headmaster a second report stating the result.

73 INDEMNITY BOND

For every Member's ticket reported lost but not traced out, the Member should give an indemnity bond in the prescribed form and pay a fee of one Rupee to the headmaster.

74 ISSUE OF DUPLICATE TICKET

On the receipt of the Indemnity Bond and the fee thereof, a duplicate Member's Ticket will be given to the member.

75 VIGILANCE ABOUT LOST TICKET

The Circulation Section will keep a Black List of the Members Tickets reported lost. On any of them being presented by any person at the charging counter, the ticket will be confiscated by the circulation assistant; and the person concerned will be sent to the headmaster along with a report on the case.

8 Conditions of Loan

81 SOUNDNESS OR OTHERWISE OF THE COPY TAKEN OUT ON LOAN

Before leaving the counter, a Member shall satisfy himself as to whether the book lent to him is in sound condition, and if not, he shall immediately bring the matter to the notice of the circulation assistant. Otherwise at the time of the returning of the book he is liable to be asked to pay the cost for purchasing a new copy of the book.

82 DOCUMENTS NOT AVAILABLE FOR LOAN

Periodical publications, dictionaries, and such other documents declared by the headmaster as reference books, cannot be taken on loan, except with the permission of the headmaster in any particular case.

83 BOUND VOLUME OF PERIODICAL

Notwithstanding Sec UA82 each Teacher-Member can take a bound volume of a periodical on loan.

84 SUB-LENDING

No member shall sub-lend any book taken on loan from the library.

85 PERIOD OF LOAN

Any book taken on loan from the library should be returned on or before the end of a fortnight.

851 *Books in Unusual Demand*

Any book in unusual demand may be lent out for a short period fixed by the headmaster, including issue for overnight only. As an alternative, a book in extraordinarily unusual demand — such as a text-book during examination season — may be declared by the headmaster to be a reference book until a prescribed date. A book lent for overnight only shall be deemed to be due for return at or before 10 a. m. on the next day.

86 OVER-DUE CHARGE

On a book not being returned on the due date, an over-due charge of five paise per day shall be levied till its return.

87 Renewal of Loan

A Loan may be renewed for a further period of one fortnight provided:

1 The renewal application reaches the circulation assistant not less than three and not more than six clear days before the due date of the book; and

2 No other member has applied for the book in the meantime.

Not more than three consecutive renewals shall be allowed for the same book without its production in the library for inspection.

In the case of condition 2 in Sec UA87 not being satisfied, the circulation assistant shall cause a letter to that effect to be sent to the Member. And the Member should return the book on or before the due date.

9 Disability from Loan

A Member owing any sum of money to the school is liable to be refused loan of books from the library.

CHAPTER UB

MODERNISING CIRCULATION METHOD

1 Law 4 of Library Science Against Old Method of Circulation

The apparatus of circulation work in a school library stands in urgent need of modernisation. Law 4 of Library Science "Save the time of the reader" would protest against the old leisurely way of circulating books on loan. For, it adversely affects the psychological tempo of each student just developing a wish to use the library.

2 Result of Not Having "Open Access"

There is no justification to perpetuate any longer the old method of :

1 Keeping the books in locked cupboards;

2 Keeping the students far away from them by severe barriers;

3 Asking them to apply for books in specific forenoons with the aid of the catalogue; and

4 Giving out the books in the afternoon to an impatient crowd elbowing at one another.

Often some of them have to go away in disappointment on account the books asked by them being not available. Their specified forenoon for applying for an alternative book will come only next week! Nor is it proper that the time of the do-all school librarian be consumed in writing the old ledger books and cancelling the entries in them during most of the day.

3 Advantage of New Method of Circulation

Due to the urge of the Laws of Library Science, the library profession has, during the last five decades, evolved a new circulation method. The new method is simplicity itself. At the same time it secures lightning speed and fool-proof accuracy. It further keeps a student actively engaged while in library. It leaves no moment to be spent by him in waiting with impatience. It knocks off the long interval to be spent in day-dreaming while in the class-room, about his getting or not getting in the afternoon the book applied for in the forenoon. The new method may be described as that of "Open access *cum* Book-Card and Member's-Ticket."

4 Open Access System and Freedom

41 Freedom for the Student

The democratic spirit of modern library gives each student the same freedom and privilege as his teacher gets. Like the teacher he can:

1 Walk amidst the book stacks;

2 Browse round examining the books;

3 Pull out any book at will;

4 Dip into it; and

5 Select the books wanted by him by actually "tasting" it even in the stack room.

This is denoted by the term "Open Access System."

42 Safeguards for Open Access System

The extreme freedom in the inside of the library needs extreme vigilance at the entrance and exit gates of the circulation counter, forming the control region of the library. The exit and entrance gates are to be fitted with wicket gates. To make any of them open out the circulation assistant should press the pedal under his feet. The circulation assistant must be all vigilance. The school authorities should keep the wicket gate arrangement ever in good repair. Any breakdown in the counter equipment should be immediately set right without harassing delay by red-tape.

5 New Method of Circulation

The new method of circulation — Book Card Members Ticket method — is described in the successive chapters. The details of the method are given elsewhere (54).

CHAPTER UC

TICKET WORK FOR STUDENT-MEMBER

1 Work of Getting Students' Names

The following are the routines:

1 Nominal roll of students (*Annual Job*).— About a week after the beginning of the school year, get from the school office a complete nominal roll of the students of each class and division.

2 Supplementary nominal roll of students (*Annual Job*).— Ask the office to give on a specified day of each week any supplementary nominal roll of newly admitted students.

2 Work of Preparation of Tickets for Student Members

The following are the routines:

1 Picking out the Blank Tickets (*Annual Job*).— From the stock of blank green tickets for Student-Members pick out twice as many tickets as the number of students in the nominal roll, and place them in the Working Tray for Blank Tickets.

2 Writing out Tickets for Student-Members (*Annual Job*).— For each student write out each of the two tickets due to him, in the successive lines or block of lines, as the case may be, beginning from near the top, the following:

21 Ticket Number.— Consisting successively of,

211 His class number in Roman numeral;

212 His division number, if any, in Roman Cap;

213 The last digit of the year of issue, in Indo-Arabic numeral;

214 The roll number of the student in Indo-Arabic numerals;

215 A full stop;

216 The digit "1" in the case of the first Ticket, and digit "2" in the case of the second Ticket; and

217 The Colon Class Number of the Main Optional Subject of the student, if any, and otherwise the digit "a".

22 Name of Student.— Consisting successively of,

221 The entry element in the name of the pupil, last substantive word in the name, along with any irremovable attachment to it, in Roman Caps;

222 The secondary element in the name of the student, the remaining words in the name preceding the entry element, written in the sequence of their occurrence and enclosed within circular brackets, in Roman Caps and Smalls.

23 Your initial and date at the left hand bottom corner.

Example

IV B31212.2G
JAYARAJAN NAIR
(Parappurath)

PJR
3.6.1973

3 Work of Temporary Filing of Tickets Prepared for Student Members

The following are the routines:

1 Arranging the Tickets (*Casual Job*).— Arrange the tickets alphabetically by the names of the students in a tray — having in its front side the label "unsorted tickets" — putting tickets 1 and 2 together, one behind the other.

2 Transferring to Temporary Tray (*Casual Job*).—Transfer the alphabetised tickets into a tray — one for each class and division having in its front side a label showing the class and division.

3 Preparation of Overdue Sheet (*Annual Job*).— Prepare for each student member an overdue sheet.

4 Work of Handing Over the Tickets to Student Member

The following are the routines:

1 Notifying the Class Teacher (*Annual Job*).— According to a time table notify the teacher of the different classes about the

tickets of student members being ready for issue, asking him to send the students for collecting their respective tickets;

2 Handing over the Ticket (*Immediate Job*).— On demand by a student pick out his two tickets and hand them over to him.

3 Taking the Signature (*Immediate Job*).— Take his dated signature against his name in the nominal roll.

5 Work of Changing Tickets of Student-Member

A student may be changed from one division to another in the course of the year. On getting notification about this, the following are the routines to be done:

1 Calling the Student (*Casual Job*).— Send a note to his class teacher asking the student to come to the library with his Member's Tickets in order to collect new Member's Tickets.

2 Canceling the Ticket (*Immediate Job*).— On the student producing his old tickets, cancel them and put them in the Cancelled Ticket Tray in alphabetical sequence;

3 Preparing New Tickets (*Immediate Job*).— Prepare new tickets and hand them over to the student.

4 Taking Signature (*Immediate Job*).— Take the signature of the student, in the letter of notification of his transfer from one division to another.

5 Correcting in the Overdue Register (*Daily Job*).— Towards the closing hours of each day with the aid of the cancelled tickets in the Cancelled Tickets Tray, correct in the Overdue Register the old Ticket Numbers into the new Ticket Numbers of each student.

6 Work of Annual Cancelling of Tickets of Student-Member

The following are the routines:

1 Notify for the Annual Return of Tickets (*Annual Job*).— About the end of the academic year, request the headmaster to notify the students asking them to return their respective tickets to the librarian.

2 Cancelling the Ticket (*Immediate Job*).— On the receipt of the tickets, cancel them and put them in the Cancelled Tickets Tray for the year in the alphabetical sequence of their names.

3 Cancelling in the Overdue Register (*Daily Job*). — Towards the closing hours of each day score the Ticket Numbers of the Tickets in the page of the student concerned;

4 Transferring of the Scored Overdue Sheets (*Daily Job*).— While correcting the Ticket Numbers in the Overdue Register take out the corrected sheet. Alphabetise all the sheets scored in the day. Insert them in alphabetical sequence in a new overdue binder for use in the next year.

5 Notifying Defaulters (*Annual Job*).— About a week before the closing of the school send to the headmaster a list of the names of the students not having returned their Tickets.

6 Supplementary Cancelling of Tickets (*Immediate Job*).— On the return of tickets by a defaulter, follow the analogy of the routines described above.

7 Supplementary Listing of Defaulters (*Annual Job*).— From the Overdue Register of the year, prepare a list of the names with class and division of each student with his overdue sheet found still in the overdue binder;

8 Supplementary Notifying (*Annual Job*).— On the penultimate day of the closing of the school send to the headmaster a supplementary list of the names of the students not having returned their Members Tickets.

7 Work on the Tickets of a Student Leaving the School

A student may leave the school at the end of the year or at any time. Then the following are the routines:

1 Standing notification to headmaster (*Annual Job*).— Leave with the headmaster a standing notification not to allow a student to leave the school or to take a transfer certificate either at the end of the year or at any time during the year, without getting a clearance certificate from the librarian after returning the Members Tickets of the student to the library.

2 Other routines.— Other routines analogous to those in Sec UC5.

CHAPTER UD

TICKET WORK FOR TEACHER-MEMBER

1 Work of Getting Teachers' Names

The following are the routines:

1 Standing request (*Annual Job*).— Make a standing request to the headmaster to send you at the beginning of each year a list of the names of the teachers of the school with their respective designations or the classes in their charge;

2 Newly appointed teacher (*Annual Job*).— Make a standing request to the headmaster to send you the name of each new teacher appointed in the course of the year with his designation or the class in his charge;

3 Teacher leaving in the Course of the Year (*Annual Job*).— Make a standing request to the headmaster to send you the name of each teacher leaving the school at any time in the course of the year.

4 Keeping uptodate the list of teachers (*Daily Job*).— Keep the list (*See* routine 1) of teachers in service uptodate by adding the new names to the basic list (*See* routine 2) and by cancelling the names of resigned teachers from the basic list (*See* routine 3).

2 Work of Preparation and Handing over Tickets for Teacher-Member

The following are the routines:

1 Receiving Application for Membership (*Immediate Job*).— At the request of a teacher for enrolment as Member, give him an application card for membership and get it filled up by him;

2 Picking out the Blank Tickets (*Immediate Job*).— From the stock of blank red tickets for teacher members, pick out six tickets;

3 Writing out Tickets for Teacher-Member (*Immediate Job*).— Write out on each of the tickets, in the successive lines or block of lines, as the case may be, beginning with the topmost line, the following:

31 Ticket Number.— Consisting successively of ;

311 The Colon Class Number of his Main Subject of teaching, if any, and otherwise the number "a";

312 The serial number of the member, in Indo-Arabic numerals;

313 A full stop;

314 The digit "1" in the case of the first ticket, the digit "2" in the case of the second ticket, and so on.

32 Name of the Teacher. (On the analogy of Subsection 22 in Routine 2 in Sec UC2)

33 Designation of the Teacher; and

34 Your initial and date at the left hand bottom corner.

4 Preparation of Overdue Sheet.— (*Immediate Job*).— Prepare for each teacher-member an overdue sheet.

5 Handing over of the Ticket (*Immediate Job*).— Hand over to the teacher-member the tickets prepared for him.

6 Taking the Signature (*Immediate Job*).— Take under the printed appropriate line in the Application Card of the teacher — reading "Received my six tickets" — the dated signature of the teacher.

7 Filing the application Card of Teachers (*Casual Job*).— File the application card of the teacher in the proper alphabetical place in the 125 × 75 cm box having the label "Application Cards of Teachers."

8 Filing of Overdue Sheet (*Casual Job*).— File the overdue sheet of the teacher-member in the proper alphabetical place, by the name of the teacher, in the binder having the label "Over-due Register Binder of Teachers."

3 Work of Cancelling of Tickets of Teacher-Member

The following are the routines:

1 Standing request (*Annual Job*).— Request the headmaster to inform you immediately about the termination of the service of a teacher.

2 Requesting the Resigning Teacher-Member to surrender

his Tickets (*Immediate Job*).— On receipt of the information from the headmaster about the termination of the service of a teacher, request him to surrender his tickets to the library immediately.

3 Cancelling of Tickets (*Immediate Job*).— On the receipt of the tickets from the teacher-member, cancel each of them and put them in the Cancelled Tickets Tray.

4 Cancelling in the Overdue Register (*Daily Job*).— Towards the closing hours of each day, remove the Overdue Sheet of the teacher-member from the Overdue Register and cancel it.

5 Informing the Headmaster in case of Non-Surrender of Tickets (*Casual Job*).— On your hearing about a teacher-member leaving the school or three days after receiving information about the termination of a teacher-member from the headmaster, whichever is earlier, inform the headmaster about the non-surrender, if any, of Tickets and also about the non-return of library book, if any, and requesting him to withhold his last pay until the teacher-member surrenders his Tickets and/or returns the library book.

6 Informing the Headmaster in case of Surrender of Tickets or of Library Book (*Immediate Job*).— On a teacher-member surrendering his Member's Tickets and/or returning the library book, send a clearance certificate to the headmaster.

CHAPTER UE

TICKET WORK FOR OUTSIDE MEMBER

1 Work of Preparation and Handing Over of Tickets for Outside Member

The following are the routines:

1 Receiving Application for Membership (*Immediate Job*).— On the receipt of a recommendation from the headmaster to admit an outsider as a Member of the library, give him an Application Card for Membership and get it filled up by him.

2 Collecting deposit amount (*Immediate Job*).— Collect from the outsider the deposit amount prescribed by the Rules of the library, and give him the receipt.

3 Picking out the Blank Tickets (*Immediate Job*).— From the stock of blank yellow tickets for Outside Members, pick out two tickets.

4 Writing out Tickets for Outside Member (*Immediate Job*).— Write out on each of the tickets, in the successive lines or block of lines, as the case may be, beginning with the topmost line, the following:

41 Ticket Number.— Consisting successively of—

411 The capital letter "O" indicating his being an outside member;

412 The Colon Class Number representing the Main Subject of his interest;

413 The last digit of the year of issue of the ticket, in Indo-Arabic numeral;

414 The receipt number of his deposit;

415 A full stop; and

416 The digit "1" in the case of the first ticket, and the digit "2" in the case of the second ticket;

42 Name of the outside member (on the analogy of Subsection 22 in Routine 2 in Sec UC2);

43 Private address of the outside member;

44 Official designation and address if any; and

45 Your initial and date at the left hand bottom corner.

5 Preparation of Overdue Sheet (*Immediate Job*).— Prepare an overdue sheet for each outside member;

6 Handing over of the Ticket (*Immediate Job*).— Hand over to the outside member the tickets prepared for him.

7 Taking the Signature (*Immediate Job*).— Take under the appropriate line in the application card of the outsider — reading "Received my two tickets" — the dated signature of the member.

8 Filing of the Application Card (*Casual Job*).— File the Application Card of the outsider, in the proper alphabetical place in the 125 × 75 cm box having the label "Application Cards of Outsider-Members."

9 Filing the Overdue Sheet (*Casual Job*).— File the overdue sheet of the outside member in the proper alphabetical place, by his name in the binder having the label "Overdue Register Binder of Outsider Members."

2 Work of Cancelling the Tickets of Outside Member

The following are the routines:

1 Requesting the Outside Member to fill up the Application Form (*Immediate Job*).— Request any outside member desiring to cancel his membership to fill up the prescribed Application form for Cancellation of Membership;

2 Cancelling Tickets (*Immediate Job*).— Collect from the Outside Member his two tickets, cancel each of them, and put them in the Cancelled Tickets Tray.

3 Scrutinising the Overdue Register (*Immediate Job*).— Find out from the Overdue Register for Outside Members any amount due from the Member.

4 Collecting the Outstanding Amount (*Immediate Job*).— Collect from the Outside Member the outstanding amount due from him and give him the receipt for it.

5 Repaying the deposit amount (*Immediate Job*).— Send a clearance certificate to the headmaster requesting for the repayment of the deposit money to the Outside Member, also ask the Outside Member to meet the headmaster and take the refund of his deposit amount.

CHAPTER UF

BOOK CARD MEMBERS TICKET METHOD OF CIRCULATION

1 Book Card

In the "Book Card, Member's Ticket" method of circulation, each volume in the library has a small book card made of white thick card board. The book card is generally $7 \times 4 \times 0.1$ cm. It is prepared by the Maintenance Section; and it is put inside the book pocket. It gives successively,

1 The Call Number of the book;
2 The name of its author; and
3 Its title

At its back the coat-of-arms of the library is printed.

2 Member's Ticket

Each member is given members' tickets. The number of tickets given to a reader is same as the number of volumes loanable to him at one time. The ticket is made of white thick cardboard lined with cloth in the back, to prevent its being easily foldable. It is generally $6 \times 4 \times 0.2$ cm. This is prepared by the Circulation Section.

3 Due Date Label

Further the book has a date label pasted on the very first page.

4 Circulation Work

The routines involved in the Circulation Work have been described in the succeeding Chapters.

CHAPTER UG

WORK AT THE ENTRANCE POINT OF THE COUNTER

1 Locker for Each Student

To keep his private books and other materials, provide for each student a locker. Train each student into the habit of keeping his books, etc, in his locker before entering the library.

2 Member Bringing Private Property

In spite of the provision for locker, occasionally a student may be obliged to carry with him some material, such as an umbrella or even a book, while entering the library. This will also happen in the case of a teacher or an outside person.

3 Private Property Custody Work

The following are the routines:

1 Taking the Umbrella and/or Stick into Custody (*Immediate Job*).— Put the umbrella and/or stick into one of the vacant holes in the stand in the counter enclosure, find out at the same time the number of the hole.

2 Handing over the Token (*Immediate Job*).— Hand over to the reader the corresponding token, asking him to keep it safe and surrender it to the circulation assistant to claim his umbrella and/or stick, while leaving the library.

3 Keeping Book (*Immediate Job*).— In the case of a book, put it on the table inside the counter enclosure reserved for it.

4 Handing over the Token (*Immediate Job*).— Pick out a token pair, put one of them on the book and hand over the other token to the reader with a request similar to that for an umbrella and/or stick.

Do similarly with any other material taken for custody.

4 Discharging Work

41 The Work of Discharging a Not-Overdue Book

The routines are as follows:

1 Locating the due date guide (*Immediate Job*).— Taking the due date from the date label of the book, locate the due date guide in the Charged Tray

2 Picking out the Charged Pocket (*Immediate Job*).— From behind the due date guide, pick out the Charged Pocket with the Call Number of the book

3 Verifying Call Number (*Immediate Job*).— Verify the Call Number of the book, with that in the Charged Pocket

4 Inserting the Book Card inside the Book Pocket (*Immediate Job*).— Insert the book card inside the book pocket

5 Examining plates, maps etc (*Immediate Job*).— In the case of there being any special note on the due date label about plates, maps, etc in the book, rapidly examine their being in tact

6 Examining fresh damage (*Immediate Job*).— Examine also there being any fresh damage to the book;

7 Verifying Name (*Immediate Job*).— In case of there being no damage etc, verify the name in the Member's Ticket in the Charged Pocket just discharged with the name of the reader returning the book;

8 Handing over the Member's Ticket (*Immediate Job*).— Hand over the Member's Ticket to the member;

91 Keeping Book on Temporary Replacing Table (*Immediate Job*).— Keep the book on the Temporary Replacing Table inside the counter enclosure;

92 Placing the Book on Bespoken Books Sequence (*Immediate Job*).— In case of the Charged pocket just discharged containing a coloured slip attached to it, place the book in the Bespoken Books Sequence;

93 Disposing Damaged Book (*Immediate Job*).— In case of there being any damage, etc to the book, send the book to the headmaster along with a note and the Member's file and also request the Member to meet the headmaster immediately.

42 Work of Discharging an Overdue Book

The following are the routines additional to those mentioned in Sec UG41:

1 Informing the Member about the Overdue (*Immediate Job*).— Inform the Member about the amount of the overdue charge;

2 Releasing of Book Card (*Immediate Job*).— Release the book card on payment of the overdue charge;

3 Returning of the Ticket (*Immediate Job*).— Ask the Member to get in. Tell him that his Ticket will be returned along with the receipt for the overdue amount;

4 Attaching Slip to Ticket (*Immediate Job*).— In case the preparation of the receipt for the overdue charge being not possible immediately, attach a slip to the Member's Ticket mentioning the amount of overdue charge collected;

5 Attaching a slip in case of non-payment (*Immediate Job*).— In case of non-payment, prepare a slip showing the amount due, put the initial and date it, clip it to the Member's Ticket, and file in the Kept Tickets Tray;

6 Charging (*Immediate Job*).— Charge the Member's Ticket in case of renewal being sought and allowed;

7 Posting the Date of Return in the Overdue Register (*Immediate Job*).— Post the date of return in the Overdue Register.

43 Old Overdue Charge Work

The following are the routines, additional to those mentioned in Sec UG41 and UG42:

1 Picking out Charged Pocket (*Immediate Job*).— Pick out the charged Pocket from the Kept Tickets Tray;

2 Finding out the Total Amount Due (*Immediate Job*).— Find out the total amount due, tally it with that shown in the Overdue Register;

3 Collecting the Amount (*Immediate Job*).— Collect the amount and issue receipt.

5 Entrance Gate Releasing Work

The following is the routine:

1 Releasing of Entrance Gate (*Immediate Job*).— After the

completion of all the routines mentioned in Sec UG41 to UG43, release the entrance gate and allow the reader to enter the library.

2 Enforcing Queue System (*Immediate Job*).— Attend first to the first reader reaching you. Till he is let into the library do not begin work with any other readers. Whenever necessary inform the readers waiting near the entrance gate to observe the rule of queue.

6 Query Answering Work

The following are the routines:

1 Giving the answer (*Immediate Job*).— Give to any reader the answer to any question in a few words immediately, if possible;

2 Sending the Reader to Reference Section (*Immediate Job.*).— In case of the question of a reader requiring long investigation or not being within your competence, admit him into the library, and send him to the person doing reference service to get the answer.

7 Work With Conscience Box As an alternative

The following are the routines:

1 Maintaining the Conscience Box (*Annual Job*).— At a convenient place on the counter top, fix a Conscience Box consisting of a glass cylinder with a metal cap. It should be locked, with the key in your custody.

2 Collecting the Overdue Amount (*Immediate Job*).— When a member returns an overdue book, tell him the amount due and ask him to drop the amount into the Conscience Box.

3 Sending the amount in the Conscience Box to the Accountant (*Daily Job*).— At the end of the day, collect the amount in the Conscience Box and send it to the accountant along with the chalan book stating the amount sent in both copies of the chalan book, asking the accountant to tear off the second copy of the challan for his own use and to return the challan book to you.

The advantages of the Conscience Box method are:

1 Saving the time and labour of maintaining Overdue Register,

giving receipts for the amount collected, and maintaining an Overdue Accounts book.

2 A common advantage is developing civic sense and responsibility in the members.

8 Work of Returning Readers' Articles in Custody

The following are the routines:

1 Returning Personal Property to Reader (*Immediate Job*).—Return to the reader any material of his left at the counter for custody, on his returning the token.

CHAPTER UH

WORK AT THE EXIT POINT OF THE COUNTER

1 Counter Vigilance Work

The following are the routines:

1 Asking the reader to Return all the Books (*Immediate Job*).— Ask the reader wishing to get out of the library to return at the counter all the books used by him within the library.

2 Examining the readers carrying away any volume (*Immediate Job*).— Examine carefully, the readers carrying away any volume of the library either forgetfully or surreptitiously. Particularly, look for bulging pockets of each reader and secure any such volume discovered before releasing the exit gate.

3 Informing the Headmaster (*Immediate Job*).— Send the reader to the Headmaster. Also send to him the book secured from the reader.

2 Work on Books Returned After Consultation

1 Examining any fresh damage (*Immediate Job*).— Examine any fresh damage in each book returned by a reader after consultation within the library.

2 Sending the book to the Headmaster (*Immediate Job*).— In case of any fresh damage, send the reader to the Headmaster. Also, send to him the damaged book.

3 Placing book without damage near at hand (*Immediate Job*).— Place aside, but near at hand, every book without damage. This is necessary for preparing the statistics about the books consulted.

4 Placing damaged books near at hand (*Immediate Job*).— Place every damaged book also, along with the books not damaged on its being received back from the Headmaster.

3 Work on the Preparation of Statistics for Books Consulted

The following are the routines:

1 Entering in Statistics Sheet (*Casual Job*).— During free

moments, enter in the Statistics Sheet for Daily Consultation, by putting against the Class Number of each book consulted, in the column of the hour concerned, a vertical stroke; for every fifth book with the same Class Number and in the same column of the hour put the fifth stroke horizontally across the preceding four vertical strokes.

2 Counting the books, with different Class Numbers, Consulted and Returned (*Hourly Job*).— At the end of each hour count the number of books consulted and returned in each subject in the preceding hour and enter the number in Indo-Arabic numerals and encircle it.

3 Totalling, for each Class Number, the Books Consulted and Returned during the day (*Daily Job*).— At the end of the day, enter in the "Vertical Total Column," in Indo-Arabic numerals, the total number of books returned after consultation in each subject during the day.

4 Totalling, for each Hourly Column, the Number of Books Consulted and Returned (*Daily Job*).— At the end of the day, enter in the "Horizontal Total Column," in Indo-Arabic Numerals, the total number of books returned after consultation during the day.

5 Totalling the number in the last Vertical Column (*Daily Job*).— At the end of each day add up the numbers in the last Vertical Column and put, in Indo-Arabic Numerals, in the last Horizontal Column the total number of volumes returned after consultation during the day.

6 Totalling the numbers in the last Horizontal Lines (*Daily Job*).— At the end of each day, add up the numbers in the last horizontal lines and verify if the total agrees with the number already entered in the last column of the horizontal line. If not, investigate the cause for the difference and set it right.

7 Totalling for the Week (*Weekly Job*).— As early as possible on the first day of each week, enter in the Statistics Sheet for Weekly Consultation, in Indo-Arabic Numerals, in the column of the week of the month, the number of volumes consulted in each class number and also the total number.

8 Totalling the numbers in the last Vertical Column (*Weekly Job*).— At the end of each week add up the numbers in the last Vertical Column, and put in Indo-Arabic Numerals, in the last Horizontal Column the total number of volumes returned after consultation during the week.

91 Totalling the numbers in the Last Horizontal Line (*Weekly Job*).— At the end of each week add up the numbers in the last horizontal lines and verify if the total agrees with the number already entered in the last column of the horizontal line. If not investigate the cause for the difference and set it right.

92 Totalling for the Month (*Monthly Job*).— As early as possible on the first day of each month, enter in the Statistics Sheet for Monthly Consultation, in Indo-Arabic Numerals, in the column of the month, the number of volumes consulted in each class number, and also the total number.

93 Totalling the numbers in the last Vertical Column (*Monthly Job*).— At the end of each month add up the numbers in the last vertical column and put, in Indo-Arabic Numerals in the last Horizontal Column the total number of volumes returned after consultation during the month.

94 Totalling the Numbers in the last Horizontal Line (*Monthly Job*).— At the end of each month, add up the numbers in the last horizontal lines and verify if the total agrees with the number already entered in the last column of the horizontal line. If not, investigate the cause for the difference and set it right.

95 Totalling for the Year (*Annual Job*).— As early as possible on the first day of each year, enter in the Statistics Sheet for Yearly Consultation, in Indo-Arabic Numerals the number of volumes consulted in each class number, and also the total number.

96 Totalling the numbers in the last Vertical Column (*Annual Job*).— At the end of each year, add up the numbers in the last vertical column and put, in Indo-Arabic Numerals, in the last horizontal column the total number of volumes returned after consultation during the year.

97 Totalling the Numbers in the last Horizontal Line (*Annual Job*).— At the end of each year, add up the numbers in the last horizontal lines and verify if the total agrees with the number already entered in the last column of the horizontal line. If not, investigate the cause for the difference and set it right.

98 Tallying for Ten Years (*Decennial Job*).— As early as possible, after every ten years, enter in the Statistics Sheet for Decennial Consultation, in Indo-Arabic Numerals, in the column of the ten years, the number of volumes consulted in each class number, and also the total number.

991 Totalling the numbers in the last Vertical Column (*Decennial Job*).— At the end of every ten years, add up the numbers in the last vertical columns and put in Indo-Arabic Numerals, in the last horizontal column, the total number of volumes returned after consultation during the ten years.

992 Totalling the Numbers in the last Horizontal Lines (*Decennial Job*).— At the end of every ten years, add up the numbers in the last horizontal lines and verify if the total agrees with the number already entered in the last oolumn of the horizontal line. If not, investigate the cause for the difference and set it right.

4 Work Preliminary to Charging

The reader may be a member of the library; and he may bring a library book for charging. In that case, the following are the routines:

1 Verifying the owner of the book (*Immediate Job*).— See if the owner of the Member's Ticket himself presents the Ticket; in case of doubt, ask the reader politely about his being the owner of the Member's Ticket.

2 Asking for letter of Authorisation (*Immediate Job*).— In case of his not being the owner of the Ticket, ask for the letter of authorisation given by the owner of the Member's Ticket.

3 Sending the reader to the Headmaster (*Immediate Job*).— Send the reader to the Headmaster in case of suspicion, send also the book and the file of the member concerned, along with a note explaining the ground for suspicion, to the Headmaster.

4 Issuing the book (*Immediate Job*).— Issue the book only after the Headmaster directing to do so.

5 Charging Work

In case of an admissible loan the following are the routines:

1 Stamping the due date (*Immediate Job*).— Stamp the due date of return in the last vacant compartment of the due date label of the book.

2 Tallying the call number (*Immediate Job*).— While stamping the due date, tally the call number in the due date label and in the book card; in case of their agreeing,

3 Pulling out the book card (*Immediate Job*).— Pull out the book card from the book pocket.

4 Getting of the Member's Ticket (*Immediate Job*).— Get one of the Member's Tickets of the member from him.

5 Coupling the book card with the Members Ticket (*Immediate Job*).— Couple the book card with the Member's Ticket, with the first in front.

6 Putting the Coupled Book Card and Member's Ticket in a pocket (*Immediate Job*).— Put the coupled book card and with Member's Ticket in a pocket; short enough to allow the reading of the words in the book card. Such a pocket containing Book Card and Member's Ticket will be denoted by the term 'Charged Pocket.'

7 Filing the Charged Pockets (*Immediate Job*).— File the charged pockets in the sequence of the call numbers in a Charged Tray.

6 Exit Gate Releasing Work

The following are the routines:

1 Releasing the exit gate.— After completing all the routines mentioned in Sec UH3 to UH4, release the exit gate and allow the member to leave the library.

Attend to the readers only one at a time. Request politely any reader attempting to go out before his turn to observe the rule of queue.

7 Loan Issuing Work

The following is the routine:

1 Handing over the book charged (*Immediate Job*).— Hand over to the reader the books charged for him only after his passing out of the exit gate.

8 Work on the Preparation of Issue Statistics

Routines analogous to those described in Sec UH3.

CHAPTER UJ

CHARGED TRAY WORK

1 Work of Charged Tray Tightening

The following is the routine:

1 Tightening the Charged Pockets (*Casual Job*).— Close up carefully, at frequent intervals, the Charged Pockets, so as to make them stand erect and with comfortable tightness.

2 Work of Charged Pockets Filing

The following are the routines:

1 Placing of Due Date Guide (*Daily Job*).— At the end of each day, place at the end of the Charged Pockets in the Charged Tray, the Due Date Guide for the issues of the day; and

2 Transferring Charged Pockets (*Daily Job*).— Transfer to behind the Due Date Guide all the Charged Pockets in the Temporary Charged Tray of the day.

3 Guide Changing Work

The following are the routines:

1 Releasing the old Overdue Guide (*Daily Job*).— Insert, behind the Overdue Guide showing the highest amount, the Overdue Guide showing the next higher amount and release the old Overdue Guide. Do similarly in the case of each one of the Overdue Guides, in case of there being any undischarged Charged Pockets behind it.

2 Inserting Five Paise due guide (*Daily Job*).— Insert the Five Paise overdue guide behind the due date bearing the date of the day, in case of there being any undischarged Charged Pockets behind it.

3 Removing Date Guides and Overdue Guides (*Daily Job*).— Remove each of the Date Guides and Overdue Guides having no Charged Pocket behind it.

4 Putting guides in the Unused Guides Tray (*Daily Job*).— Put such Date Guides and Overdue Guides in proper sequence in the Unused Guides Tray.

4 Overduing Work

The following are the routines:

1 Alphabetising Five Paise overdue charged pockets (*Daily Job*).— As early as possible, in the morning transfer each of the Charged Pockets standing charged behind the five paise overdue guide, to a Tray, and alphabetise them by the names of the Members;

2 Entering in the Overdue Register (*Daily Job*).— Make an entry, for each such Charged Pocket, in the Overdue Register of the member concerned "Call number due date."

3 Rearranging the Charged Pockets (*Daily Job*).— Rearrange then, the Charged Pockets by their Call Number.

4 Retransferring the rearranged Charged Pockets (*Daily Job*).— Retransfer the rearranged Charged Pockets to the Charged Tray to behind the Five Paise overdue guide.

5 Work of Overdue Noticing

The following are the routines:

1 Preparing Overdue List (Five Paise) (*Daily Job*).— At the end of each day but before beginning the guide changing work, prepare for each class and division separately a list of the members, the tickets being charged behind the overdue guide of five paise.

2 Distributing Overdue List to teacher (*Daily Job*).— As soon as the school reopens on the next day, distribute the Overdue Lists to the respective class teachers for necessary action.

3 Preparing Overdue List (35 Paise) (*Weekly Job*).— Prepare a similar list for the names of the students, the tickets stand charged behind 35 paise overdue guide.

4 Sending Overdue Sheet to Headmaster (*Weekly Job*).— Send

the above mentioned list on the next day to the Headmaster for necessary action.

5 Sending Overdue Notice to teacher (*Daily Job*).— In the case of a teacher, send a separate note to him on the first day as well as on the seventh day, if need be, about his overdue.

6 Sending weekly Reminders (*Weekly Job*).— Further, send weekly Reminder Notices to the Headmaster in the case of each student and to each teacher themselves, in the case of teacher, till the recovery of the overdue charge.

CHAPTER UK

WORK OF RENEWAL OF LOAN

1 Renewal Noting Work

A member or his representative may request, orally or through a letter, for the renewal of a book. Then the following are the routines:

1 Finding out the details about the loan (*Immediate Job*).— Find out from the person asking for the renewal of a book or from the letter, the due date, name of author and title, and the call number of the book.

2 Locating the Charged Pocket (*Immediate Job*).— From behind the due date guide in the Charged Tray locate the Charged Pocket.

3 Renewing the book due that day (*Immediate Job*).— The book being due on that day itself, renew it in accordance with the routine described in Sec UJ2.

4 Renewing the book due on a later date (*Immediate Job*).— The book being due on a later date, attach a white slip to the Charged Pocket having your signature and date.

5 Renewing an overdue book (*Immediate Job*).— The book being overdue, collect the overdue charge according to the Rules prescribed by the library. Then renew the book in accordance with the routine described in Sec UJ2.

(*Note.*— It is desirable to do the renewal noting in the presence of the person asking for it).

6 Declining renewal (*Immediate Job*).— The book being bespoken or the maximum number of times renewal being already done, decline renewal.

7 Requesting to return the book (*Immediate Job*).— In the case of a non-renewable book. request the person asking for renewal to return the book immediately, if that day itself is the due date, or on or before the due date.

2 Renewing Work

The following are the routines:

1 Picking out the Renewable Charged Pockets (*Daily Job*).— Before the closing hour of each day, pick out each of the charged pockets having a white slip attached to it and standing behind the date guide of the day.

2 Transferring the renewable Charged Pockets to Charging Tray (*Immediate Job*).— Transfer each of the renewable Charged Pockets into the Charging Tray.

3 Putting a dash on the white slip (*Immediate Job*).— Put a horizontal dash on the white slip attached to each of the renewable Charged Pockets. In case of the last possible renewal being made, put a vertical stroke across the earlier horizontal dashes.

4 Disposing of the Renewed Charged Pockets (*Daily Job*).— Dispose the renewed Charged Pockets as if it were a fresh Charged Pocket (*See* Sec UH4).

CHAPTER UL

BESPEAKING WORK

1 Bespeaking Card Receiving Work

The following are the routines:

1 Requesting the Member to fill up the Bespeaking Card (*Immediate Job*).— To a member desiring to bespeak a book, give a Bespeaking Card. Ask him to fill up the Card, to write his own address in the proper place, and to affix the proper postage stamp.

2 Receiving the filled up Bespeaking Card (*Immediate Job*).— In case of a Bespeaking Card being filled up correctly by a Member, put your initial at the left hand bottom corner and put the date and time of receipt of the Card just near the left hand top corner, and place it in the Temporary Bespeaking Tray.

2 Bespeaking Noting Work

The following are the routines:

1 Picking up the Bespeaking Cards (*Casual Job*).— As a pick up work, at odd moments of leisure, take out each of the Bespoken Cards one by one from the Temporary Bespeaking Tray.

2 Attaching a Red Slip to the Charged Pocket in the case of the Book Card being in the Charged Tray (*Immediate Job*).— The Charged Pocket containing the Book Card of the bespoken book may be in the Charged Tray behind some due date guide. Then attach to the Charged Pocket a red slip with your signature and date.

3 Attaching a Red Slip to the Book Card of a book in the Bespoken Collection (*Immediate Job*).— The concerned pocket may not be in the Charged Tray, but the book may be in the Bespoken Collection. Then attach to the book card of that book a red slip with your signature and date.

4 Asking the Maintenance Section to investigate the Untraceable Book (*Immediate Job*).— The book may not be traceable

in the Charged Tray or in the Bespoken Collection or among the books returned either at the exit counter or at the entrance counter. Then ask the Maintenance Section to investigate the case.

5 Searching for the Book (*Immediate Job*).— A member of the Maintenance Section should look for the book,

1 In the stack room;

2 In the binding sequence; and

3 In the list of books sent to the binder.

In case of its not being found in any of these places, have a quick walk through the reading room to find out its being actually in use by any reader. Finally communicate the result to the circulation assistant at the entrance gate for taking further action.

51 In case of the book being on the shelf, call for it and give it to the reader if still present, or go through the usual routine.

52 In case of the book being in the Binding Sequence attach a red slip with your signature and date to the book card concerned.

53 In case of the book being with the Binder send to the Binder a red slip with your signature and date for attachment to the book card concerned.

54 In the case of the book being in use by a reader in the reading room, insert a red slip, with signature and date below the book card of the book. Inform the circulation assistant about this having been done and ask him to be vigilant to locate this book and hand it over to the circulation assistant at the entrance counter.

3 Work of Arranging Bespeaking Cards

The following are the routines:

1 Inserting the Bespeaking Card (*Daily Job*).— Before the closing hour of each day, insert each of the Bespeaking Cards in the proper place in the classified sequence in the Permanent Bespeaking Box.

2 Arranging the Bespeaking Cards in case of there being two or more for the same book (*Immediate Job*).— There may be a book with two or more bespeaking cards. Then arrange them among themselves in the sequence of the date and time, put at the left hand top corner of the card.

4 Work of Bespeaking Card Picking

The following are the routines:

1 Picking out the Bespeaking Card (*Daily Job*).— Towards the end of the day, but in good time to catch the last mail of the day, for each of the books added in the course of the day to the Bespoken Books Sequence, pick out the appropriate Bespeaking Card from the Permanent or the Temporary Bespeaking Cards Box, as the case may be.

2 Attaching a Red Slip to the Charged Pocket (*Immediate Job*).— A book may have two or more Bespeaking Cards. Then the card presented earliest, as indicated by the date and time, is to be picked out. Attach a red slip to the book card of that book (At the time of issuing that book, attach this red slip to the Charged Pocket)

3 Tallying the Book with the Book mentioned in the Bespeaking Card (*Immediate Job*).— Tally the book, after taking it out of the Bespoken Books Sequence, with the book mentioned in the bespeaking card.

4 Keeping the volume in the Bespoken Books Sequence (*Immediate Job*).— In case of the book taken out of the Bespoken Books Sequence being the same as that mentioned in the Bespeaking Card, keep the book back in its original place in the Bespoken Books Sequence.

5 Work of Bespeaking Card Forwarding

The following are the routines:

1 Signing the Bespeaking Card (*Immediate Job*).— Put your dated signature in each Bespeaking Card.

2 Despatching the Bespeaking Card (*Immediate Job*).— On finishing each of the routines mentioned above, despatch each of the Bespeaking Cards.

PART V

LIBRARY CLASSIFICATION

CHAPTER VA

SCHEME FOR LIBRARY CLASSIFICATION

1 Need for a Classified Arrangement of Books

Books in a library should be put to use to the maximum possible extent. This is possible only if they are arranged on the shelves in a classified sequence according to their subject matter. This is because in the majority of cases it is the subject-approach to books that recurs. A reader usually requires some book or all the books on a specific topic. His requirements can be satisfied without loss of time and without an undue strain on the memory of the staff if and only if all the books on the said topic are kept together on the shelf and the position of this topic among thousands of other topics represented on the shelves is a filiatory one. Again, the task of finding this position while reshelving should not involve the restudy of the book determining its filiatory place *ab initio*, but should be rendered mechanical. To secure this result, books in a library are classified by a scheme for library classification. It is fitted with a notation, capable of expressing the subject matter of a book in terms of ordinal numbers — class numbers as they are called — according to a well-tried standard schedule. In effect, class numbers constitute an artificial language designed to secure filiatory sequence among topics and to mechanise their arrangement. Such an attangement alone will satisfy the Five Laws of Library Science (*See* Chap SA).

2 Important Schemes for Library Classification

There are several schemes for library classification in the field. The following seven are the more important ones:

S N	Year of invention	Name of scheme	Name of Author	Country of origin
1	1873	Decimal Classification	Mevil Dewey	USA
2	1891	Expansive Classification	Charles Ammi Cutter	USA

S N	Year of invention	Name of scheme	Name of Author	Country of origin
3	1904	L C Classification	Library of Congress	USA
4	1906	Subject Classification	James Duff Brown	UK
5	1933	Colon Classification	S R Ranganathan	India
6	1935	Bibliographical Classification	Henry Evelyn Bliss	USA
7	1961	International Classification	Fermont Rider	USA

Of these, the second, the third, the fourth, the sixth and the seventh may be passed over as they are not much in vogue and for other reasons.

CHAPTER VB

DECIMAL CLASSIFICATION

1 Defects of Decimal Classification

The Decimal Classification (DC) has been the only influential scheme in the field for nearly seven decades. It has too much of American bias. Without detracting from its pioneer status, it has to be said that naturally because of that, it has been outmoded. Its structure is based on a constricted base. Its notation is not sufficiently mnemonic. Its hospitality has been outgrown by the growth of the universe of subject. Its treatment of Linguistics and Geography disqualify it particularly for school libraries. Its treatment of the Sciences disqualify it particularly for college libraries.

2 Bliss on Decimal Classification

Bliss devotes a whole chapter to the proof of the thesis "The Decimal Classification is disqualified...both structurally and functionally. It does not embody the natural, scientific, logical, and educational orders (sequences). It fails to apply consistently the fundamental principles of classification...It is inefficient in classifying the modern literature of specific topics...Nor is its vogue among librarians and even among scientists and businessmen especially significant, except of the fact that there was nothing else readily available. It is an antiquated and inadaptable product ...And now it is hopelessly beyond reconstruction" (10).

3 Out-of-dateness of Decimal Classification

According to E B Schofield "Owing to lack of adaptation to changed conditions "Dewey" is out of touch with modern knowledge, it has also lost contact with the stock and demand of the libraries which use it (32). This had led some of the Western schools and colleges (like those at Bristol and Cheltenham) to give it up and improvise their own schemes.

4 Indological Subjects

The feeble treatment of Indological subjects makes it still more unsuited to Indian schools and colleges. Attempts to thrust Indology into it tend to mangle it beyond recognition.

5 Difficulty in Using One's Own Scheme

It has to be stated, at the same time, that individual schools inventing their own schemes or modifying a standard scheme will soon land themselves in difficulties. They may get on all right with their outline serving for a moderate number of books. But it is by no means easy to ensure that their answer equally well in a growing library. Hence the proper course is to adopt a tried, published scheme having infinite hospitality and providing devices to meet in a unique way every new subject created from time to time.

CHAPTER VC

COLON CLASSIFICATION

1 Basis of Colon Classification

The Colon Classification (CC) is of Indian Origin. Apart from reasons of patriotism its acknowledged merit is its recommendation. According to Bliss, "The system is constructed on valid principles...The 'Basic' classification is logical in most of its divisions, scientific in its details, and scholarly in its elaboration" (11). Its basis is utterly different from that of DC. It is based on the Meccano principle. Hence its hospitality is virtually infinite. Indeed, it has been remarked that every new subject creates its own class number in the scheme" (33).

2 Indological Subjects

W Howard Phillips says: "The objects sought through this synthetic method are minuteness of classification — extending to the individualising of every book in the library — a high mnemonic value, hospitality, and elasticity, combined with great brevity as to the printed schedules...The process of subdividing by topic is normally simple, and figures are used decimally, but there are many divisions where a succession of characteristics is applied in order. These are really minor schedules, and the principle involved is familiar to most students of other schemes...It should be of maximum service in classifying a world bibliography" (44). Further Indological subjects are fully worked out. W C Berwick Sayers says, "It has an admirable scheme for arranging the Indian literatures, the fullest I know (78).

3 School Libraries in India

It may be further stated that CC has by now found its way into text-books on library classification all the world over. This is evidence of its being well established and trustworthy. Since most libraries in India — particularly school libraries — are yet to be classified, it will be an advantage to adopt this highly hospitable and thoroughly scientific scheme.

4 Schedules of Colon Classification

The CC is not a scheme giving ready-made class numbers, but one giving schedules of fundamental constituent classes, and leaving it to the classifier to construct the class numbers of derived compound subjects as and when they come up, in accordance with prescribed rules. However in view of the fact that few of our school and college libraries are now manned by trained librarians, some of the schedules of common isolates frequently in demand in constructing class numbers are given in this part. Further, a brief schedule of ready made class numbers for subjects which most frequently figure in school libraries is also given. This is only a select schedule of an illustrative nature. To deal with subjects not finding a place in the illustrative schedule and even to understand and apply the scheme accurately and to the most advantageous extent one should use the original books — the *Colon classification* (49) and the general theory of library classification given in the companion volume *Prolegomena to library classification* (59).

My book *Library classification: Fundamentals and procedure* (57), giving 1,008 graded examples and exercises and illustrating also the application of DC, will be also of help.

5 CC Notation

The digits in the notational system of CC are the following as they would stand arranged according to the increasing ordinal values:

← ") & ' . : ; , — = → +

a b c d e f g h j k m n p q r s t u v w x y z 0 1 2 3 4 5 6 7 8 9
A B C D E F G H J K L M Δ N O P Q R S T U V W X Y Z (

Just as any idea can be expressed in the English language by words formed with the letters of its alphabet, the Colon translation of the name of any subject can be effected by class numbers formed with the above digits.

The place values of the digits in a class number are as in decimal fractions. For example, 233 will come between 23 and 24.

CHAPTER VD

MAIN SUBJECTS AND PARTIAL COMPREHENSIONS IN COLON CLASSIFICATION

The following schedule gives the main subjects and partial comprehensions in CC:

z	Generalia
1	Universe of subjects: Its structure and development
2	Library science
2V	Library service
2YT	Librametry
3	Book science
3T	Reading material
3V	Reading method
3X	Notes writing
4	Journalism
5	Exhibitionology
6	Museology
7	Systemology
8	Management science
9b	Career
9c	Metrology
9d	Standardisation methodology
9e	Specification methodology
9f	Research methodology
9g	Evaluation methodology
9p	Conference methodology
9s	Seminar methodology
9t	Commission methodology
9P	Communication theory
9Q	Symbolism
9Z	Sciences (Natural & Social)
9ZZ	Pure
9ZZZ	Applied
A	Natural science
A1	Pure
A2	Applied
A9C	Microtechnique
AZ	Mathematical sciences
B	Mathematics
BT	Statistical calculus
BTT	Operations research
BV	Cybernetics
BWZ	Astronomical sciences
BX	Astronomy
BYC	Astrophysics
BYE	Astrochemistry
BYG	Astrobiology
BZ	Physical sciences
C	Physics
CV	Space physics
CZ	Engineering and technology
D	Engineering
DYT	Engineering statistics
DYV	Engineering cybernetics
DX	Draughtsmanship
DZ	Chemical sciences
E	Chemistry
EX	Chemical engineering
F	Technology
FV	Foundry
FX	Welding
FZ	Biological sciences
G	Biology
GT	Cytology
GTT	Histology
GV	Microbiology

GWA Molecular biology
GWC Biophysics

GX Biochemistry
GYT Biometry
GYV Biocybernetics

GZ Geological sciences

H Geology
HUB Geodesy
HV Geophysics
HVT Geochemistry
HX Mining

HZ Plant sciences

I Botany

IZ Agriculture and Forestry

J Agriculture
JX Forestry
JYT Agrometry

JZ Animal sciences

K Zoology
KX Animal husbandry

KZ Medical sciences

L Medicine
LU5 Public health
LU5Z Hospital and sanitorium
LU6 Hospital
LU7 Sanitorium
LUD Medical technology
LX Pharmacognosy
LY1 Nursing
LY7 Anaesthesiology
LYT Medicometry
LYV Medical cybernetics
LYX Medical jurisprudence
M Useful arts

△ Mysticism and spiritual experience
△X Astrology

△Z Fine arts and literature

N Fine arts

NZ Language and literature

O Literature
P Linguistics
PW3 Calligraphy
PW5Z Typewriting and shorthand

PW6 Typewriting
PW7 Shorthand
PYT Linguametry
PYV Linguistic cybernetics

PZ Religion and philosophy
PZZ Religion and ethics

Q Religion

QZ Philosophy and psychology

R Philosophy

RZ Behaviorial sciences
RZZ Psychology and education

S Psychology
SX Applied psychology

SYT Psychometry
SYV Psycho-cybernetics

SZ Social sciences

T Education
TYT Educametry
TYV Educo cybernetics

TZ Geography and history

U	Geography
UZ	History, political science, and economics
UZZ	History and economics
V	History
VX	Historical source (as a pure discipline)
W	Political science
WX	Geopolitics
X	Economics-in-theory
XV	Economics-in-action
XX	Economics of business enterprise
XYT	Econometrics
XYV	Econimico-cybernetics
Y	Sociology
YX	Social work
YYT	Sociometry
YYV	Socio-cybernetics
Z	Law
ZT	International law
ZV	Law of War
ZX	Jurisprundence

CHAPTER VE

STEPS IN CLASSIFYING

1 Determination of Main Subject

The first step in classifying is to determine the main subject to which the subject-matter of the book belongs. The numbers representing the main subject are taken from the schedule given in Chap VD. Consider the following two groups of examples:

Group 1		*Group* 2	
1	Medicine	1	Education
2	Human anatomy	2	Educational organization
3	Human physiology	3	Educational measurement
4	Digestive system	4	Marking
5	Anatomy of the digestive system	5	University education
6	Physiology of the digestive system	6	University organization
7	Intestines	7	Measurement in university education
8	Anatomy of the intestines	8	Marking in university examinations
9	Physiology of the intestines	9	Marking in honours examinations

The subjects of Group 1 belong to the main subject "Medicine" and the number representing it is "L." If classification stopped here, we should find all the books on the diverse subjects occurring in Group 1 bearing the same class number and getting mixed together on the library shelves. The main subject "Medicine" is therefore divided further. In fact a book on Medicine may present more facets — such as Organ, Property, Effect, Action, Agent, and Method. The Medicine schedule of the CC is accordingly headed by the facet formula:

L, [1P1]; [1MP1]; [1MP2]; [1E], [2P1]; [2MM1].

This facet formula may be explained as

L, [Organ]; [Property]; [Effect]: [Action], [Agent]; [Method].

2 Second Step in Classifying

The next step in classifying is to replace these general terms by the particular terms warranted by the name of the subject classified. Let us take subject 9 in Group 1. In its case the formula will become

L, [Intestine]; [Physiology]. It is usual to speak of "Intestine" as the focus in the organ facet and of "Physiology" as the focus in the property facet.

3 Final Step in Classifying

The final step is to translate these terms into numbers with the aid of the Organ and the Property schedules given in the chapter on Medicine. Thus we get the class number "L,25;3"

4 Class Number for the Subject given in Sec VE1

The subject 6 in Group 1 has an organ facet as well as a property facet. The focus of the organ facet is "Digestive System" and that of property facet is "Physiology." Hence its class number will be L, 2; 3. The subject 9 in Group 1, also has an organ facet as well as a property facet. The focus of the organ facet is "Intestine" and it is a sharper focus than the one in subject 6. Hence its class number is L, 25;3. The examples given in Sec VE1 belong to the following Main Subjects:

Medicine; and Education;

The facet formula relevant to the present context, for there Main Subjects are, respectively as follows:

L, [1P1]; [1MP1] and T, [1P1]; [1MP1]

With these facet formulae, and with the help of the schedules concerned, we will get the following class numbers for the different subjects mentioned in the two groups in Sec VE1.

	Group 1		*Group* 2
1	L	1	T
2	L; 2	2	T; 4
3	L; 3	3	T; 47
4	L, 2	4	T; 475
5	L, 2; 2	5	T, 4
6	L, 2; 3	6	T, 4; 4
7	L, 25	7	T, 4; 47
8	L, 25; 2	8	T, 4; 475
9	L, 25; 3	9	T, 43; 475

CHAPTER VF

SCHEDULE OF ANTERIORISING COMMON ISOLATES

The following is a Schedule of Anteriorising Common Isolates, generally required while classifying general books:

a	Bibliography
c	Concordance
d	Table
e	Formula
f	Atlas
k	Cyclopaedia
m	Periodical
n	Serial
p	Conference Proceedings
q	Code
v	History
w	Biography of Specialist
w1	Autobiography
w2	Ana
w4	Letters
wT	Biography of Mystic
x	Works (Collection or Selection)
y1	Programme of instruction
y2	Syllabus
y3	Synopsis
y4	Scope
y7	Case study
y8	Digest
yP	Technical glossary

CHAPTER VG

SCHEDULE OF SPACE ISOLATES

The following is an extract from the Schedule of Space Isolates, generally required while classifying general books:

1	World
2	Mother country
3	Favoured country
3Z	Eurasia
4	Asia
418	Penghu
41U1	Korea
41V	Formosa (Taiwan)
41W1	Tibet
41X	Sinkiang
41Y1	Mongolia
41Y5	Hong Kong
42	Japan
431	Vietnam
431T	North Vietnam
431V	South Vietnam
431W1	Laos
431X	Cambodia
433	Thailand
434	Philippines
436	Indonesia
437	Malaysia
438	Burma
44	India
4411	Tamil Nadu (formerly Madras)
441111	Madras
441115	Chingleput
441121	South Arcot
441125	Tiruchirapalli
441131	Thanjavur
441135	Ramanathapuram
441141	Tirunelveli
441145	Kanyakumari
441151	Madurai
441161	Coimbatore
441165	Nilgiris
441171	Salem
441175	Dharmapuri
441181	North Arcot
4411T	Pondicherry
4412	Kerala
441211	Trivandrum
441221	Quilon
441225	Alleppey
441231	Kottayam
441241	Ernakulam
441251	Trichur
441261	Palghat
441267	Malappuram
441271	Kozhikode
441281	Cannanore
4412U1	Laccadive, Minicoy, and Amindive Islands
4413	Mysore State
441311	Kolar
441313	Bangalore
441321	Tumkur
441322	Chitradurga
441331	Mandya
441335	Mysore (district)
441337	Coorg
441341	Hassan
441345	Chikkamagalur
441347	Shimoga
441351	South Kanara
441355	North Kanara
441361	Belgaum
441365	Dharwar
441367	Bellary
441371	Raichur

441375	Bijapur
441381	Gulburga
441385	Bidar
4415	Andhra Pradesh
441511	Srikakulam
441515	Vishakapatnam
441521	East Godavari
441525	West Godavari
441531	Krishna
441535	Guntur
441541	Nellore
441543	Chittoor
441545	Cuddapah
441547	Anantapur
441551	Kurnool
441553	Mahbubnagar
441555	Hyderabad
441561	Medak
441563	Nizamabad
441565	Adilabad
441571	Karimnagar
441575	Warrangal
441581	Khamman
441585	Nalgonda
4417	Andaman and Nicobar Islands
44171	Andaman Islands
44175	Nicobar Islands
4433	Goa
4435	Maharashtra
443511	Ratnagiri
443513	Kolaba
443515	Bombay
443517	Thana
443521	Kolhapur
443523	Satara
443525	Sangli
443527	Sholapur
443531	Poona
443533	Ahmednagar
443535	Nasik
443541	Dhulia
443543	Jalgaon
443545	Buldhana
443546	Akola
443548	Amravati
443551	Wardha
443553	Nagpur
443555	Bhandara
443557	Chanda
443561	Yeotmal
443563	Nanded
443564	Osmanabad
443571	Bheed
443575	Aurangabad
443581	Parbhani
4436	Gujarat
443611	Dangs
443613	Bulsar
443615	Surat
443621	Broach
443625	Baroda
443631	Panchamahals
443635	Kaira
443641	Ahmedabad
443645	Mehsana
443651	Banaskantha
443655	Sabarkantha
443661	Bhavnagar
443665	Amreli
443668	Junagadh
443671	Jamnagar
443675	Rajkot
443677	Surendranagar
443681	Kutch
4437	Rajasthan
443711	Barmer
443715	Jalore
443717	Sirohi
443721	Pali
443725	Jodhpur
443727	Jaisalmer
443731	Bikaner
443733	Nagaur
443741	Ganganagar
443745	Chura
443747	Sikar

443751	Jhunjhunu
443753	Alwar
443755	Bharathpur
443758	Jaipur
443761	Ajmer
443765	Tonk
443767	Sawai Madhavapur
443771	Jhalawar
443773	Kota
443775	Bundi
443777	Bhilwara
443781	Chittorgarh
443783	Banasware
443785	Dungarpur
443787	Udaipur
4441	Delhi
4442	Haryana
44421	Gurgaon
44422	Mahendragarh
44423	Hissar
44425	Rohtak
44426	Karnal
44427	Ambala
4442Y1	Chandigarh
4443	Punjab
444311	Patiala
444321	Sangrur
444323	Bhatinda
444331	Ferozepore
444335	Amritsar
444341	Gurdaspur
444351	Kapurthala
444355	Jullundar
444361	Ludhiana
444371	Rupar
444381	Hoshiarpur
4445	Jammu and Kashmir
444511	Kathua
444515	Jammu
444521	Mirpur
444525	Phoonch
444531	Riasi
444535	Udhampur
444541	Anantnag
444545	Srinagar
444551	Baramulla
444555	Muzaffarabad
444561	Gilgit
444571	Chilas
444581	Ladakh
4447	Himachal Pradesh
444711	Sirmur
444721	Simla
444731	Mahasu
444735	Kinnaur
444741	Lahaul and Spiti
444745	Chamba
444751	Kangra
444761	Kulu
444771	Mandi
444781	Bilaspur
4452	Uttar Pradesh
445211	Jalaun
445212	Kanpur
445213	Etawah
445214	Mainpuri
445215	Agra
445216	Mathura
445217	Farrukabad
445221	Etah
445222	Aligarh
445223	Bulandashahar
445224	Budaun
445225	Shahjahanpur
445226	Moradabad
445228	Meerut
445231	Bijnaur
445232	Muzaffarnagar
445233	Sahranpur
445234	Tehri-Garhwal
445235	Dehra Dun
445237	Garhwal
445241	Uttar Kashi
445242	Chamoli

445243	Pithorgarh
445245	Almora
445246	Nainital
445247	Rampur
445251	Pilbhit
445252	Bareilly
445253	Kheri
445255	Sitapur
445256	Hardoi
445258	Lucknow
445261	Mirzapur
445262	Varanasi
445263	Jaunpur
445264	Ghazipur
445265	Ballia
445267	Azamgarh
445268	Basti
445271	Gorakhpur
445273	Deoria
445274	Gonda
445275	Bahraich
445276	Barabanki
445277	Faizabad
445278	Sultanpur
445281	Pratapgarh
445287	Allahabad
445283	Fatehpur
445284	Unnao
445285	Rae Bareilly
445286	Banda
445287	Hamirpur
445288	Jhansi
4455	Madhya Pradesh
445511	Raipur
445513	Bastar
445515	Durg
445521	Balaghat
445522	Seoni
445523	Chindwara
445524	Narasimhapur
445525	Sagar
445526	Damoh
445527	Jabalpur
445528	Mandla
445531	Betul
445532	Hoshangabad
445533	Sehore
445534	Raisin
445535	Vidisha
445536	Rajgarh
445537	Shahajapur
445541	East Nimar
445543	West Nimar
445545	Dhar
445547	Jhebua
445551	Ratlam
445553	Mandasor
445555	Ujjain
445556	Indore
445558	Dewas
445561	Guna
445563	Shivapur
445565	Morena
445556	Bhind
445567	Gwalior
445568	Datia
445571	Tikamgarh
445572	Chattarpur
445573	Panna
445574	Satna
445575	Rewa
445576	Sidhi
445577	Sahadol
445581	Surguja
445583	Raigarh
445585	Bilaspur
4471	Bihar
447111	Singbhum
447115	Ranchi
447121	Palamau
447125	Hazaribag
447127	Dhanbad
447131	Shahabad
447133	Patna
447135	Gaya
447141	Saran
447145	Muzaffarpur

447147 Champaran
447151 Darbhanga
447155 Saharsa
447161 Purnea
447165 Bhagalpur
447171 Malda
447175 Santalparaganas
447181 Monghyr

4473 Orissa
447311 Koraput
447315 Kalahandi
447321 Bolangir
447325 Baudhkhondmals
447331 Sambalpur
447335 Sundargarh
447341 Keonajhar
447345 Mayurbhanj
447351 Balasore
447355 Dhenkanal
447361 Cuttack
447471 Puri
447381 Gunjam

4475 West Bengal
447511 Midnapore
447515 Bankura
447521 Purulia
447525 Birbhum
447527 Burdwan
447531 Hooghly
447435 Howrah
447541 Twenty-four paraganas
447545 Calcutta
447551 Nadia
447555 Murshidabad
447561 West Dinajpur
447565 Darjeeling
447571 Jalpaiguri
447581 Cooch Bihar

4477 Assam
447711 Mizo hills
447717 Cachar
447721 United District of Mikir and North Cachar Hills
447731 United Khasi and Jaintia Hills
447741 Garo Hills
447751 Goalpara
447761 Kamarup
447765 Darrang
447771 Nowgong
447775 Sibsagar
447781 Lakhimpur

4477T Nefa
4477T1 Kameng
4477T3 Subansiri
4477T5 Siang
4477T7 Luhit
4477T8 Tirap

4477U1 Manipur
4477V Tripura

4478 Nagaland
44781 Kohima
44783 Tuensang
44785 Mokokchung

44T Nepal
44TT Sikkim
44TV Bhutan
44V Ceylon
44X1 Bangla Desh
44X5 Pakistan

45 Iran
46 Arabian Peninsula
461 Iraq
462 Kuwait
463 Saudi Arabia
464 Federation of South Arabia
464T Yemen
4651 Jordan
4653 Israel (Palestine)
4654 Lebanon
467 Syria

47 Turkey (Asia)

48	Russia (Asia)
5	Europe
51	Turkey (Europe)
51T	Cyprus
51V	Greece
52	Italy
52T	San Marino
52U1	Monaco
52X	Liechtenstein
52Y1	Switzerland
53	France
53U1	Andorra
54	Spain and Portugal
541	Spain
541T	Gibraltar
542	Portugal
55	Germany
551	West Germany
553	East Germany
55T	Luxemburg
55X	Netherlands
56	United Kingdom
561	England
562	Wales
563	Scotland
565	Northern Ireland
56V	Ireland (Eire)
57	Scandinavia
571	Sweden
572	Denmark
573	Norway
574	Iceland
57T	USSR
58	Russia (Europe)
591	Poland
592	Czechoslovakia
593	Austria
594	Hungary
595	Rumania
596	Bulgaria
597	Yugoslavia
598	Albania
5991	Malta
6	Africa
611	Tanzania
613	Zambia
615	Malawi
622	Mozambique
625	Swaziland
626	Lesotho
633	South Africa
636	Botswana
642	Namibia
643	Angola
645	Democratic Republic of Congo
646	Congo Republic (Brazzaville)
647	Gabon
651	Cameroon
652	Central African Republic
654	Nigeria
655	Dahomey
656	Togo
657	Ghana
658	Upper Volta
661	Mali
662	Ivory coast
663	Liberia
664	Sierra Leone
665	Guinea
666	Portuguese Guinea
667	Senegal
668	Gambia
668T	Equitorial Guinea
668V	Mauritania
668X	Spanish Sahara
671	Morocco
671T	Ifni
671V	Centa
671X	Melina
672	Algeria
673	Tunisia
674	Libya
676	Chad
677	United Arab Republic (Egypt)
678	Sudan

681	Ethiopia
683	French Territory of the Afras and the Issas
685	Somalia
687	Kenya
688	Uganda
688T	Rwanda
688V	Burundi
688X	Malagasy
7	America
71	North America
72	Canada
72T	Greenland
73	United States
74	Mexico
75	Central America
77	South America
78	West Indies
8	Australia
81	Queensland
82	New South Wales
82T	Australian Capital Territory (Canberra)
83	Victoria
84	South Australia
85	Western Australia
86	Northern Territory
87	Tasmania
8V	New Guinea
8V1	Netherlands New Guinea (West Irian)
8V3	Papua
8X	New Zealand
8Z	Other Islands
92	Atlantic Islands
93	Land within Pacific Ocean
934	Melanesia
935	Micronesia
936	Polynesia
943	Antarctica
947	Arctic Islands
94Z	Oceans
95	Indian
96	Atlantic
97	Pacific

CHAPTER VH

SCHEDULE OF LANGUAGE ISOLATES

The following schedule is an extract from the Schedule of Language Isolates, generally required while classifying general books:

1	Indo-European
11	Teutonic
111	English
11173	American English
112	Dutch
113	German
113Z	Scandinavian
114	Swedish
115	Norwegian
116	Danish
117	Icelandic
12	Latin
121	Italian
122	French
123	Spanish
124	Portuguese
128	Celtic
13	Greek
14	Slavonic
141	Lethic
142	Russian
143	Bulgarian
144	Illyrian
1441	Slav
1442	Servian
145	Polish
146	Bohemian
147	Ukrainian
14Z	Sanskritic
15	Sanskrit
151	Prakrit
1511	Pali
1515	Maharashtri
1516	Ardhamagadhi
1518	Apabhramsa
156	Gujarati
157	Bengali
158	Assamese
16	Iranian
161	Avestic
162	Pahlavi
164	Persian
165	Afghan (Pushtu)
168	Urdu
17	Armenian
18	Albanian
2	Semitic
25	Hebrew
28	Arabic
31	Tamil
32	Malayalam
33	Kannada
35	Telugu
38	Brahui
391	Toda
4	Asian languages
41	Chinese
42	Japanese
44	Indian languages
467	Sumerian
5	European languages
575	Finnish
594	Hungarian

6	African languages
6B	Bantu
7	American languages
7334	Cuddom (originated in Nebraska)
74	Aztec
8	Australian languages
83	Victorian family
8Z	Languages of small islands
936	Polynesian languages
99A	Artificial languages
99M	Solresol
99M7	Lingualumina
99M8	Volapuk
99M84	Blaia Zimondal
99M86	Cabe Aban
99M87	Esperanto

CHAPTER VJ

SCHEDULE OF TIME ISOLATES

The following is an extract from the Schedule of Time Isolates, generally required while classifying general books.

A	By Geological age (Before 9999 B C)	E	1000 to 1099 A D
		F	1100 to 1199 A D
AO1	Eozoic	G	1200 to 1299 A D
A1	Palaeozoic	H	1300 to 1399 A D
A2	Mesozoic	J	1500 to 1599 A D
A3	Cainozoic	K	1600 to 1699 A D
		M	1800 to 1899 A D
AZ	By Calendar time	N	1900 to 1999 A D
B	9999 to 1000 B C	Q	2100 to 2199 A D
C	999 to 1 B C	S	2300 to 2399 A D
D	1 to 999 A D	Z	Future

CHAPTER VK

SCHEDULE OF SELECT READY-MADE CLASS NUMBERS

a	Bibliography
a,14	Bibliography of Printed books
k	Encyclopaedias
m	Periodical
n	Year book
w	Biography
x	Works, Essays
z	Generalia
2	Library science
2,5	Classification
2,6	Cataloguing
2,7	Reference service
2,8	Administration
2V,J	Academic library
2V,J1	School library
2V,J3	College library
2V,M1	Children's library
B	Mathematics
B-1	Arithmetic
B-1;08	Fraction
B-1;081	Vulgar
B-1;082	Decimal
B-1,11	Numeration
B-1,12	Notation
B-1,13	Arithmetical operation
B-1,14	Approximation
B-2	Algebra
B-2,13	Fundamental operation and law
B-2,15	Ratio and proportion
B-2,16	Progression
B-2,17	Permutation and combination
B-2,3	Equation
B-2,31	Simple (Linear)
B-2,32	Quadratic

B-3	Analysis
B-3,2	Calculus
B-3,21	Differential
B-3,25	Integral
B-4	Group theory
B-4,6	Finite group
B-4,7	Infinite group
B-5	Trigonometry
B-5,2	Plane
B-5,3	Spherical
B-6	Geometry
B-6;3	Differential
B-6;6	Pure
B-6;7	Projective
B-6;8	Mapping
B-6,2	Plane
B-6,21	Straight line configuration
B-6,27	Algebraic cure
B-6,276	Cone
B-6,3	Three dimensions
B-6T	Topology
B-7	Mechanics
B-7;2	Statics
B-7;3	Dynamics
B-7,1	Solid
B-7,1;2	Solid statics
B-7,1;3	Solid dynamics
B-7,5	Liquid
B-7,5;2	Hydrostatics
B-7,5;3	Hydrodynamics
B-7,7	Gas
B-8	Physico-mathematics
B-85	Wave function
BX	Astronomy
BX;1	Chronology
BX;17	Calendar

BX;18	Era
BX;57	Eclipse
BX;8	Cosmogony
BX,1	Earth
BX,2	Moon
BX,3	Sun
BX,4	Planet
BX,5	Meteor and comet
BX,6	Star
C	Physics
C-1	Fundamentals
C-1,3	Space
C-1,32	Areas
C-1,33	Volume
C-1,5	Energy
C-1,7	Matter
C-2	Properties of matter
C-2;1	Density
C-2;2	Elasticity
C-2,1	Solid
C-2,16	Crystal
C-2,3	Fluid
C-2,5	Liquid
C-2,5;4	Surface tension
C-2,5;47	Capillarity
C-2,5;62	Viscosity
C-2,8	Gas
C-2,8;71	Vacuum
C-3	Sound
C-3;21	Velocity
C-3;1	Frequency
C-4	Heat
C-4;282	Calorimetry
C-4;284	Specific heat
C-4;3.	Thermometry
C-4;7	Expansion
C-4;8	Change of state
C-5	Light (Radiation)
C-5;3	Spectroscopy
C-6	Electricity
C-6,2	Static electricity
C-6,3	Current electricity
C-7	Magnetism
C-92	Transport phenomena
C-8B	Molecular physics
C-9C	Atomic physics
C-9D	Nuclear physics
C-9E	Elementary particles
C-K	Gravitation theory
C-M	Kinetic theory
C-N	Quantum theory
CNO	Special theory of relativity
C-N1	General theory of relativity
C-N2	Wave mechanics (Quantum mechanics)
D	Engineering
D-1	Civil engineering
D-2	Building engineering
D-2Z	Hydraulic engineering
D-3	Irrigation engineering
D-4	Track engineering
D-41	Land track
D-43	Railway track
D-44	Bridge
D-45	Water way
D-47	Air way
D-5	Sanitary engineering
D-55	Water supply
D-56	Sewage
D-58	Pollution
D-5Z	Production engineering
D-6	Power engineering
D-61	Mechanical power
D-62	Hydraulic power
D-63	Pneumatic power
D-64	Thermal power
D-66	Electrical power
D-7	Service engineering
D-73	Communication engineering

D-73,33	Telephone	E-2;11	Atomic weight
D-73,34	Telegraphy	E-2;12	Molecular weight
D-73,3G	Broadcasting	E-2,2	Solution
D-73,3H	Radio		
D-73,3M	Television	E3	Analytical chemistry
		E-3;M	Volumetry
D-74	Transport engineering	E-3;N	Gravimetry
D-75	Illumination engineering	E-3;Q	Qualitative
		E-3;R	Quantitative
D-76	Ventilation engineering		
		E-4	Synthetic chemistry
D-77	Airconditioning engineering	E-7	Macromolecular chemistry
D-772	Refrigeration engineering	E-8	Polymer chemistry
D-78	Control engineering	F	Technology
D-8	Commodity production engineering	F,b	Metallurgy
		F,c	Iron
D-8,3Z	Vehicle	F,d	Steel
D-8,4	Land vehicle	F,1	Fertilizer
D-8,4A	Motor	F,3	Food
D-8,4J	Motor car	F,4	Beverage
D-8,52	Railway vehicle	F,46	Alcohol
D-8,6	Water vehicle	F,462	Wine
D-8,6K	Ship	F,463	Beer
D-8,7	Air vehicle	F,7	Fabrics
D-8,7B	Aeroplane	F,8	Dye
D-8,7P	Helicopter	F,9f	Paint
D-8,8	Space vehicle	F,9g	Enamel
D-8,92	Rocket	F,94	Fuel
D-8,9Z	Machine	F,9415	Coal
D-8,D4	Heat engine	F,9453	Petroleum
D-8,D46	Steam engine	F,95	Explosive
D-8,D4A	Internal combustion engine	F,95Y	Matches
		F,9M5	Plastics
		F,M.	Soap
E	Chemistry	F,T	Perfume
E-1	General chemistry	F,V	Cosmetics
E-1:4	Preparation		
E-1,b	Metals	G	Biology
E-1,d	Non-metals	G;5	Ecology
E-1,1	Inorganic chemistry	G;6	Genetics
E-1,3	Acid	G;61	Heredity
E-1,4	Salt	G;66	Evolution
E-1,5	Organic chemistry	G;67	Reproduction
E-2	Physical chemistry	G;7	Development

H	Geology
H-1	Mineralogy
H-1,9A	Precious stone
H-2	Petrology (Rocks)
H-3	Structural geology
H-4	Geomorphology
H-5	Stratigraphy
H-6	Palaeontology
H-61	Palaeobotany
H-7	Economic geology
HV	Geophysics
HV-3	Volcanology
HV-35	Geyser
HV-4	Seismology
HV-4,3	Earthquake
HV-5	Hydrology
HV-57	Oceanology
HV-8	Atmospherology
HV-86	Ionosphere
I	Botany
I,23	Fungi
I,5	Flowering plant
I,5;13.2	Indian flowering plants
I,5;13.211	Flowering plants of Tamil Nadu
I-9K2	Creeper
I-9K3	Climber
I-9Uk2	Desert plants
I-9U3	Tropical plants
J	Agriculture
J;1	Soil
J;2	Manure
J;3	Propagation
J;4	Disease
J;5	Development
J;6	Breeding
J;7	Harvest
J,1	Horticulture
J,16	Floriculture
J,251	Grass
J,311	Sugarcane
J,37	Fruit

J,371	Apple
J,3722	Orange
J,3731	Plantain
J,374	Grape
J,3751	Mango
J,3794	Tomato
J,38	Cereals and grains
J,381	Rice
J,382	Wheat
J,451	Tea
J,452	Tobacco
J,481	Coffee
J,561	Rose
J,581	Groundnut
J,582	Cocoanut
J,711	Rubber
J,741	Jute
J,742	Flax
J,771	Cotton
JX	Forestry
JX,21	Pine
JX,53	Teak
JX,54	Sandalwood
JX,55	Rosewood
K	Zoology
K;12	Natural history of animals
K,1	Invertebrata
K,7	Mollusca
K,8	Arthropoda
K,86	Insecta
K,8Z	Vertebrata
K,92	Pisces (Fishes)
K,94	Reptila
K,96	Aves (Birds)
K,96;13.2	Indian birds
K,97	Mammalia
K,97;13.2	Indian mammals
KX	Animal husbandry
KX,142	Aquarium fish
KX,2	Cattle

KX,31	Milk-giving animals
KX,311	Cow
KX,311;71	Milk
KX,311;73	Butter
KX,311;75	Butter milk
KX,311;76	Cheese
KX,332	Fish
KX,4	Traction animals
KX,442	Horse
KX,446	Camel
KX,447	Elephant
KX,448	Reindeer
KX,5	Pet animals
KX,541	Dog
KX,542	Cat
KX,546	Parrot
KX,611	Bee
KX,711	Silkworm
L	Medicine
L;2	Anatomy
L;3	Physiology
L;4	Disease
L;4:5	Prevention of disease
L;4:6	Treatment of disease
L;4:7	Surgery
L;4:91	After-care
L;4;2	Etiology
L;5	Personal hygiene
L;51	Residence
L;512	Water supply
L;513	Ventilation
L;515	Light
L;518	Drainage
L;53	Food
L;536	Fasting
L;542	Stimulant
L;544	Intoxicant
L;555	Bath
L;557	Toilet
L;558	Cleanliness
L;56	Regulation of habit
L;57	Clothing
L;58	Sleep

L,177	Throat
L,183	Ear
L,185	Eye
L,2	Digestive system
L,21	Mouth
L,214	Tooth
L,25	Intestine
L,25;4232	Typhoid
L,25;4232-416	Dysentery
L,25;4362	Hook worm
L,2722;452	Constipation
L,291;455	Jaundice
L,293;452	Diabetes
L,35;4261	Malaria
L,44;455	Asthma
L,7	Nervous system
L,7;4235	Rabies
L,7;45	Cholera
L,72	Brain
L,82	Bone
L,87	Skin
L,881	Hair
L,883	Nail
L-9C	Child medicine
L-9C,73;4232	Poliomyelitis
L-9C,82;471	Rickets
L-9F	Old-age medicine
L-9H	Female medicine
L-9Ux	Space medicine
L-9U3	Tropical medicine
L-B	Ayurveda
L-C	Siddha
L-D	Unani
L-L	Homeopathy
L-M	Naturopathy
LX	Pharmacognosy
LX-3	Pharmacology
LX-5	Pharmacopoeia
LX-6	Pharmacy
LX-7	Drug manufacture
M	Useful arts

M-1	Book production
M-15	Composition
M-16	Printing
M-2	Carpentry
M-3	Masonry
M-7	Textile
M-7:2	Spinning
M-7:7	Weaving
M-7,41	Cotton
M-7,53	Wool
M-7,55	Silk
M-8	Dress-making
M-92	Tailoring
M-97	Laundry
M-9F	Photography
M-A3	Home science
M-KZ	Physical exercises, Games, and Amusement
M-L	Physical exercises and Games
M-La	Physical exercise
M-Lc	Gymnastics
M-Le	Acrobatics
M-Lg	Trapeze work
M-Lj	Rope and wire walking
M-Lm	Athletics
M-Lp	Field Sports
M-Lq	Jumping
M-Ls	Running
M-Lt	Cycling
M-Lz	Game
M-L1	Ball game
M-L2	Foot ball
M-L3	Tennis
M-L5	Cricket
M-L6	Base ball
M-L7	Golf
M-L8	Billiards
M-L92	Basket ball
M-LB	Tug of war
M-LC	Throwing game
M-LE	Aiming
M-LF	Chasing
M-LG	Hunting

M-LH	Attack and defence
M-LJ	Fighting
M-LK	Boxing
M-LM	Ice and snow
M-LM 2	Skating
M-LN	Water sports
M-LN1	Canoeing
M-LN2	Rowing
M-LN3	Sailing (Navigation)
M-LN4	Yachting
M-LN6	Motor boating
M-LN7	Swimming
M-LN8	Water polo
M-LP	Aviation
M-LR	Hiking
M-LS	Animal riding
M-LT	Vehicle riding
M-M	Mental games and Entertainments
M-M1	Mental game
M-M3	Skill game
M-M4	Betting game
M-M5	Horse race
M-M7	Cards play
M-M92	Watching game
M-MA	Occupational amusement
M-MB	Hobby
M-MC	Book collecting
M-ME	Stamp collecting
M-MJ	Gardening
M-MN	Entertainment
M-MP	Carnival
M-MR	Circus
M-MS	Indoor game
M-MT	Outdoor game
M-MX	Special games
M-MXC	Children
M-MXF	Old
M-MXH	Female
M-MXJ	Invalid

M-MK	Cripple
M-ML	Sports material
M-NR	Musical instruments
M-NT	Theatre equipments
M-NW	Cinema production engineering
M-NX	Talkie production engineering
M-U8	Tourism
M-V	War science
M-V1	Land
M-V5	Naval
M-V7	Air
M-X4	Traffic regulation
Δ	Spiritual experience and mysticism
Δ;34	Breath control
Δ;8	Occultism
Δ;86	Prophecy
Δ;861	Numerology
Δ;862	Physiognomy
Δ;8628	Phrenology
Δ;8692	Omen
Δ;87	Magic and witchcraft
Δ,2	Hindu yoga
Δ,73	Sufism
N	Fine arts
N-b	Ornament
N-c	Gold ornament
N-d	Silver ornament
N-e	Precious stone
N-f	Diamond
N-g	Ruby
N-h	Sapphire
N-j	Opal
N-k	Topaz
N-s	Lapidary art
N-t	Bead work
N-v	Numismatic art
N-1	Graphic art
N-3	Calligraphy

N-5	Drawing
N-6	Painting
N-7	Glyptic art (Engraving)
N-8	Etching
N-91	Needle work
N-93	Embroidery
N-95	Lace work
N-97	Tapestry
N-A	Architecture
N-B	Furniture
N-C	Town planning
N-D	Plastic art
N-E	Sculpture
N-G	Ceramic art
N-H	Artistic glass
N-L	Mosaic art
N-M	Inlay art
N-P	Toy making
N-R	Music
N-R,22	Flute
N-R,291	Harmonium
N-R,31	Veena
N-R,32	Violin
N-R,34	Piano
N-R,38	Guitar
N-R,41	Drum
N-R,97	Vocal music
N-R(44)	Indian music
N-R(5)	European music
N-S	Dance
N-T	Theatre
N-U	Puppet play
N-V	Shadow play
N-W	Cinema
N-X	Talkie
O	Literature
O,111;v	History of English literature
O,111	English literature
O,111,1 H40	Chaucer
O,111,1H40,C	Canterbury Tales
O,111,1I65	Malory

O,111, 1J52	Spenser
O,111,1J52	Faerie Queene
O,111,1K08	Milton
O,111,1K08, P+L	Paradise lost
O,111,1K08, P+R	Paradise regained
O,111,1K79	Parnell
O,111,1K79,H	Hermit
O,111,1L16	Gray
O,111,1L16,E	Elegy
O,111,1L28	Goldsmith
O,111,1L28,D	Deserted village
O,111,1L59	Burns
O,111,1L70	Wordsworth
O,111,1L88	Byron
O,111,1L88,C	Childe Harold
O,111,1M07	Longfellow
O,111,1M07,E	Evangeline
O,111,1M07,H	Hiawatha
O,111,1M09	Tennyson
O,111,1M09, I+K	Idylls of the King
O,111,1M09, I+M	In memoriam
O,111,1M22	Arnold
O,111,1M22,S	Sohrab and Rustum
O,111,1M56	Toru Dutt
O,111,1M61	Tagore
O,111,1M61,C	Crescent moon
O,111,1M61,GA	Gardener
O,111,1M61,GI	Gitānjali
O,111,1M79	Sarojini Naidu
O,111,2	English drama
O,111,2J64	Shakespeare
O,111,2J64,M	Macbeth
O,111,2M61	Tagore
O,111,2M61,C	Chitra
O,111,2M61, C+S	Cycle of spring
O,111,2M61,K	King of the dark chamber
O,111,2M61,P	Post office
O,111,2M61,S	Sacrifice
O,111,3	English fiction
O,111,3K59,R	Robinson Crusoe
O,111,3K67,G	Gulliver's travels
O,111,3L28,V	Vicar of Wakefield
O,111,2L48,H	History of Sanford and Merton
O,111,2L71	Scott
O,111,3M12	Dickens
O,111,3M57	Ghosal
O,111,3M59	Doyle
O,111,3M61	Tagore
O,111,3M65	Kipling
O,111,3M74	Ramakrishnapillai (T)
O,111,3M76	Madhaviah (A)
O,111,3M91	Venkataramani (K S)
O,111,6	English prose
O,111,6L75	Lamb
O,111,6M00	Macaulay
O,111,6M12	Smiles
O,111,6M12,C	Character
O,111,6M12,D	Duty
O,111,6M12,S	Self-help
O,111,6M12,T	Thrift
O,111,6M61	Tagore
O,111,6M61,P	Personality
O,15	Sanskrit literature
O,15,1	Sanskrit poetry
O,15,1A1	Rāmāyana
O,15,1A2	Mahābhārata
O,15,1D40	Kālidāsa
O,15,1D40,K	Kumārasambhava
O,15,1D40,M	Megaduta
O,15,1D40,R	Raghuvamsa
O,15,1D60	Bhartrihari
O,15,2	Sanskrit drama
O,15,2D10	Sudraka
O,15,2D10,M	Mricchakatika
O,15,2D30	Bhāsa
O,15,2D30,V	Vāsavadattā
O,15,2D40	Kālidāsa
O,15,2D40,M	Mālavikāgnimitra
O,15,2D40,S	Sākuntala

O,15,2D40,V	Vikramorvasiya
O,15,2D68	Harsha
O,15,2D68,R	Ratnāvali
O,15,2D70	Bāna
O,15,2D70,K	Kādambari
O,15,2D79	Bhavabhuti
O,15,2D79,M	Mahāviracharita
O,15,2D79,U	Uttararāmacharita
O,15,2D80	Bhatta Nārāyana
O,15,2D80,V	Venisamhāra
O,15,2D81	Visākhadatta
O,15,2D81,M	Mudrārākshasa
O,15,3	Sanskrit fiction
O,15,3D20	Vishnusarma
O,15,3D20,P	Panchatantra
O,15,3E60	Somadeva
O,15,3E60,K	Kathā Saritsāgara
O,15,3H00	Nārāyana Pandita
O,15,3H00,H	Hitopadesa
O,15,6	Sanskrit prose
O,15,6D59	Dandin
O,15,6D59,D	Dasakumāracharita
O,15,6D70	Bāna
O,15,6D70,H	Harsha charita
O,15,6E10,B	Bhoja charita
O,15,6M60	Lakshmana Suri
O,15,6M60,N	NalopakhyānaSangraha
O,15,7	Sanskrit champu
O,15,7D91	Trivikrama bhatta
O,15,7D91,N	Nala champu
O,31,1	Tamil poetry
O,31,1A	Ettuttokai
O,31,1A1	Narrinai
O,31,1A2	Kuruntokai
O,31,1A3	Aingurunuru
O,31,1A4	Patirruppāttu
O,31,1A5	Paripadai
O,31,1A6	Kalittokai
O,31,1A7	Agananuru
O,31,1A8	Purananuru
O,31,1B1	Padinen Kizhk-kanakku
O,31,1B21	Naladiyar
O,31,1B22	Nanmankkatikai
O,31,1B3	Nanarppatu
O,31,1B31	Inna narpatu
O,31,1B32	Iniyavai narpatu
O,31,1B33	Kar narpatu
O,31,1B34	Kalavashi narpatu
O,31,1B4	Aintinai
O,31,1B41	Aintinai aimpatu
O,31,1B42	Aintinai ezhupatu
O,31,1B43	Tinaimozhi yaimpatu
O,31,1B44	Tinaimalai nurraimbatu
O,31,1B5	Tirukkural
O,31,1B51	Aratruppal
O,31,1B52	Porutpal
O,31,1B53	Kamattuppal
O,31,1B61	Tirukatukam
O,31,1B62	Acarakkovai
O,31,1B63	Pazhamozhi
O,31,1B64	Cirupanca mulam
O,31,1B65	Mutumozhikkanchi
O,31,1B66	Eladi
O,31,1B67	Kainilai
O,31,1B7	Pattupāttu
O,31,1B711	Tirumurukarruppadai
O,31,1B712	Porunararruppadai
O,31,1B721	Cirupanarruppadai
O,31,1B722	Perumpanarruppadai
O,31,1B731	Mullaippattu
O,31,1B732	Maturaikkauchi
O,31,1B741	Nedunalvadai
O,31,1B742	Kurunchippāttu
O,31,1B751	Pattinappalai
O,31,1B752	Malaipatu Katam
O,31,1B8	Pancha Kāvyam
O,31,1B81	Civaka cintāmani
O,31,1B82	Cilappadikāram
O,31,1B83	Manimekalai
O,31,1B84	Valaiyapati
O,31,1B85	Kundalakeci
O,31,1B91	Cirupancha Kāvyam
O,31,1B911	Yasodhara Kāvyam
O,31,1B912	Culamani
O,31,1B913	Udayana Kāvyam

O,31,1B914	Nagakumara Kavyam	O,31,1B951	Neelakesi

Note.— For any work of any author in any language, proceed as follows:

Start with O. Put after it a ", " (comma) and then the number for the language of the literature, taking from the Schedule of language isolates given in chap VH. Put a ", " (comma) after the language number and thereafter put the number for the form of the literature, remembering that 1 is poetry, 2 is drama, 3 is fiction, 6 is prose etc. After the form number, put down the chronological number for the year of birth of the author of the book using the Schedule of Time Isolates given in Chap VJ. After the author number, if necessary, put a "," (comma) and add thereafter the Roman Capital(s) representing that particular work, got by Alphabetical Device. The language number need not be written, but taken as understood, in the case of favoured language of the library.

P	Linguistics	P,111;76	Essay writing
P,111	English language		
P,111;1	Phonetics	P,111,35	Verb
P,111;2	Morphology	P,111,4;k	Dictionary of idioms
P,111;3	Syntax	P,111,6;k	Dictionary of proverbs
P,111;4;k	Dictionary	P,111,78	Precis
P,111;7	Composition	P,111,8	Punctuation
P,111;71	Verse Writing	P,111,97	Practice material (Reader)
P,111;72	Drama writing	P,111=D	Anglo-Saxon English
P,111;73	Story writing	P,111=E	Middle age English
P,111;74	Letter writing	P,111=J	Modern English

Note.— Books on the linguistics of other languages are to be classified similarly. The number "111" representing English language being replaced by the number representing the other languages taken from the Schedule of Language Isolates given in Chap VH. Here are some examples:

15=A	Vedic Sanskrit	31=J	Modern Tamil
15=B	Epic Sanskrit	31=A	Ancient Kannada
15=C	Classical Sanskrit	31=E	Halegannada
31=A	Ancient Tamil	31=J	Hosagannada
31=D	Middle Tamil		

Note.— For the Classics in Indian languages, readymade class numbers are given in the original book *Colon classification*. Here are some examples:

P,15=C"x1,1	Pānini: Astādhyāyi
P,15=C"x1,1,2	Patanjali: Mahābhāsya
P,15=C"x1,1,6	Bhattoji Diskita: Siddhāntakaumudi
P,15=C;4"x1,1	Amara-simha: Amara-Kosa
P,31=A"x1	Agattiyar
P,31=D"x1,1	Tolkāppianar: Tolkāppiam
P,31=D"x1,1,1	Ilampūranar: Commentary
P,31=D"x1,1,2	Kallādanār: Commentary
P,31=D"x1,1,3	Perasiriyar: Commentary
P,31=D"x1,1,4	Senā-varaiyar: Commentary
P,31=D"x1,1,5	Naccinārkkiniyar: Commentary
P,31=D"x,1,11	Ezhut-adhikāram
P,31=D"x1,13	Sol-adhikāram
P,31=D"x1,14	Porul-adhikāram
P,31=J"x1,1	Pava-nandi Munivar: Nannūl
P,31=J"x1,1,3	Subrahmanya Diksitar: Prayoga-vivekam
P,31=J"x1,1,4	Swāmi-nātha Deskiar: Illakkanak-Kottu
P,33=E;4"x,1,1	Nāga-varma: Abhidhāna-vastu-kosa
P,35=E"x1,1	Nannaya-bhattācharya: Andhra-bhāsā-cintāmani
P,35=E"x1,1,1	Ahobala-pandita: Ahobala-panditiyamu or Kavi-siro-bhūsanamu
35=E"x1,1,2	Narasimha-rāja Simhudu Balāri-simha: Kavi-jnānānjanamu
P,35=E"x1,1,3	Appa-kavi: Appa-kaviyamu
P,35=E"x3,1	Ketana-kavi: Andhra-bhāsā-bhūsanamu
P,35=E"x4,1	Peddanna: Kāvyā-lankāra-cūdāmani
P,35=E"x5,1	Timmaya: Sarva-laksana-sāra-san-grahamu
P,35=E"xM60,1	Cinnaya Sūri (Parva-vasu): Bālavyā-karanamu
P,35=E;4"x3,1	Venkanna (Koti): Andhra-bhāsār-navamu
P,35=E;4"x6,1	Sūrya (Adidamu): Andhra-nāma sesamu
Q	Religion
Q;1	Mythology
Q;2	Scripture
Q;25	Saying
Q;26	Tradition
Q;3	Theology
Q;31	God
Q;311	*Avasara*
Q;315	*Avatara*
Q;32	Angel and devil
Q;321	Angel
Q;324	Devil
Q;33	Founder of religion
Q;4	Religious practice
Q;41	Personal
Q;417	Hymn
Q;4173	*Nāmāvali*
Q;418	Sacred formula (Incantation)
Q;4198	Pilgrimage
Q;42	Sacrament
Q;43	Holy day
Q;45	Public religious practice
Q;454	Worship
Q;457	Festival
Q;494	Sacrifice
Q;495	Holy Water

Q;5	Social religious practice
Q;6	Religious institutions
Q;7	Religious sect
Q,1	Hinduism (Vedic)
Q,1;2	Scripture
Q,1;21	Samhitā
Q,1;22	Brāhmana
Q,1;23	Āranyaka
Q,1;24	Upanishad
Q,11	Ṛigvedic
Q,12	Yajurvedic
Q,13	Sạmavedic
Q,14	Atharvavedic
Q,2	Hinduism (Post-vedic)
Q,2;2	Scripture
Q,2;21	Relevant selection from Vedas
Q,2;22	Relevant selection from Purānas
Q,2;24	Upaṇishad
Q,21	Smārtaism
Q,21;2251	Adhyātma Rāmāyana
Q,21;226	Yoga-vāsistha Rāmāyana, Jnānavāsistha
Q,21;227	Ānanda Rāmāyana
Q,21;228	Adbhuta Rāmāyana
Q,22	Vaisnavism
Q,22″w1	Life of Ālwārs
Q,22;223	Bhāgavata
Q,22;417″x1	Nālāyira-divya-prabandhaṃ
Q,22;4173″x1	Vishnu-sahasra-nāma
Q,23	Saivism
Q,23″w″x1	Sekkizar: Periyapurānam
Q,23;226	Skāndapurānam
Q,23;417″x1	Tevāram
Q,23;417″x2	Sambandar
Q,23;417″x3	Appar
Q,23;417″x4	Sundarar
Q,23;417″x5	Mānikka-vācagar
Q,23;417″x8	Tirumūlar: Tirumandiram

Q,24	Ganapatyism
Q,26	Saktaism
Q,25″x1,1	Sankara: Saundarya-lahari
Q,26	Sanmukhaism
Q,27	Sauraism
Q,286	Hanumatseva
Q,288	Village god worship
Q,3	Jainism
Q,31	Svetāmbara
Q,32	Digambara
Q,4	Buddhism
Q,41	Hinayāna
Q,42	Mahāyāna (Indian & general)
Q,43	Lamaism
Q,44	Mahāyāna (China)
Q,45	Mahāyāna (Japan)
Q,5	Judaism
Q,6	Christianity
Q,6;21	Bible
Q,6;22	Old testament
Q,6;23	New testament
Q,6;231	St. Matthew
Q,6;232	St. Mark
Q,6;233	St. Luke
Q,6;234	St. John
Q,62	Roman catholic
Q,63	Protestant
Q,64	Presbyterian
Q,65	Puritan
Q,66	Quaker
Q,7	Islam
Q,71	Sunnis
Q,72	Shi'ah
Q,73	Mu'tazilite
Q,77	Wahabi
Q,8412	Confucianism
Q,8413	Lao-Tseism Taoism
Q,8441	Sikhism
Q,8451	Zorastrianism

R	Philosophy
R-1	Logic
R-1,1	Induction
R-1,2	Deduction
R-2	Epistemology
R-3	Metaphysics
R-4	Ethics
R-4,OZ,8(Q)	Religious ethics
R-4,OZ,8(Q,2)	Hindu ethics
R-4,1	Personal ethics
R-4,111	Truth
R-4,114	Falsehood
R-4,121	Humility
R-4,122	Modesty
R-4,124	Pride
R-4,125	Egoism
R-4,13	Temperance
R-4,141	Gentleness
R-4,142	Kindness
R-4,143	Sweetness
R-4,144	Anger
R-4,145	Cruelty
R-4,146	Envy
R-4,147	Tolerance
R-4,151	Chastity
R-4,154	Adultery
R-4,161	Gratefulness
R-4,164	Ungratefulness
R-4,171	Diligence
R-4,174	Sloth
R-4,181	Courage
R-4,182	Firmness
R-4,184	Cowardliness
R-4,185	Weakness
R-4,2	Family ethics
R-4,211	Husband
R-4,212	Wife
R-4,221	Parent
R-4,225	Child
R-4,3	Social ethics
R-4,321	Truth
R-4,324	Slander
R-4,331	Philanthropy
R-4,335	Humaneness
R-4,34	Etiquette
R-4,341	Entertainment
R-4,344	Games and sports
R-4,371	Friendship
R-4,3W	State ethics
R-4,4	Professional ethics
R-4,6	Ethics of leisure and amusement
R-4,7	Conduct towards animal
R-6	Indian philosophy
R-61	Hindu philosophy
R-62	Vaisesika and Nyāya
R-621	Vaisesika
R-625	Nyāya
R-63	Sānkhya and Yoga
R-631	Sānkhya
R-635	Yoga
R-64	Purva mimāmsā
R-641	Bhātta mimāmsā
R-645	Prābhākara mimāmsā
R-65	Vedānta
R-66	Advaita
R-663	Pratyabhijnā (Kashmirism)
R-6634	Virasaiva
R-667	Visistādvaita
R-672	Vaisnava
R-673	Saivasiddhānta
R-68	Dvaita
R-6891	Bhedābheda
R-6892	Dvaitādvaita
R-6893	Suddhādvaita
R-691	Cārvāka
R-693	Jaina
R-694	Buddhistic
R-6941	Hinayāna
R-6942	Vaibhāsika
R-6943	Sautrāntika
R-6945	Mahāyana
R-6946	Yogācāra

R-6947	Mādhyamika
R-7	Greek philosophy
R-71	Pre-Socratic
R-711	Milesian
R-712	Pythagoreans
R-713	Eleatic
R-714	Sophist
R-715	Megarian
R-72	Socratic and Platonic
R-721	Socratic
R-722	Cynics
R-723	Platonic
R-725	Aristotelian
R-73	Post-Aristotelian
R-731	Peripatetic
R-732	Stoic
R-734	Epicurean
R-74	Sceptic
R-741	Pyrrhonism
R-75	Eclecticism
R-77	Alexandrian
R-8(41,C4)	Confucianism
R-N	Existentialism
S	Psychology
S;1	Sensation
S;31	Attention
S;343	Work
S;344	Fatigue
S;357	Habit
S;4	Cognition
S;41	Idea concept
S;432	Memory
S;433	Remembering
S;434	Forgetting
S;435	Imagination
S;442	Thinking
S;443	Reasoning
S;447	Judgement
S;47	Opinion
S;5	Emotion
S;52	Feeling
S;523	Joy
S;524	Anger
S;525	Fear
S;531	Affection
S;534	Hatred
S,537	Ego
S;55	Love
S;56	Anxiety
S;571	Sentiment
S;572	Interest
S;595	Sex
S;6	Conation
S;64	Conscience
S;7	Personality
S;74	Character
S;8	Meta-psychology
S;81	Sleep
S;811	Dream
S;851	Hypnotism (Mesmerism)
S;G	Psycho-genetics
S,1	Child psychology
S,1;31	Attention in children
S,1;357	Habit in children
S,1;432	Memory in children
S,11	New-born
S,12	Toddler
S,13	Infant
S,15	Pre-adolescent
S,2	Adolescent
S,3	Adult
S,35	Middle age
S,38	Old age
S,4	Sick and infirm
S,5	Sex
S,55	Female
S,56	Male
S,6	Abnormal
S,61	Mentally disordered
S,621	Idiot
S,64	Genius
S,65	Criminal

S,66	Physically handicapped
S,662	Stammerer
S,663	Cripple
S,67	Deaf and dumb
S,68	Blind
S,7	Family
S,83	Left-handed
T	Education
T,b	Teaching profession
T;2	Curriculum
T;3	Teaching technique
T;31	Audio-visual technique
T;313	Audio
T;3133	Sound record
T;3136	Radio
T;3137	Television
T;315	Visual
T;316	Picture
T;3163	Motion picture
T;318	Excursion
T;32	Computer-assisted
T;33	Medium of teaching
T;331	Mother tongue
T;332	Bilingualism
T;335	Foreign language
T;338	Classical language
T;33Z	Method of teaching
T;341	Heuristic
T;35	Catechism
T;37	Case study
T;38	Experiment
T;382	Observation
T;384	Laboratory
T;387	Project
T;3871	Individual
T;3877	Team work
T;391	Direct
T;392	Dramatisation
T;393	Story
T;394	Recitation
T;395	Play
T;396	Pictorial
T;397	Lecture
T;398	Discussion
T;3982	Seminar
T;3984	Conference
T;3(A)	Teaching of science
T;3(B)	Teaching of mathematics
T;3(B-6)	Teaching of geometry
T;3(K)	Teaching of zoology
T;3(K)-38	Experimental method in teaching zoology
T;3(P,O1)	Teaching of mother tongue
T;3(P,O5)	Teaching of foreign language
T;3(P,O8)	Teaching of classical language
T;3(V)	Teaching of history
T,3(V)-398	Teaching of history by discussion
T,4	Student's work
T;41	Home work
T;42	Library work
T;43	Study method
T;431	Programmed learning
T;435	Independent study
T;44	Field work
T;45	Examination work
T;46	Competition
T;47	Group work
T;48	Correspondence course
T;492	Part-time course
T;494	Vacation course
T;5	Educational measurement
T;51	Intelligence test
	Divisions by (CD) (Illustrative)
T;51N	Binet Simon
T;51N1	Terman
T;51N2	Block-design
T;51N24	Form board and performance test
T;51N26	Drawing test
T;51N3	Brain test
T;51N31	Merrill-Palmer test

T;52	Achievement test
T;55	Examination
T;551	Entrance examination
T;552	Marks
T;56	Written test
T;57	Viva voce
T;58	Diploma
T;6	Physical education
T;61	Measurement
T;64	Medical inspection
T;65	Games
T;7	Student's life
T;71	Students organisation
T;711	International
T;712	National
T;714	Local
T;717	Alumni
T;72	Public relation
T;723	Teacher-student relation
T;7237	Student guidance
T;725	Teacher-parent relation
T;74	Student's unrest
T;75	Student exchange
T;76	Students aid
T;762	Stipend
T;764	Scholarship
T;765	Fellowship
T,1	Education of children
T,13	Nursery
T,15	Elementary education
T,2	Secondary education
T,2;2	Curriculum for Secondary school
T,2;3	Teaching technique in secondary schools
T,2;311	Audio-visual method of teaching in Secondary schools
T,2;3(A)	Teaching methods for science in Secondary schools
T,2;3(A)-311	Audio-visual method of teaching Science in Secondary schools
T,25	Intermediate
T,3	Adult
T,33	Literate
T,34	Illiterate
T,342	Semi-literate
T,343	Neo-literate
T,4	University
T,43	Honours
T,45	Post-graduate
T,47	Research
T,5	Sex
T,55	Female
T,56	Male
T,58	Co-education
T,6	Abnormal
T,61	Under-developed
T,614	Idiot
T,62	By Intelligence quotient
T,7	Backward class
T,72	Orphan
T,76	Pauper
T-J	Commenius: object teaching
T-L	Rousseau's school
T-L2	Kant's school
T-L5	Pestalozzi's school
T-L6	Fichte's school
T-L7	Herbart's school
T-L3	Froebel's Kindergarten
T-L9	Mann's school
T-M	Manual training
T-N	Plantoon school
T-N1	Montessori school
T-N3	Wardha scheme
U	Geography
U.1	Geography of the world

U.2	Geography of India	U.73	Geography of USA

Similarly by putting the Space Isolate Number of any region, taken from Chap VG, we get the geography of that region. For example, "U.213 Geography of Mysore State."

U-1	Mathematical geography
U-1,1	Cartography
U-1,2	Map projection
U-1,5	Marine cartography
U-1,7	Aerial cartography
U-2	Physical geography
U-2,1	Physiography
U-2,5	Hydrography
U-2,57	Oceanography
U-2,7	Climatography
U-2,71	Weather
U-2,72	Wind
U-7,755	Rain fall
U-2,76	Season
U-2,761	Spring
U-2,762	Summer
U-2,763	Autumn
U-2,764	Winter
U-3	Biogeography
U-3,4	Plant
U-3,5	Animal
U-3,6	Paleogeography
U-5	Anthropogeography
U-5,1	Race
U-5,3	Population
U-5,5	Human geography
U-5,8	Migration
U-5,81	Inland
U-5,85	Emigration
U-5,86	Immigration
U-6	Political geography
U-6,1	Military geography
U-6,5	Naval geography
U-6,7	Aerial geography
U-6,8	Historical geography
U-7	Economic geography
U-7,4	Trade route
U-7,41	Land route
U-7,415	Railway route
U-7,457	Oceanic route
U-7,47	Air route
U-8	Travel, Expedition, Voyage

Add after the number "U-8" a dot (.) and then the Space Isolate Number, taken from the Schedule in Chap VG, for the region, then a "single inverted comma" (') and then the Time Isolate Number, taken from the Schedule in Chap VJ, for the decade of the commencing of the travel. For example:

U-8.1'L4	Anson's voyage round the world
U-8.42'N1	James Cousin's *New Japan: Impressions and reflections.*
U-8.72'N2	*Canada today* 1924.

V	History
V,1'N7	World history brought up to 1970s
V,1-1N19	League of Nations
V,2	Indian History
V,2'D0	Hindu period
V,2'G0	Ghazni period
V,2'H0	Delhi Sultans
V,2'L0	Moghul period
V,2'M5	British period (East India Company)
V,2'N4	British period (Direct rule)
V,2;18'N7	India's Foreign policy in 1970s
V,2;2	Constitution of India
V,2;51	Fundamental rights of Indian citizens
V,2,1;3	Functions of the President of India
V,211'I2	Vijayanagar period
V,3	British History
V,3'D0	Anglo-Saxon period
V,3'F5	Norman period
V,3'I0	Plantagenet period
V,3'I8	Lancastrian period
V,3'K0	Tudor period
V,3'L1	Stuart period
V,3'N1	Hanoverian period
V,3'N4	Windsor period
V,3;11'N6	Home policy of Britain in 1960s
V,3;18'N7	Foreign policy of Britain in 1970s
V,3;3	Constitution of UK
W	Political science
W,4	Monarchy
W,6	Democracy
W,6,21	Prime minister in a democracy
W,6,21;3	Functions of prime minister in a democracy

W,64	Dictatorship
W,691	Communism
W,691,5	Citizens of a communistic country
W,7	Utopia
W,81	Revolution
W,87	Passive resistance
X	Economics-in-Theory
X,1	Consumption
X,2	Resources
X,3	Distribution
X,4	Value
X,46	Price
X,5	Money
X,6	Finance
X,61	Individual finance
X,62	Family finance
X,68	Corporate finance
X,7	Public finance
X,71	Budget
X,72	Tax
XV	Economics-in-Action
XV,3'N7	Economics of India in 1970s
XV,2,5'N71	Money in India in 1971
XV,2,72'N71	Tax in India in 1971
XV,2,A'N7	Economics-in-Action of business enterprise in India in 1970s
XV,2,B'N7	Communication in India in 1971
XV,2,B1'N70	Postal communication in India in 1970
XV,211(J)'N71	Agriculture industries in Tamil Nadu in 1971
XX	Economics-in-Theory of business enterprise
XX,(D)	Engineering industry
XX,(J)	Agricultural industry
Y	Sociology

Y;1	Civilization and culture
Y;3212	Marriage
Y;34	Ceremony
Y;351	Folklore
Y;354	Superstition
Y;356	Custom
Y;36	Festival
Y;38	Symbolism
Y;4	Social pathology
Y;41	Intemperance
Y;411	Alcoholism
Y;412	Tobacco habit
Y;413	Opium habit
Y;42	Degeneration
Y;421	Physical degeneration
Y;424	Mental degeneration
Y;425	Moral degeneration
Y;426	Spiritual degeneration
Y;43	Destitution
Y;431	Widowhood
Y;432	Orphanhood
Y;433	Unemployment
Y;434	Poverty
Y;438	War
Y;44	Social evil
Y;45	Crime
Y;46	Short life
Y;48	Disunion
Y;482	Tension
Y;484	Espionage
Y;492	Slavery
Y;5	Demography
Y;512	Under-population
Y;514	Over-population
Y;53	Birth and death
Y;58	Migration
Y;7	Personality
Y;8	Equipment
Y;81	Habitat
Y;82	Utensil
Y;83	Implement
Y;86	Ornament
Y;87	Furniture
Y;88	Apparel

Y,1	Children
Y,12	Youth
Y,12;411	Alcoholism in youth
Y,13	Adult
Y,15	Woman
Y,16	Man
Y,2	Family
Y,31;3213	Marriage ceremony in rural residents
Y,391	Gypsy
Y,394	Refugee
Y,394;42	Degeneration in Refugees
Y,47	Leader
Y,492	Slave
Y,55	Alien
Y,5923	Brahman
Y,5924	Kṣhatriya
Y,5925	Vaisya
Y,5926	Sudra
Y,5927	Harijan
Y,82	Indians
Y,82;3213	Marriage among Indians
Y,844V	Ceylonese
Y,872	Canadians
YX	Social work
YX;4:5	Prevention of social pathology
YX,11;411:5	Prevention of alcoholism among children
Z	Law
Z,2	Indian law
Z,3	British law
Z,(Q;2)	Hindu law
Z,(Q,7)	Muslim law
Z,2,111	Indian law regarding minors
Z,2,111,2	Indian law of property of minors
Z,2,3	Indian law of contract
Z,2,4	Indian tort
Z,2,5	Criminal law in India

CHAPTER VL

EXAMPLES OF ANTERIORISING COMMON ISOLATES

0 Introduction

For amplifying each of the anteriorising common isolates, special Rules are given in *Colon Classification* (51). A few examples showing the construction of class numbers warranting Anteriorising Common Isolates are given in the succeeding Sections.

1 Maps and Atlases

BX"f	Astronomical atlas
BX,6"f	Star atlas
U.1"f	World atlas
U.2"f	General atlas of India
U-2.1"f	Atlas of the physical features of the world
U-2,7.1"f	Meteorological atlas of the world
U-3,5.1"f	Zoogeographical atlas of the world
U-6,8.2"f	Historical atlas of India
U-7,457.1"f	Atlas of the marine routes in the world

2 Encyclopaedia and Dictionary

A. "K Scientific encyclopaedia M-A3" K Encyclopaedia of domestic science

P,111;4"k	N26	Cassel's new English dictionary (1926)
P,111;4"k	35N28	English-Telugu dictionary (1928)
P,111;4"k	152N01	Student's Anglo-Hindi dictionary (1901)
P,15;4"k	N26	Sanskrit-English dictionary (1926)
P,15;4"k	15N33	Sanskrit-Sanskrit dictionary (1933)
P,15;4"k	31N33	Sanskrit-Tamil dictionary (1933)
P,157;4"k	N24	Bengali-English dictionary (1924)
P,157;4"k	157M88	Bengali-Bengali dictionary (1888)
P,157;4"k	168N07	Bengali-Urdu dictionary (1907)
P,33;4"k	N23	Kannada-English dictionary (1923)
P,33;4"k	33N41	Kannada-Kannada dictionary (1924)
Q;31"k		Dictionary of deities
Q,6"k		Dictionary of Christianity
Q,62"k		Catholic encyclopaedia

3 Biography

The common Anteriorising Isolate Number "w" representing "Biography" may be amplified by chronological number representing the year of birth of the biographee.

2w"M92	Biography of Ranganathan
Lw"k	Dictionary of medical biography
MY214w"k	Who's Who in world cricket
0,111,2J64"w	Biography of Shakespeare
0,157,1M61"w	Biography of Tagore
0,31,1M15"w	Biography of Minakshisundaram Pillai

4 Special Cases of Biography

Q,2;x"w Biographical stories from puranas

(To be individualised by Alphabetical Device)
(Illustrative)

Q,2;x"wD	Dhruva charita
Q,2;x"wJ	Jadabharata Charita
Q,2;x"wK	Krishna Charita
Q,2;x"wM	Markandeya Charita
Q,2;x"wP	Prahlada Charita
Q,2;x"wR	Rama Charita

Note.— Biographies of individual Alwars and individual Nayanmars other than the five mentioned in Chap VK are to be individualised by Alphabetical Device. Here are a few illustrations:

Q,22"wTN	Nammalwar
Q,22"wTP	Peyalwar
Q,22"wTT	Tirumanpayalwar
Q,23"wTK	Kannappanayanar
Q,23"wTN	Nandanar
Q,23"wTS	Siruthondanayanar
R-66"w1	Life of Sankaracharya
R-67"w2	Life of Ramanuja
R-68"w1	Life of Madhwa
R-6893"w1	Life of Vallabhacharya
V,2,21"wTM8	Life of Jawaharlal Nehru
V,3,21"wTM65	Life of George V
V,53,21"wTL69	Life of Napoleon

(*Note.*— In the case of lives of mystics, the anteriorising common isolate "w" should not be used, but "wT" should be used):

Δ"wT,M36	Life of Sai Baba
Δ,2"wT,M36	Life of Sri Ramakrishna
Δ,2"wT,M79	Life of Ramana Maharishi
Δ,6"wT,F82	Life of St Francis of Assisi
Δ,6"wT,M89	Life of Sadhu Sundar Sing
Δ,73"wT,M89	Life of Gazzali

5 Collections, Selections, and Anthologies

0,111,1"x	Selections from English poetries
0,111,1"x(G)	Nature anthology from English poetries.
0,111,1"x(J,6)	Anthology of flowers from English poetries
0,111,1"x(Δ)	Anthology from mysticism from English poetries
0,111,6"x"k	Dictionary of English prose quotations
0,15,1"x(R-4)	Moral maxims from Sanskrit poetries

CHAPTER VM

BOOK NUMBER

1 Need for Book Number

The number derived with the aid of the schedules in a scheme for classification is denoted by the term "Class Number." It is a translation into ordinal number of the subject of the book. It represents the class of the least extension and greatest intention. This class is denoted by the term is 'Ultimate Class' of the book. Now, several books will have the same ultimate class and hence they will have the same class number. To distinguish them from one another, the 'Book Number' is used. This number cannot have anything to do with the subject of the book; for all the books in the same class have, by assumption, virtually the same subject and hence the subject cannot distinguish them.

2 Characteristics for the Construction of Book Number

The book number is constructed with the aid of certain other characteristics of the book — such as language and the year of publication (50). The language of the book is translated into symbols with the aid of the language schedule given in Chap VH. The translation into numbers, of the year of publication of the book, is added after the language number. This translation is made with the aid of schedule given in Chap VJ.

3 Favoured Language

If the language of the book is the favoured language of the library, its number need not be written but may be taken as understood.

4 Accession Part of Book Number

An ultimate class may contain more than one book in one and the same language published in the same year. Then the year of publication number is augmented by the addition of '1' in the case of the second book, '2' in the case of the third book,

'3' in the case of the fourth book, and so on. This added number is denoted the term 'accession part of the book number.'

5 Multi-volumed Book

A book may be in two or more volumes. Then the volumes are individualized by adding a decimal point after the year of publication number or the accession part of the book number, as the case may be, and writing thereafter the serial number of the volume.

6 Linguistic Dictionary

In the case of a linguistic dictionary, the language part of the book number will be the number of the language in which the meaning appears.

7 Examples of Book Number

1 Assuming that English is the favoured language of the library, a book written in English on a given subject and published in 1946, will have its book number N46.

2 If it is in Hindi and not in English, its book number will be 152N46.

3 If it is in Urdu its book number will be 168N46.

4 If it is in Tamil, its book number will be 31N46.

5 The second book on the same subject in the library, written in English and published in 1946, and in fact even a second copy of this book itself, will have its book number N461.

6 If it is in three volumes, the book numbers of the volumes of the first set will be N46.1, N46.2 and N46.3 while those for the volumes of the second set will be N461.1, N461.2 and N461.3.

7 If the language of the book is not the favoured language of the library, the language number should be prefixed to the numbers given in categories 5 and 6.

8 Style of Writing

The book number is written either below the class number or to the right of it, after leaving some intervening space. The class number and the book number taken together is denoted by the term 'Call Number.' The Call Number for this book may be written as follows:

2,J1 or 2,J1 N73
N73

PART W

LIBRARY CATALOGUE

CHAPTER WA

PHYSICAL FORM OF LIBRARY CATALOGUE AND LIBRARY HAND

1 Printed Catalogue

The printed catalogue is a waste of funds in a school library necessarily ever-growing. "Growing" implies addition of new Entries for new books added and withdrawal of existing entries for existing books weeded out. Often an argument used in support of the printed catalogue is, "Library fund is not affected by printing. For, each student is obliged by the Rules to buy a copy of the printed catalogue." This argument has only to be stated to be condemned. Any money collected from each student by a school by the fiat of Rules, need not be wasted on the unwanted and ever-out-of-date anachronism called the "Printed Catalogue of the Library." Why should not that money be added to the never-too-flourishing book fund? Again, the libraries are notoriously understaffed or not separately staffed at all; then it is nothing short of callousness or even crime to waste the time of the person in charge of the library to prepare the press copy of the Catalogue and see it through the press, and thus take him away from direct service to each student. The Victorian tradition of printing catalogues in libraries should stop without any ado.

2 Paste-Down Catalogue

Another physical form of library catalogue found in occasional use is denoted by the term 'Paste-Down Catalogue.' Its base is a bound volume of thick blank sheets. Each typed or printed entry is pasted, in the correct sequence on the successive right hand pages, leaving space for at least five more entries to be inserted between any two consecutive pages. The left hand page is left blank for pasting down any new entry, not finding its due place vacant on the right hand page, in a corresponding position. In this physical form of library catalogue, new entries can be inserted in their correct places to a limited extent. But, the removal of the old entries for weeded-out books is not easy.

Often they are struck out. This is a clumsy form of library catalogue. Fortunately, it is fast going out of date.

3 Card Catalogue

In a card catalogue, there is only one Entry in one card. Each card is of 125 × 75 mm. The cards are arranged in trays and held in their relative positions by a rod passing through holes near their bottom edge. The trays are all built into a cabinet. A specification for the catalogue cabinet is given by the Indian Standards Institution (31). Small schools may change the size of the cabinets by having only three drawers in each column. In this arrangement, new cards can be inserted at any point without disturbing or having to rewrite any of the already existing cards. So also cards of weeded-out books can be removed. All the schools should adopt the card form for their library catalogue.

4 Library Hand

The catalogue cards should be written in black indelible ink. In writing a catalogue card all individuality in hand-writing should be suppressed. An impersonal "Library Hand" has been developed by the library profession for writing catalogue entries. It consists of an upright hand with the letters of a word written independently of one another — that is, without running into one another. It is not difficult to acquire the habit of writing in library hand. Many of my old students have learned to write in this way after a practice of a month or two. Anything written in library hand is easy to read. It also presents a pleasant appearance. After habit, writing in Library Hand does not take more time than writing in the personal way. I know of some librarians writing even their letters in library hand. This makes the reading of the letters easy and free from any mis-reading. A library catalogue is a permanent record, lasting through many generations. Naturally the entries will have to be written by different cataloguers. Each cataloguer writing in the cards in his own personal hand will make the library catalogue ugly.

CHAPTER WB

LIBRARY CATALOGUE FREED FROM THE FUNCTION OF STOCK REGISTER

1 Advent of Shelf Card

11 LIBRARY CATALOGUE USED ALSO AS STOCK REGISTER

Generally each book in a library has been given only one entry in a library catalogue. It was given under the name of its author. This type of Catalogue is denoted by the term 'One document, One entry' catalogue. In this case the entries in the catalogue of a library and the corresponding books on the shelves in the stack room have been arranged in parallel sequences. This has been helping the use of the catalogue for inventory work — that is, as stock register also.

12 INTRODUCTION OF SHELF CARD

Now, as a result of the experience and modernisation of ideas:

1 The library catalogue has many entries for each book:

2 As a result of open access system the books in the stack room have to be arranged in several sequences — such as those for reference books, under-sized books (pamphlets), over-sized books, art books and other books with poor physique; but

3 The catalogue entries have all to be arranged in a single sequence, in order to facilitate their use.

Therefore, the file of catalogue cards is not fit for use in stock verification. This has led to the writing of one additional card for each book to be used only for stock verification. This additional card is denoted by the term 'Shelf Card.' The Shelf Cards are arranged exactly parallel to the arrangement of the books on the shelves of the stack room. The new card is called "Shelf Card" on account of this fact.

2 Effect of the Advent of Shelf Card on Library Catalogue

The advent of shelf card has liberated the library catalogue from the effect of its use for stock verification. Now its sole function is to disclose to the reader — and for that purpose to the staff also — all the holdings of the library on his subject of interest at the moment. The catalogue should disclose to the reader pin-pointedly, exhaustively, and expeditiously all the books, parts of books, and papers in periodicals, bearing on his subject of interest.

3 Function of Library Catalogue

Varied are the lines of approach of a reader to the documents (books or parts of books or papers in periodicals) needed by him. He may be asked to know all the resources of the library:

1 On a particular subject;

2 By a particular author; or

3 Edited or translated or commented upon or illustrated by a particular person; or

4 In a particular publisher's series; or

5 In a publisher's series edited by a particular person.

Alternatively the reader may also ask for a book by its title or by a vague description of its subject without any other information. Even with the slightest clue it must be possible for a reader to get his document in the shortest possible time.

4 "One Document, Many Entries" in the Library Catalogue

The functions of the library catalogue enumerated in Sec WB3 are many. All these functions cannot be carried out by a library catalogue of the kind, "One document, one entry." On the other hand, obviously it must be of the kind "One document, many entries."

5 One Kind of Name of an Entry

One usual way of naming an entry in a library catalogue is

naming it after the occupant of the first line of an entry — for example, "Class number entry," "Author entry," "Editor entry," "Series entry," and "Alternative-name-Entry."

6 Classified Catalogue

A Classified Catalogue can serve the readers better than a Dictionary Catalogue. The entries in the succeeding Chapters are made in accordance with the Rules of my *Classified catalogue code* (47).

CHAPTER WC

MAIN ENTRY

Note.— In each Entry in this and in the succeeding Chapters, the name of each Section in an Entry is given in the right hand margin for the benefit of the Librarians. But in the library catalogue, these names of entries should not be given.

1 Justification of the Name 'Main Entry'

One of the many catalogue entries given to a book gives more information about the book than the others — the fullest intended by the catalogue. All the other Entries are derived from this Entry. For these reasons this Entry is denoted by the term 'Main Entry.'

2 Examples of Main Entry

21 EXAMPLE 1

Entry	*Name of Section*	
2,J1	Class Number	
Library Science, School library.	Name-of-Class	
N73 RANGANATHAN (Shiyali Ramamritam) (1892).	Heading	
New Education and School Library	Title	
(Sarada Ranganathan Endowment for Library Science Series. 4).	Series Note	Note Section
"*Previously published as* School and college libraries".	Change-of-Title Note	
3657	Accession Number	

22 EXAMPLE 2

Entry	*Name of Section*
T.1'N7	Class Number
Education. World Brought upto 1970s.	Name-of-Class
N68 JOHNSON (RR) (1897–1970).	Heading
World history of education. Ed by B Robertson (1932)	Title
(History of Education Series. Ed by C Wells. 2)	Series Note
3156	Accession Number

3 Function of Main Entry

The function of a Main Entry is to bring the book to the notice of the reader, remembering its subject. It may therefore be denoted also by the term 'Subject Entry' of the book. Of course, the reader will know the name of the subject only in a natural language used by the library. By looking up the name of the subject in the alphabetical part of the catalogue, he will get its translation into Class Number. He will then look up the Entries, in the classified part of the catalogue, with that Class Number in the Class Number Section.

4 Sections of Main Entry

In the examples given in Sec WC21 and WC22 the usual name of each Section of the Main Entry is given against it in the right hand margin of the Entry. The first section is also denoted by the term 'Leading Section.' The names of the sections are descriptive and self-explanatory.

5 Number Entry

The Main Entry gives a Class Number in its Section 1. Therefore it may also be denoted by the term 'Number Entry.'

CHAPTER WD/WJ ADDED ENTRY

CHAPTER WD

CROSS REFERENCE ENTRY OR SUBJECT ANALYTICAL ENTRY

1 Example 1

11 Genesis

To understand the genesis of the idea denoted by the term 'Cross Reference Entry' and its equivalent term 'Subject Analytical' we shall consider the book represented by the Main Entry given in Sec WC21, as Example 1. According to its Class Number its chief subject or focus is "School Library." It occupies parts F to Y. But, Parts B to E are on "School Education." "School Education" may then be regarded as a subsidiary subject or focus of this book. This subsidiary subject is not brought out by the name of the main subject "School Library." Therefore, it is necessary to bring out, in another Entry, the treatment of the subsidiary subject "School Education" in Part B to E. This additional entry is denoted by the term 'Cross Reference Entry.' According to this term, this Entry does not by itself represent a book. It only "Cross refers" to some part of another book. The alternative name "Subject Analytical" is perhaps a little more self-explanatory. This is the genesis of the idea of "Cross Reference Entry" or "Subject Analytical."

12 Justification by the Laws of Library Science

The Cross Reference Entry fulfills Law 2, Law 3, and Law 4 of Library Science. According to Law 2, the library catalogue should disclose to a reader pinpointedly all the books and even parts of books and papers in periodicals on the subject of his interest at the moment. According to Law 3, the library catalogue should disclose exhaustively not only all the books but also all the parts of books and papers in periodicals available in the library. Then only each of them will have a chance to get its reader to the satisfaction of Law 3. According to Law 4, the reader should not be obliged to spend time in looking through all the books in the library in order to spot out all the materials of his interest, available in the library. The time of the reader should be saved. This is the justification for giving Cross Reference Entries or Subject Analyticals. In fact the Laws of Library Science demand them.

13 CROSS REFERENCE OR SUBJECT ANALYTICAL ENTRY

Sec WD11 and WD12 give rise to the following Cross Reference or Subject Analytical Entry:

Entry	*Name of Section*
T,2	Class Number
Education, School	Name-of-Class
See also	Directing
2,J N73	Call-Number
Ranganathan: New education and School library, Parts B to E	Host and Locus

14 ADDED ENTRY, KIND 1

Obviously the above is not a Main Entry. It is only an Added Entry — that is an additional or extra entry for the book. This is one kind of added entry. This Entry is a Class Number Entry. In other words it is a Subject Entry. Obviously, it is also a Number Entry, even as the Main Entry.

2 Example 2

21 GENESIS

The analogy of Sec WD11 is followed here. Part P of the book is on "Under-production of school books in India." This may then be regarded as another subsidiary subject or focus of the book. This subsidiary subject is not brought out by the name of the main subject "School Library." Therefore, it is necessary to bring out, in another entry, the treatment of the subsidiary subject in Part P. This forms example 2 of a Cross Reference Entry or Subject Analytical.

22 Justification by the Laws of Library Science

All the arguments given in Sec WC22 hold good also in the case of this Cross Reference or Subject Analytical Entry. Perhaps there may be another reason in this case. There is every chance for the library to have a separate book wholly on "T,2 School Education." But the chance is very poor — almost negligible — for the library to have a separate book only on "Under-production of school books in India."

If so, without a Cross Reference Entry from this subject, the library may fail to serve a reader needing information on this subject. If so, the Library will be sinning against the Laws of Library Science.

23 Cross Reference or Subject Analytical Entry

	Name of Section
3V,44,Zc;2'N7	Class Number
Book Science-in-action, India, School book; Under-production, 1970s	Name of subject
See also	Directing
2,J1 N73	Call-Number
Ranganathan: New education and school library, Part P.	Host and locus

CHAPTER WE/WJ ALPHABETICAL INDEX ENTRY

CHAPTER WE/WJ BOOK INDEX ENTRY

CHAPTER WE

AUTHOR INDEX ENTRY

1 Example 1

The book represented by the Main Entry given in Sec WC21 admits of the following Author Index Entry.

Entry	*Name of Section*
RANGANATHAN (Shiyali Ramamritam (1892).	Author
New education and school library.	Title
2,J1 N73	Index Number

2 Example 2

The book represented by the Main Entry in Sec WC22 admits of the following Author Index Entry.

Entry	*Name of Section*
JOHNSON (RR) (1897–1970).	Author
World history of education.	Title
T.1'N7 N07	Index Number

3 Function of Author Index Entry

The function of an Author Index Entry is obviously to help a reader bringing up his requirements by mentioning the name of the Author of the book needed by him. This is necessary to satisfy Law 2 and Law 4 of Library Science. In a library with other books by the same Author, the Author Index Entries will also satisfy Law 3, by bringing to the notice of the reader all the books by the same author.

CHAPTER WF

EDITOR INDEX ENTRY

1 Example

The book represented by the Main Entry given in Sec WC22 admits of the following Editor Index Entry.

Entry	Name of Section
ROBERTSON (B) (1932), *Ed.*	Editor
Johnson: World history of education	Author and Title
T.1'N7 N67	Index Number

2 Function of Editor Index Entry

The purpose of an Editor Index Entry is to help a reader bringing up his requirements by mentioning the name of the Editor of the book needed by him. This is necessary to satisfy Law 2 and Law 4 of Library Science. In a library with other books by the same Editor, the Editor Index Entries will also satisfy Law 3, by bringing to the notice of the reader all the books by the same editor.

CHAPTER WG

SERIES INDEX ENTRY

1 Example 1

The book represented by the Main Entry in Sec WC21, admits of the following Series Index Entry.

Entry	Name of Section
SARADA RANGANATHAN ENDOWMENT FOR LIBRARY SCIENCE SERIES.	Series
9 Ranganathan: New education and school library 2,J1 N73	Author and Title Index Number

2 Example 2

The book represented by the Main Entry in Sec WC22 admits of the following Series Index Entry.

Entry	Name of Section
HISTORY OF EDUCATION SERIES.	Series
2 Johnson: World history of education. T.1'N7 N67	Author and Title Index Number

3 Function of Series Index Entry

A Series Index Entry helps a reader bringing up his requirements by the name of the Publishers Series of the book needed by him. This is necessary to satisfy Law 2 and Law 4 of Library Science. In a library having other books belonging to the same Publishers Series, the Series Index Entry will also satisfy Law 3, by bringing to the notice of the reader all the books belonging to the same Publishers series. This will give a chance to each of those books to find its reader.

CHAPTER WH/WJ GENERAL ADDED ENTRIES

CHAPTER WH

CLASS INDEX ENTRY

1 Example 1

The book represented by the Main Entry given in Sec WC21 admits of the following Class Index Entries:

11 CLASS INDEX ENTRIES DERIVED FROM THE MAIN ENTRY

Entry	*Name of Section*
SCHOOL LIBRARY, LIBRARY SCIENCE.	Subject
For documents in this Class and its Subdivisions see the Classified Part of the catalogue under the Class Number	Directing
2,J1	Index Number

Entry	*Name of Section*
ACADEMIC LIBRARY, LIBRARY SCIENCE.	Subject
For documents in this Class and its Subdivisions see the Classified Part of the catalogue under the Class Number	**Directing**
2,J1	**Index Number**

Entry	*Name of Section*
LIBRARY SCIENCE.	**Subject**
For documents in this Class and its Subdivisions see the Classified Part of the catalogue under the Class Number	**Directing**
2	**Index Number**

12 CLASS INDEX ENTRY DERIVED FROM THE FIRST CROSS REFERENCE ENTRY

The Cross Reference Entry given in Sec WD13 admits of the following Class Index Entries:

Entry	Name of Section
SCHOOL, EDUCATION.	Subject
For documents in this Class and its Subdivisions see the Classified Part of the catalogue under the Class Number	Directing
T,2	Index Number

Entry	Name of Section
EDUCATION.	Subject
For documents in this Class and its Subdivisions see the Classified Part of the catalogue under the Class Number	Directing
T	Index Number

13 CLASS INDEX ENTRY DERIVED FROM THE SECOND CROSS REFERENCE ENTRY:

The Cross Reference Entry in Sec WD23 admits of the following Class Index Entries:

Entry	Name of Section
UNDER-PRODUCTION, SCHOOL BOOK, INDIA.	Subject
For documents in this Class and its Subdivisions see the Classified Part of the catalogue under the Class Number	Directing
3V,44,Zc;2	Index Number

	Name of Section
SCHOOL BOOK, INDIA, BOOK SCIENCE-IN-ACTION.	Subject
For documents in this Class and its Subdivisions see the Classified Part of the catalogue under the Class Number	Directing
3V,44,Zc	Index Number

	Name of Section
INDIA, BOOK SCIENCE-IN-ACTION.	Subject
For documents in this Class and its Subdivisions see the Classified Part of the catalogue under the Class Number	Directing
3V,44	Index Number

	Name of Section
BOOK SCIENCE-IN-ACTION.	Subject
For documents in this Class and its Subdivisions see the Classified Part of the catalogue under the Class Number	Directing Section
3V	**Index Number**

2 Example 2

The book represented by the Main Entry in Sec WC22 admits of the following Class Index Entries:

	Name of Section
WORLD, EDUCATION.	Subject
For documents in this Class and its Subdivisions see the Classified Part of the catalogue under the Class Number	Directing Section
T.1	Index Number

EDUCATION. *For documents in this Class and its Subdivisions see the Classified Part of the catalogue under the Class Number* T	*Name of Section* Class Index Directing Index Number

Note.— The above Class Index Entry is redundant because it has been already given in Sec WH12.

3 Function of Class Index Entry

A reader may not know the Class Number of the Subject he is interested in at the moment. The alphabetical index to the class numbers — the Class Index Entries — directs the reader to the entries with the particular class number in the classified part of the catalogue. The Class Index Entries satisfy Laws 2, 3 and 4 of Library Science.

4 Other Methods of Giving Class Index Entries

Strictly speaking a reader may be expected to bring up to the Alphabetical Part of the Catalogue any one of the Facet terms in the name of the subject. He may mention the other Facet Terms in any sequence. To satisfy him in all possible cases, the number of Class Index Entries should be factorial n, where n is the number of Facet Terms in the subject. This would multiply the Class Index Entries enormously — almost to the point of hiding away the substantial entries. The choice made above is just to prevent this. For in this case the number of Class Index Entries will be n.

CHAPTER WJ

EDITOR OF SERIES ENTRY

1 Example

The book represented by the Main Entry given in Sec WC22 admits of the following Editor of Series Entry:

Entry	*Name of Section*
	(Referred from)
WELLS (C), *Ed.*	(Editor of Series)
See	Directing
HISTORY OF EDUCATION	(Referred to)
SERIES.	(Name of Series)

2 Cross Reference Index Entry

An Editor of Series Entry is one type of Cross Reference Index Entry, the other kinds of Cross Reference Index Entries being:

1 Alternative Name Entry;
2 Variant-Form-of-Word Entry;
3 Pseudonym–Real-Name Entry; and
4 Generic-Name Entry.

3 Function of Cross Reference Index Entry

As the name indicates, a Cross Reference Index Entry merely refers from one term to another. A Cross Reference Index Entry satisfies the Law of Parsimony. In a Publishers Series there may be 20 volumes. By giving a full Series Index Entry for each of the 20 volumes under the name of the Editor of the Series the number of entries will have to be 20. These entries will run exactly parallel to the entries under the name of the series. No purpose is served by this repetition. Therefore according to the Law of Parsimony a single Cross Reference Index Entry is sufficient under the name of the Editor of the Series.

CHAPTER WK

TRACING SECTION

1 Record of Added Entries

The back of the Main Entry Card gives the "Tracing Section." "Tracing Section" means a section showing all the added entries arising out of the Main Entry or the Cross Reference Entry, if any, found on the front of the card.

2 Number of Items in the Tracing Section

The items in a Tracing Section may fall into the following four groups:

1 Class Numbers of the Cross Reference Entries. These are written on the Left half of the right hand side of the back of the Main Entry Card. in the sequence of the Class Numbers;

2 Headings of the Class Index Entries. These are written on the Uppermost part of the back of the Main Entry Card in the alphabetical sequence;

3 Headings of the Book Index Entries. These are written on the Middle part of the right hand side of the back of the Main Entry Card in the alphabetical sequence; and

4 Headings of the Cross Reference Index Entries. These are written on the Lowest part of the right hand side of the back of the Main Entry Card in the alphabetical sequence.

3 Example 1 of Tracing Section

The following will be the items in the back of the Main Entry Card for the book mentioned in Sec WC21.

3V,44,Zc	Part P	Academic library, Library Science. Book science-in-action. Education.

T,2 Part B to E India, Book science-in-action.
Library science.
School, Education.
School book, India, Book science-in-action
School Library, Library science.
Ranganathan (Shiyali Ramamritam) (1892)
Sarada Ranganathan Endowment for
Library Science Series. 4.

---

4 Example 2 of Tracing Section

The following will be the items in the back of the Main Entry Card for the book mentioned in Sec WC22.

Education.
World, Education
History of education series. 2.
Johnson (RR) (1897–1970)
Robertson (B) (1932). *Ed.*
Wells (C), *Ed.*

---

5 Function of Tracing Section

The Tracing Section is a record of the added entries made for a particular book. The Tracing Section helps the staff in finding out the different added entries made for a book for purposes such as correction of entries and withdrawal of entries as a result of the weeding out of any book.

PART X

MAINTENANCE WORK

CHAPTER XA

FUNCTIONS OF MAINTENANCE SECTION

1 Five Laws and Maintenance Section

The stack room will be under the complete charge of the Maintenance Section. In an Open Access Library the readers directly go into the stack room. The browsing facility provided helps them to make a careful selection of their books. To facilitate browsing, the Maintenance Section should keep the books always arranged strictly by their Call Numbers. Otherwise, all the relevant books may not catch the eyes of the readers; and at any rate, time will be wasted by readers.

2 Functions of the Maintenance Section

The following are the main functions of the Maintenance Section:

1 Shelving of each new book in its appropriate place;

2 Reshelving of each book returned after consultation or loan;

3 Shelf rectification;

4 Periodical weeding out of each of the completely worn out or outmoded books;

5 Arranging for the binding of books and attending to all other work related to it;

6 Transfer of books from one collection to another whenever needed;

7 Periodical rearrangement of the sequence of the subjects in the stack room;

8 Rearrangement of the Shelf Register Cards in accordance with the Principle of Parallel Movement;-

9 Stock verification.

3 Work of Maintenance Section

The succeeding Chapters of this Part describe the routines of the work of the Maintenance Section. A detailed account of the routines is given in my *Library administration* (55).

CHAPTER XB

COLLECTION FORMATION

1 Need for Formation of Collection

11 Differentiated Popularity of Main Subjects

The rigid arrangement of books on different subjects according to their Main Subject sequence in the scheme for Classification results in wastage of time and energy of both the readers and the reference staff. In such an arrangement, the reader may have to waste his time and energy in unnecessarily walking long distances to get at his books. The reference staff also are affected in the same way, their movement depending on the movement of the readers. Therefore, it is necessary to break the schedule sequence and judiciously re-permute the Main Subjects on the shelves.

12 Peculiarity in the Physique of Books

The peculiarities of the physique of books also call for the formation of parallel classified collections — for example undersized or pamphlet collection, oversized collection, collection of art books and books kept on closed shelves or otherwise denied open access (this may be denoted by the term 'Closed collection,' and 'Worn-out Collection'). Indicate a book of Undersized Collection by underlining its Book Number in the book itself, in all its catalogue entries, and in every other record. So also indicate a book of the Oversized Collection by overlining its Book Number. Indicate a book of the Closed Collection by both underlining and overlining the Book Number. Indicate a book of the Worn-out Collection by encircling its Book Number. Indicate a book in the Reference Collection by inserting the letter pair "RR" over its Book Number.

2 Collection by Standard

21 Need for Distinguishing Standards

The amplitude of variation in standard is far more pronounced in a school library than in a library for adults. In a high school at least three distinct standards must be distinguished. The rate of mental growth, between the ages ten and sixteen, is very abrupt. Therefore, keep the books belonging to each of the three standards in different parallel sequences.

22 Collection Number for Standards

Indicate a book in the collection of Standard I by putting the Roman Numeral "I" above its Book Number. Indicate a book in the collection of Standard II by putting the Roman Numeral "II" above its Book Number and so on.

23 Shelving of Collections of Different Standards

The rate of physical growth is high during school age. Therefore keep the books of Standard I in the lowermost plank of each shelf all along the stack room. The books of Standard II in the second plank from bottom of each shelf all along the stack room. The books of Standard III in the third plank from bottom of each shelf all along the stack room. Keep all other books — mainly suited to teachers and outsiders — without any Collection Number, in the planks above the third left over all through the stack room.

3 Class Library

The modern tendency is to have a central library in each school. All the advantages of class room libraries can be derived from an open access central library. Still a school may prefer to have a class library for each class. Then indicate a book of the library of a particular class, by putting above its Book Number, the number and the Division of the Class — example IIIB as the Collection Number for the library in Division B of Class 3.

4 Topical Collection

Form temporary topical collection from time to time. This will facilitate class room work. In other words, this will bring about effective correlation between library work and class room teaching. This will also save the time of the students. Indicate a book in the Topical Collection by putting on the last vacant line of the due date label of the book, the date for the release of the book from the Topical Collection and encircle that date. This will enable the Circulation Section to disallow its being taken on loan. This may also be of help to prevent its being shelved in its normal place.

5 Collection According to the Interest of Readers

Form the following collections based on the frequency of use by Readers:

1 Primary Collection.— The collection of books in most demand;

2 Secondary Collection.— The collection of periodicals and serials; and

3 Tertiary Collection.— The collection of books of infrequent demand.

Collection Numbers are not necessary for a book belonging to the primary or secondary collection. No Collection Number means Primary Collection. A volume of a periodical and a serial is recognised by its very title. Therefore no Collection Number is necessary. To indicate a book in the Tertiary Collection put the digit "T" over its Book Number.

6 Temporary Collection

Form the following Temporary Collections whenever necessary:

1 Correction Collection.— Call Numbers and Catalogue Entries may require correction. On segregating sets of books for these corrections, form a separate collection of such books. This may be denoted by the term 'Correction Collection.'

2 Binding Collection.— Form a separate collection of books in the different stages of binding work. This may be denoted by the term 'Binding Collection.'

7 Principle of Parallel Movement

Having been obliged to disturb the schedule sequence and to arrange the books in many collections, it is a great responsibility for the Maintenance Section to keep a book in its Collection and within each Collection to keep the books in the strict classified sequence. Need may arise now and again to change a book from one Collection to another — not temporarily but as if permanently. The mechanical apparatus invented by the library profession to secure this is the Shelf Register. It is made up of standard 125 × 75 mm cards, written on the Principle "One Title, One Card" with the Call Number in the leading line, having the collection number written above its Book Number. The Shelf Register Cards are sorted out into different Collections in accordance with the Collection Number. These Shelf Register Cards are kept absolutely parallel to the books on the shelves. Except on a book leaving its proper place on the shelf to get into the hands of a reader, every movement of that book will be controlled and imitated by an exactly parallel movement by its Shelf Register Card. For example, the Shelf Register Card of a book transferred from the Reference Collection to the Worn-out Collection will have its Collection Number "RR" removed and its Book Number encircled. Then the Shelf Register Card will be transferred in the Shelf Register Cabinet from among the Reference Collection Cards to among the Worn-out Collection Cards. This process is denoted by the term 'Principle of Parallel Movement.'

CHAPTER XC

PREPARATION OF BOOK

Note.— 1 All the routines in Sec XC1 and routines 1 to 4 in Sec XC2 should be left to be done by an attendant trained to do these routines.

2 All the other routines in this Chapter should be done by the Maintenance Assistant.

1 Preliminary Work

The following are the routines:

1 Cutting open the pages (*Weekly Job*).— Take each volume and cut open the pages with a cutting bone. In certain formes, the bottom edge may have also to be cut open.

2 Easing the back of the volume (*Weekly Job*).— Ease the back of each volume by opening it somewhere in the middle and placing it on a flat table and gently running the thumb from the top to the bottom along the inner margin. Do this easing work very carefully to avoid breaking of the back of the book.

2 Work of Stamping, and Fixing of Tag, Pocket and Due Date Label

The following are the routines:

1 Stamping work (*Weekly Job*).— Put the stamp of the library, in the conventional places in the book. Here is a model convention about the places for stamping:

11 The lower half of the back of the title page;

12 The top of the first Chapter or Introduction, as the case may be;

13 The bottom of the last page of the volume;

14 The bottom of the last page of the first Chapter ending after the middle of the volume; and

15 Each plate, map, and any other sheet not included in pagination.

Take particular care to see that the stamp does not fall upon any printed matter, plate or map. Again, put the stamp in proper alignment.

2 Tagging work (*Weekly Job*).— Stick up a tag on the back of each volume. Remove the book jacket, if any, temporarily, before tagging and replace it after tagging is over. Put the tag exactly one inch above the bottom of the volume. In case of the back of the volume being too thin to put the tag, fix it on the front cover close to the back at a distance of one inch from the bottom. For this purpose, a narrow metal plate bent into two arms at right angles to each other, each one inch in size, should be used to mechanise the fixing of the place for applying the tag.

3 Pasting of due date label (*Weekly Job*).— Paste a due date label, on the very first page after the cover of each book.

4 Making the book pocket (*Weekly Job*).— Fold over the bottom of the due date label so that the crease of the fold comes a little above the bottom edge of the book. At a distance of about 4.2 cm from the left edge of the page apply a thin line of gum and press. Allow it to dry sufficiently. Then use this as the book pocket. For this purpose, the due date label should be of tough paper not easily tearable. Otherwise, the book card would tear the bottom of the book pocket.

5 Preparing Book Card (*Weekly Job*).— Write in library hand, in the successive lines or block of lines, as the case may be, beginning from near the top the following:

1 The Call Number of the book;

2 Name of the author or authors, consisting successively of

21 The entry element in the name, the last substantive word in the name, along with any irremovable attachment to it, in Roman caps; and

22 The secondary element in the name, the remaining words preceding the entry element, written in the sequence of their occurrence and enclosed within circular brackets, in Roman caps and smalls;

3 Title of the book; and

4 Accession Number of the book

A book card is generally made of white cardboard of the size 7 × 4 × 0.1 cm

V,2;1'N7 N71
RAMASWAMY (KV)
History of India
3191

6 Inserting Book Card (*Weekly Job*).— Insert each of the Book Cards in the Book Pocket of the corresponding book.

3 Work of Volume Numbering

The following are the routines:

1 Numbering on the Jacket (*Weekly Job*).— Write the call number in ink on the jacket, if any, at a place corresponding approximately to the position of the tag on the back of the book. In case the colour of the jacket does not admit of writing with black ink, use red ink or paste a tag on the jacket and write on it.

2 Numbering on the Tag (*Weekly Job*).— Write the Call Number in ink on the tag. Write the Book Number below the Class Number.

3 Numbering on Due Date Label (*Weekly Job*).— Write in ink the accession number and the Call Number in the appropriate places of the due date label. In the case of a book belonging to the primary sequence, write in the appropriate place the date of its release for loan. In the case of a book of any other sequence write the date of its shelving and the date of its release for loan.

4 Numbering inside the Book (*Weekly Job*).— Write in ink the accession number, and in pencil the Call Number on a conventional page inside each volume. Here is a model convention.

41 The middle of the back of the title page;

42 The last page of the Chapter ending earliest after the fiftieth page, provided it is not the last page of the volume; in case of such a page being not available—

43 The bottom margin of the verso of the middle leaf of the volume.

Note.— Along with the Book Number, put Collection Numbers, if any;

4 Work of Prepared Volumes Arranging

The following are the routines:

1 Sorting of Volumes (*Weekly Job*).— Sort out the prepared volumes by their Collection Numbers.

2 Arranging the Volumes (*Weekly Job*).—Arrange the volumes in each Collection by their Call Numbers.

CHAPTER XD

STACK-ROOM GUIDE

1 Need for a System of Guides

On entering the stack room, the reader would find the shelf arrangement of the books chaotic and un-intelligible. Naturally, he would be bewildered. He may have to waste a long time to reach the shelves containing the books on the subject required by him. To save the Time of the Reader at this stage, provide an efficient system of guides in the stack room.

2 Plan and Row Guide

21 Plan of the Stack Room

Place at the entrance of the stack room a large bold plan of that room, showing the disposition of the book racks, and the subject of books contained in them.

22 Row Guide

The term 'Row' will be used to denote any one of the parallel rows of book racks in the stack room. Put a Row Guide at the end of each row. It will consist of a thick cardboard covered by a white paper on both sides. Write on each cardboard

1 The Class Number; and

2 The Translation of the Class Number into natural language.

Each digit and letter should be one inch high. Write in Indian Ink with the help of stencils. Insert the Guide Board in a wooden frame. Fix the wooden frame near the top of the first book rack in the row. Then each Row Guide will strike the eye of the reader while walking down the long gangway between the racks and the wall. Here is an illustration of a Row Guide:

D	ENGINEERING
E	CHEMISTRY

3 Bay Guide and Shelf-Plank Guide

31 Bay Guide

Put 1 to 3 Bay Guides at the top of each bay of each book rack. The physical form and frame of a Bay Guide is similar to that of a Row Guide. Each Bay Guide should contain in succession

1 The Class Number; and

2 The Translation of the class number into natural language. This will require more than one line in a Bay Guide, and sometimes even as many as three per Bay Guide, to give full information about all the major subjects contained in the bay. Fix all the Bay Guides vertically near the top of the Bay — on the top plank of the bay. As an alternative, fix a thin stiff long metal rod from one wall to another along the top of each row just below the ceiling of the tier. The frame for Bay Guide may have a hook for suspending it on the metal rod. Thus, the Bay Guide will not hide the books on the top plank of each of the bays.

32 Shelf-Plank Guide

Provide one or more Shelf-labels for each shelf plank. A Shelf-label may consist of a white cardboard strip of the size 80 × 20 cm, cut out from Catalogue Cards. Write on each Shelf-label:

1 The Class Number; and

2 The Translation of the Class Number into natural language, of the subjects contained in the Shelf plank.

Keep the Shelf-label, beginning just below the first book with the Class Number concerned. Provide three or four Shelf-labels for each Shelf plank, when necessary. To insert a Shelf-label, to take it off, and to move it from one end of the Shelf plank to the other, it is desirable to have a suitable groove cut along the front edge of each Shelf plank.

4 Book Tag

41 Fixing the Book Tag on the Spine

A new reader would first consult the plan at the entrance of the stack room. He may not have to do this on later occasions. The row guides greeting him at the end of each gangway, will invite him into the right gangway, between adjacent rows of book racks. While passing along the gangway, his eyes will catch the successive bay guides. He will stop in front of the bay having books on the subjects required by him. Then he will scan the shelf-plank guide in the bay. This will make him examine the volumes in the right shelf plank. Then it should be made possible for him to locate without any waste of time the particular book needed by him. For this, the Call Number of the book (= Class Number + Book Number) will be of help to him. Therefore, a tag on the book containing the Call Number of the Book should be pasted on its spine. To help his glance through the pages, each book tag should be fixed just 1" above the bottom of the spine of the book. Then all the book tags will be in one line.

42 Fast Sticking Book Tag

Fast sticking book tags, according to standard specification, are now available in the market. They alone should be used. No doubt this tag will cost a little more than a home-made tag using ordinary gum. The latter will fall off in a short time. Then another book tag will have to be made and attached to the spine of the book. In the long run the use of standard book tags available in the market is more economical than the use of home-made book tag. The durability of the book tags can be increased by applying paper varnish to them after they are affixed.

43 Maintenance of the Book Tags

Even the best book tag will come off or get mutilated or become dirty by the frequent handling of the book. It should be promptly and regularly replaced by a fresh book tag. There is nothing more offensive to the eye than a dirty half-torn tag disfiguring the back of a book.

CHAPTER XE

NEW BOOKS ADDED TO THE LIBRARY

1 New Volumes Tallying Work

The following are the routines:

1 Getting Accession Cards and Shelf Register Cards from the Technical Section (*Weekly Job*).— At the appointed hour on the appointed day of a week, get from the Technical Section the Transmission Box containing the Accession Cards coupled with the related Shelf Register Cards of the new books added in the week;

2 Comparing each Accession Card with the Corresponding Shelf Register Card (*Immediate Job*).— Compare each Accession Card with its related Shelf Register Card, correcting errors if any.

3 Placing the Compared Accession Cards (*Weekly Job*).— Place each Compared Accession Card in the Transmission Box in the sequence of the Accession Numbers.

4 Placing the Compared Shelf Register cards (*Weekly Job*).— Place each of the Compared Shelf Register Card in the Shelf Register Cards Box in the sequence of the Accession Numbers

2 Work of Shelving on the Recent Additions Shelf

The following are the routines:

1 Sorting out Shelf Register Cards (*Weekly Job*).— Sort out the Shelf Register Cards by their respective Collection Numbers if any;

2 Arranging of Shelf Register Cards (*Weekly Job*).— Arrange the Shelf Register Cards in each Collection by their Call Numbers and put them in the Shelf Register Cards Box;

3 Tallying each of the Shelf Register Cards with the Corresponding Volume (*Weekly Job*).— On the appointed day of the week, take the Shelf Register Cards Box to the Technical Section.

Tally each card with the corresponding volume, in respect of Author, Title, Call Number including Collection Number, and Accession Number;

4 Verifying Book Card (*Weekly Job*).— After completing the tallying work mentioned in Routine 3 above, tally each Book card with the corresponding Shelf Register Card in respect of Call Number, Name of Author, Title, and Accession Number, and insert back the book card in the Book Pocket.

5 Shelving of Recent Additions belonging to the Primary Collection (*Weekly Job*).— Put in a classified sequence in the Recent Additions Bay, each new volume intended to be transferred from that bay to the Primary Collection in the stack room.

6 Shelving of Recent Additions belonging to a Collection other than the Primary (*Weekly Job*).— Insert each of the remaining books among the books in the correct classified sequence in the collection appropriate to it.

7 Transferring of the Shelf Register Cards of the Volumes belonging to a collection other than the Primary (*Weekly Job*).— Insert each Shelf Register Card of the volumes belonging to a collection other than the Primary Collection, in the corresponding collection of Shelf Register Cards.

8 Transmitting Accession Cards (*Weekly Job*).— Put your initial and date in the appropriate line in the related accession card, and hand over the Transmission Box containing the accession cards to the Accession Section.

3 New Volumes Releasing Work

The following are the routines:

1 Picking out from the Recent Additions Shelf the Volumes (*Weekly Job*).— As one of the last jobs on the appointed day of each week, pick out from the Recent Additions Shelf each of the volumes having the release due date of the next day. (This work will be facilitated by using the weekly additions list containing the names of the volumes to be released in the week. Tick off for

each volume its entry in the weekly additions list. For an entry in the list being left unticked, investigate the case and collect the volume).

2 Examining the Volume (*Immediate Job*).— Examine rapidly for any damage being done by readers to each volume.

3 Leaving Bespoken Volumes with Circulation Section (*Immediate Job*).— A volume on the Recent Additions Shelf may be a bespoken one. Leave each bespoken volume with the Circulation Section.

4 Shelving of Released Volumes (*Immediate Job*).— Put each of the remaining volumes in the proper place in the classified sequence on the shelves in the Primary Collection in the stack room.

5 Transferring of the Shelf Register Cards (*Immediate Job*).— Pick out the Shelf Register Card of each of the released volumes from the Recent Additions Sequence and transfer it to its permanent place in the Shelf Register.

CHAPTER XF

VOLUMES RETURNED AFTER USE

1 Work of Replacing Returned Volumes

The following are the routines:

1 Sorting of returned volumes (*Daily Job*).— At the appointed hour of each day, sort the volumes returned at the Counter and lying in the Replacing Shelf, according to their Collection Numbers.

2 Arranging the Returned Volumes (*Daily Job*).— Arrange the volumes in each Collection, taking the Collections one after another.

3 Keeping the Books on Replacing Shelf (*Casual Job*).— To secure economy of labour, do the replacing of used volumes only once in a day. Till then, keep the returned volumes in temporary shelves — Replacing Shelf. The readers may be allowed to take away books from this shelf.

4 Shelving the Returned Volumes (*Daily Job*).— Taking each time a trolly full of returned volumes, shelve each volume in its appropriate place in the concerned collection. In case of, the number of volumes to be shelved being only a few, trolly is not necessary, carry them in hand.

2 Work with Lost Volumes

The following are the routines:

1 Transferring of the Shelf Register Card (*Immediate Job*).— On receiving intimation from the Circulation Assistant about the loss of a volume by a reader, transfer its Shelf Register Card to the Lost Volumes Collection Sequence.

2 Ascertaining of the Data about Lost Volumes (*Weekly Job*).— The reader would have paid a special deposit to cover the cost of the lost volume. He might have requested the Circulation

Assistant to get a fresh copy of the volume on his behalf. On getting intimation from the Counter Assistant about this, find out from the Accession Card the necessary bibliographical data about the lost volume — such as Publisher, Price, Format, and Edition.

3 Intimating the Book Order Section to Procure a New Volume (*Weekly Job*).— Request the Book Order Section to procure a copy of the lost volume.

4 Preparing the Replaced Volume (*Weekly Job*).— Prepare the volume replaced either by the member himself or by the library — according to the routines mentioned in Chap XE.

5 Retransferring of the Shelf Register Card (*Weekly Job*).— Pick out the related Shelf Register Card from the Lost Volumes Collection Sequence and place it in its proper place in the normal collection.

6 Intimating the Circulation Section (*Weekly Job*).— Intimate the Circulation Section about the replacement of the lost volume.

7 Shelving the Replaced Volume (*Weekly Job*).— On completing all the routines mentioned above, insert the volume in the appropriate place on the shelf.

3 Work with Damaged Volume

The following are the routines:

1 Transferring of the Shelf Register Card (*Daily Job*).— On receiving intimation from the Circulation Assistant about the damage to a volume, transfer its Shelf Register Card to the Lost Volumes Collection Sequence.

2 Sending the Damaged Volume for Binding (*Weekly Job*).— In case of the volume being repairable, send it for binding.

3 Intimating the Circulation Section about the Amount (*Weekly Job*).— Write to the Circulation Section about the binding charge to be collected from the member concerned.

4 Procuring New Volume (*Weekly Job*).— The damage being beyond repair, keep the volume in the Damaged Volumes Collection. Then proceed with all the routines mentioned in Sec XF2, as if the volume were a lost one.

CHAPTER XG

SHELF-RECTIFICATION AND STOCK-VERIFICATION

1 Shelf-Rectification

In an open access library, never allow a reader to replace books on the shelves. They have freedom only to pick out books from the shelves. In spite of this convention, books do get mixed up while browsing in the stack room by the reader. Even apart from criminally minded people deliberately putting a book in quite a distant place, the unintended misplacements within the same shelf-planks might in the long run amount to very near chaos. The process of restoring the correct sequence among the books is denoted by the term 'Shelf-rectification.'

2 Stock-Verification

There is need for periodical stock-verification. This is normally done once in a year. This practice usually involves much disturbance in the rhythm of the work of the library. Some libraries go to the criminal extent of closing the library to the public for the period of stock-verification.

3 Problems in Stock-Verification

Usually an outsider is appointed as Stock-Verifier. This implies lack of confidence in the honesty of the library staff. Stock-Verification through outsiders is used also as a "Big Stick to Beat the Librarian," by the academic staff and others carrying a grudge against the librarian. This grudge originated in the days of librarians being of low intellectual capacity and virtually regarded as attenders, though called "Librarians." In those days, preservation of books, rather than use of books by readers was the main concern of the library authorities. The modern books having only a short period of value and then deserving to be discarded had not been realised. A realisation of this would make the library authorities to look upon modern books as "expendable commodities" and not as properties preservable and accountable for ever. The modern open access is founded on this principle. The UGC recommending one volume to be written off for every 500 volumes going out in circulation is also based on this principle. Many countries make even a more liberal number of volumes to be written off. But unfortunately the "old order still prevaileth" in many libraries in our country. The correct way of knowing the actual books and the number of books lost in a library is to combine shelf-rectification and stock-verification as a weekly routine to be done by the Maintenance Section all through the year.

4 Cycle for Shelf-Rectification *cum* Stock-Verification

Each of the regions of a library may not be equally prone to disturbance and loss through readers. The primary collection will be the most disturbed. The closed collection will not be disturbed at all. The Secondary and the Tertiary collections will be disturbed much less than the Primary one. Therefore shelf-rectification and stock-verification should be done in the Primary Collection at least once in a month and that for the Secondary collection may perhaps be done once in six months. It may be enough to attend to the other collections once in a year. But, the frequency of periodical dusting and cleaning of these collections should be in just the reverse sequence. This is because in the Primary Collection the books are constantly disturbed by the readers themselves and dust and insects cannot therefore accumulate very much. But in the other collections they will accumulate.

5 Daily Quota for Shelf-rectification *cum* Stock-Verification

The daily quota of the region for shelf-rectification can be arrived at by taking the total length of shelving to be rectified and the period for completing the work. Each day, take out the shelf register trays for the day's quota. As far as possible, make the end points of the quota the end points of convenient subjects. Do the rectification work by two people.

6 Shelf-rectification *cum* Stock-Verification

The following are the routines:

1 Checking with Charged Tray (*Weekly Job*).— At the begin-

ning of the appointed day of the week, take out the shelf register card trays corresponding to the weekly quota of shelf-rectification *cum* stock-verification. Take them to the counter. Inform the person in charge of the charged tray, of the range of call numbers included in the quota. Ask him to read out from the charged tray such of the call numbers in the range of the quota as stand charged. As he reads out the number, turn the related shelf register card in its position in the tray through a right angle in its own plane such that the call number end goes up, that is in the clockwise direction, and leave it there. At the end it follows that all the shelf register cards standing in the turned position correspond to the books on loan. Also request the circulation assistant to inform you about the returning of any book belonging to the weekly quota, during the week.

2 Rectifying the Sequence on the Shelves (*Weekly Job*).— As the charged tray checking is going on, ask a member of the Maintenance Section to rectify the sequence of the volumes on the shelves in the region corresponding to the shelf register tray taken out. Also ask him to pick out from the replacing shelf all the volumes belonging to the region of the quota of the day and shelve them in their proper places.

3 Checking on the Shelves (*Weekly Job*).— After completing the Checking with the charged tray, take the shelf register cards tray to the appropriate shelves. Ask another member to go on reading the call numbers on the backs of the volumes in the shelf. It will be learnt from experience that the reading of the book number alone is practically sufficient in most cases, if the Colon Classification is used. This will increase the speed of the work. This fact will result in reducing the time taken for checking considerably. As he goes on reading them, go on tallying the shelf register cards. On coming across any turned card, bring to its normal position.

4 Keeping Shelf Register Cards in Investigation Box (*Weekly Job*).— Pick out each of the shelf register cards from the tray, of the books not being traceable. Put all such cards in the Investigation Box.

5 Replacing Shelf Register Cards Tray (*Weekly Job*).— On completing all the routines mentioned above, with regard to the Weekly quota, put the Shelf Register Cards Tray back into the cabinet.

6 Investigating Work (*Weekly Job*).— On completing the shelf-rectification *cum* stock-verification on the shelves investigate the volumes corresponding to the shelf register cards accumulated in the Investigation Box. The volumes may be lying in the replacing shelf, or they may be in the hands of the readers, or they may have been misplaced in any other shelves, or they might have been lost or the related charged cards might have been slightly misplaced in the charged tray. Put the shelf register cards of the volumes traced out, back in the Shelf Register Cards Cabinet.

7 Reporting to the Headmaster (*Weekly Job*).— On completing the investigation, take all the cards still needing investigation to the headmaster and give him a report of the result of shelf-rectification *cum* stock-verification of the week.

8 Reporting to the Authority (*Quarterly Job*).— Periodically— say quarterly — the headmaster should send to the authorities of the school the list of books not traceable during the quarter.

9 Removing from the List any Traced Book (Annual Job).— At the end of each year, remove from the quarterly lists of the year, any book traced during the year.

10 Sending Estimate of Cost of Lost Books (*Annual Job*).— At the end of the year send to the authorities of the school a final list of lost books along with the cost of each.

CHAPTER XII

BINDING

1 Need for Reinforced Binding

The books in a school library should be able to stand a good deal of wear and tear. Hence, it would be a good policy to give each of them Reinforced Library Binding. The specification for Reinforced Binding is given elsewhere (56).

2 Work with Volumes for Binding

The following are the routines:

1 Collecting the Volumes for Binding (*Daily Job*).— For the daily picking up of volumes for binding, divide the stack room into convenient zones. Collect each day the volumes for binding in the zone allotted for the day. Also collect such volumes kept aside by the Circulation Section and Reference Section. Keep all the collected volumes for binding, in the Book Rack for Binding.

2 Collating the Volumes for Binding (*Daily Job*).— Collate each of the volumes in the Binding Collection. In the case of any page missing, note it down near the top of the back of the title page. In case of the number of pages missing being too many, consult the headmaster if it is worthwhile rebinding the volume. The decision of the headmaster being against the rebinding of the volume, transfer it to the Worn-Out Collection or withdraw it from the library.

3 Transferring of Shelf Register Card (*Weekly Job*).— Take the shelf register card of each of the volumes finally decided to be bound. Transfer these cards into the Binding Collection Sequence of shelf register cards.

4 Transferring of Shelf Register Cards of Worn-Out Volumes (*Weekly Job*).— In the case of a volume transferred to Worn-Out Collection, transfer its shelf register card also to the Worn-Out Collection sequence of shelf register cards.

5 Withdrawing the Shelf Register Cards of Withdrawn Volumes (*Weekly Job*).— Remove the shelf register card of each

withdrawn volume, get it 'Cancelled' over the signature of the headmaster, pick out all the connected catalogue cards, get all of them 'Cancelled' over the signature of the headmaster, couple all these cards together with the shelf register card foremost and file them in the Withdrawn Collection Cards.

6 Cancelling the Accession Entry (*Weekly Job*).— Cancel the accession entry of each of the accession cards of the withdrawn volume over the signature of the headmaster.

7 Removing of Book Card (*Weekly Job*).— Take out the book card of each volume for binding and insert it in the classified sequence in the Binding Book Cards Tray.

8 Arranging the Volumes (*Monthly Job*).— Binding work is best done on a monthly basis. On collecting the quota for the month, scrutinize the volumes from the point of view of their binding peculiarities, and form homogeneous groups. Arrange the volumes within each group in classified sequence.

9 Preparing Binding Slip (*Monthly Job*).— Prepare a Binding Slip for each of the volumes.

10 Preparing Order Copy (*Monthly Job*).— Prepare an Order Copy — fair as well as office copy — for binding, with the aid of the Binding Slips.

11 Handing over the Volumes to the Binder (*Monthly Job*).— Ask the binder to

1 Come to the library on an appointed day;

2 Collate each volume; and

3 Tally with the Binding Order List.

Take his dated signature in the office copy of the Binding Order List as a token of receipt of the volumes for binding.

12 Keeping of Binding Slips (*Monthly Job*).— Keep the Binding Slip in the Binding Box.

3 Work in the Bindery

The following are the routines:

1 Asking the Binder the Date of Forwarding (*Monthly Job*).— Ask the binder to inform you of the date for the bound book to be forwarded.

2 Inspecting in the Bindery (*Monthly Job*).— Go to the bindery on that day and inspect the conformity of the binding work done so far to the instructions given in the agreement.

3 Passing for further Work (*Monthly Job*).— Pass the satisfactory volumes for further work.

4 Asking for Rectification (*Monthly Job*).— Ask the binder to rectify the faults in the unsatisfactory volumes and show them to you. (If this inspection is not done at this stage, the faults, if any, would be hidden away by the covering material.)

4 Work with Bound Volumes

The following are the routines:

1 Examining the Bound Volume (*Monthly Job*).— On receiving the bound volumes check each of them in respect of the covering material used, the treatment of the back, and the correctness of the tooling ask the binder to rectify the faults, if any;

2 Inserting Book Card (*Monthly Job*).— Paste the due date lable, if there is not one, pick out from the Binding Book Cards Tray its Book Card and insert it in the Book Pocket of the Volume; fill up the details in the top of the due date label.

3 Putting Initials and Date (*Monthly Job*).— Put your dated initials at the left hand bottom corner of the last end paper of the volume; if the accession card is in use, pick out the one for the bound volume and put your dated initials in the proper place.

4 Transmitting Bespoken Volumes (*Monthly Job*).— Obtain from the Circulation Assistant, the Bespoken Cards Box. Pick out each of the volumes having a Bespeaking Card. Send each Bespoken Volume, along with its Bespeaking Card, to the Circulation Assistant. Send also the Bespoken Cards Box.

5 Reinserting Shelf Register Card (*Monthly Job*).— For each of the bound volumes returned by the binder and accepted, transfer its shelf register card from the Binding Collection Cards sequence to its appropriate place in the Shelf Register Cabinet.

6 Shelving of the Bound Volumes (*Monthly Job*).— The routines are similar to those mentioned in Chap XF.

PART Y

OTHER WORK

CHAPTER YA

BOOK.SELECTION WORK

1 Factors Guiding Book Selection

The following are the three factors guiding book selection:

1 The demand for books.— The demand for books should be assessed in cooperation with the teachers and in the light of the curriculum and the prescribed textbooks, and also in the light of the demand from the students.

2 The supply or the extent and nature of the availability of books in the market. Preference should always be given to sumptuous editions on good paper with large types and plenty of illustrations.

3 The total finance available and the approved allocation of the same to different subjects and standards.

2 Sources for Book Selection

The following are some of the chief sources for book selection:

1 *Publisher's circular* of UK and *Publisher's weekly* of USA — both are weeklies;

2 *Quarterly list* of publications issued by the Registrars of Books of the different Constitutent States of India;

3 The *British national bibliography* and the *Indian national bibliography;*

4 The Catalogues of individual publishers and booksellers;

5 List of books received from the authors themselves;

6 Bibliographies in books;

7 Independent bibliographies;

8 Book reviews in periodicals;

9 Book selection lists published by Governments or national organisations either periodically or occasionally.

3 Book Selection Card

A book selection card is best printed in 8 pt type on cards of size 125 × 75 mm cut from white Bristol boards. Its headings should be as shown in the diagrams in P 467–68.

4 Selection Work

A detailed account of the routines involved in Book Selection work is given in my *Library administration* (53). In this Sec, a short account is given:

1 Preparing Book Selection Card (*Daily Job*).— Scan each of the sources for book selection. Fill up a Book Selection Card for each selected item.

2 Classifying the Book Selection Card (*Daily Job*).— Roughly classify the Book Selection Card and put the Class Number.

3 Arranging the Book Selection Cards (*Daily Job*).— First group the Cards according to the Standard. Then arrange, within each group, in a classified sequence.

4 Noting in the Card the availability of an earlier edition (*Daily Job*).— If there is already an earlier edition of the same volume, note it in the Book Selection Card concerned.

5 Making the Final Selection (*Casual Job*).— Discuss the accumulated Book Selection Cards with concerned teachers at convenient intervals — preferably at a meeting of the headmaster and the teachers. Avoid any unintended duplication and keep the estimated cost of the sanctioned books within the limit of the unspent amount of the Book Fund.

6 Getting Sanction (*Weekly Job*).— Get the sanction of the headmaster for purchasing the books selected during the week.

Ac No		Don No	W1 No
Cl No			
Heading			
Title			
Size	Colln	Edn	Yr
Pubr		Pub price	
Series, etc			
Review			
Reference			

Vendor			Cost
	Date	Initials	
Seln.			Indian
Apprd.			
Order			Foreign
Recd.			
Paid			
Accnd.			Order No.
Cut.			
Clasd.			Voucher No.
Cat.			
Shld.			
Bound			
Wl.			

CHAPTER YB

BOOK ORDER WORK

1 Problems of Libraries in India

The work of book ordering in libraries of India is at present difficult. The books will have to be purchased from the

1 Publishers or booksellers of UK and USA; or

2 Publishers or booksellers of India; or

3 Authors themselves.

Further, there is not sufficient facility in India to examine the books before placing an order, nor is the practice of the bookseller bringing books on approval to the school library widely established.

2 Work of Book Ordering

The following are the routines:

1 Alphabetising the sanctioned Book Selection Card (*Weekly Job*).— Alphabetise by the name of authors, Book Selection Cards for the finally sanctioned books.

2 Checking to avoid duplication (*Weekly Job*).— To avoid unintended duplication of all kinds, carefully check each of the Book Selection Cards for books finally sanctioned with the Catalogue and other sources — such as, Outstanding Orders, and Bills on hand.

3 Preparing the Order (*Weekly Job*).— Prepare an order, with the aid of the surviving Book Selection Cards.

4 Transmitting the Order (*Weekly Job*).— Transmit to the Office the Order List for despatching to the vendor or publisher or author as the case may be.

5 Keeping the Book Selection Cards (*Weekly Job*).— Keep the Book Selection Cards, now turned Book Order Cards, in the Books Order Tray.

3 Work of Receiving Supply

The following are the routines:

1 Inserting the Book Order Card in the Book (*Immediate Job*).— On the arrival of the supply, take out the Book Order Card of each book and insert it in the book.

2 Collating the Books (*Immediate Job*).— After all of the books get their respective Book Order Cards, carefully collate each of the books.

3 Approving the Books (*Immediate Job*).— Approve each of the volumes that conform to the bibliographical details in the corresponding Book Order Cards.

4 Passing on the Book for Preparation (*Immediate Job*).— After scrutinizing and approving, pass each of the volumes for preparation (*See* Chap XC).

CHAPTER YC

PERIODICAL PUBLICATIONS WORK

1 Idiosyncrasies of Periodicals

Periodicals are prone to develop idiosyncrasies of several kinds (48). Of these, irregularity in publication and irregularity in supply are the two idiosyncrasies a school library may meet often.

2 Irregularity in Supply

The library may not get at all an issue of a periodical. Bring this to the notice of the supplier promptly. Otherwise, the library may never get that issue. Therefore, the greatest amount of vigilance and promptness is necessary in dealing with periodical publications. And this should be done without undue dependence on mere memory. This is best done by a simple Two Card System.

3 Two Card System

Watch the prompt receipt of the current issues of each periodical publication with vigilance. This is best done by a Two Card System in a school library. One of these cards is denoted by the term 'Register Card' and the other by the term 'Check Card.'

1 Register Card.— Printed. 6 point type. Bristol board. White. 7 lines in the front page and 14 lines in the back. Gift cases, black border. Back side, column headings only. The column headings are shown below:

<table>
<tr><td colspan="3">Title</td><td colspan="2">Payment</td></tr>
<tr><td colspan="3" rowspan="2">Vendor</td><td>Vol or Year</td><td>Voucher N & Date</td></tr>
<tr><td></td><td></td></tr>
<tr><td>Cl N</td><td>Period</td><td>Order N & Date</td><td>Ann Subs</td><td></td></tr>
</table>

Vol & N	Date of pub	Date of rect	Vol & N	Date of pub	Date of rect

2 Check Card.—Printed. 6 point type. Bristol board. White. 14 lines on each side. Gift cases, black border. The column headings are shown below:

Heading									Period		
Vol and N	Date of Rem	L's Initials	Vol and N	Date of Rem	L's Initials	Vol and N	Date of Rem	L's Initials	Vol and N	Date of Rem	L's Initials

4 Registering

The following are the routines:

1 Receiving the Periodical (*Immediate Job*).—On the arrival of the mail each day, after satisfying yourself that each packet is addressed to the library, open the wrapper of each and insert it in the periodical.

2 Arranging the Periodicals (*Immediate Job*).—Arrange the periodicals alphabetically by title.

3 Collating the Periodical (*Immediate Job*).—Collate each periodical. In case of there being any abnormality, note it at the top of the back of the front cover. Put each such periodical in the Deferred Tray.

4 Making the Entry in the Register Card (*Immediate Job*).—On the periodical being a sound one, pull out its Register Card, and make the necessary entry in it.

5 Putting the Class Number in the Periodical (*Immediate Job*).—Taking the class number from the Register Card, write it near the right hand top corner of the front cover of the periodical.

6 Entering the Receipt of a Later Supply (*Immediate Job*).—The periodical received may not be the immediate one after the last registered. Then make the entry not in the next vacant horizontal line but in the line appropriate to it. Write a reminder card for the earlier issue not received.

7 Reminding about Title-page, Contents and Index (*Immediate Job*).— On the title page, contents page, and index being due, write a reminder for them.

5 Vigilance Work

The following are the routines:

1 Picking out the Check Card (*Immediate Job*).— On registering a periodical, pick out its Check Card. The Check Card will be found among the cards lying behind the current week's guide.

2 Transferring of the Check Card (*Immediate Job*).— Transfer the Check Card to behind the due week guide card of the next issue.

3 Reminding about Non-receipt (*Weekly job*).— On the last day of the week, for each of the Check Card still lying behind the guide card of the week, write out a reminder card.

4 Transferring of Check Card (*Weekly Job*).— Fill up in each Check Card the details about the reminder. Then transfer each of the Check Cards to behind the next week's guide card.

6 Display Work

Display all the new periodicals, promptly registered, for the use of the readers. For this displaying, use a display table (*See* Sec JB2). The following are the routines in the display work:

1 Removing the earlier issue (*Immediate Job*).— Take out each of the earlier issues from the display table and keep each of those in the loose numbers shelf, so that they may be readily available for consultation.

CHAPTER YD

ACCESSION WORK

1 Accession Number and Donation Number

Every volume to be included in the stock of the library must receive a serial number called Accession Number. Donated books must receive a Donation Number, in addition to the accession number. Cumulated volumes of periodicals should also receive accession numbers and if necessary also donation numbers.

2 Work of Accession Numbering

The following are the routines:

1 Arranging the books (*Weekly Job*).— As soon as the classification and cataloguing of the books or the volumes of periodicals are finished,

11 Arrange the purchased books in the sequence of their entry in their related bills;

12 Periodicals and donated books in the sequence of their call numbers.

2 Assigning Accession Number (*Weekly Job*).— Use the Book Order Card of each purchased book as the Accession Card. Use green and red cards for donated books and for periodicals, respectively. Arrange also the related shelf-register cards, the accession cards, and the catalogue cards in an exact parallel sequence. Look up the accession cabinet for the last accession and donation numbers already given. Starting with the next number, assign the accession numbers, in correct numerical sequence in each of the shelf-register cards, accession cards and the main entries.

3 Accession Register

On receiving accession number, each Book Order Card attains the status of an Accession Card. Arrange all the accession cards in the sequence of their accession numbers in the Accession Cabinet. This must be kept under lock and key, these cards being the basic records of the books in the library, giving a complete history of the respective books.

CHAPTER YE

SCHOOL LIBRARY FINANCE

1 Bad Tradition

Lastly we have to deal with the question of the finance for the school library. We may refer at once to an undesirable practice that has crept into many of the schools in India. A library fee is collected from each student; this amount is amalgamated with the general funds of the school; and it is used to meet general deficit or to meet other items of expenditure. It is seldom a library gets back the full amount to its credit. The first reform that is needed is that the amount realised as library fees should be kept separately, spent only in enriching the school library, and accounted for separately. There is a precedent for this — the sports-fund. The necessary reform is entirely in the hands of the Department of Public Instruction and we earnestly make an appeal that this reform should be made without any delay.

2 Grant-in-Aid

Further, to be in keeping with the general financial traditions of our educational institutions, the library fund of each school should be credited with not only —

1 the entire library fee collected from the students; but also

2 a contribution from the management; and

3 a contribution from the State Government equal to the sum of (1) and (2).

To this fund should also be added any other gift received at any time specifically for library purpose.

3 Student-Centred Library-Centred Education

This revision is made necessary because of the increasing cost of books and increasing scale of salary. Another factor making t necessary is change in the educational policy in the relation between library work and class room work — in short, replacing syllabus-centred, curriculum-centred method of education into student-centred library-centred education.

Here is an American model of the expenditure on school libraries, about 30 years ago. The book fund was about Rs 3 per student per year. Salary of library staff was 1.6 per cent of the total salary paid by a school (2). This would roughly amount to the salary paid to a teacher with full qualifications — academic and professional. The above is recurring grant, quite apart from the capital grant needed for building, furniture and equipment.

BIBLIOGRAPHICAL REFERENCES

Note.— 1 Col 1 gives the Serial Number of the Bibliographical Reference.

2 Col 2 gives the Section Number of the text, where the reference is made.

3 Col 3 gives the Bibliographical Reference.

1	Sec RC2	ALA Bulletin. 27; 1923; 774–75.
2	Sec YE3	—. —. 34; 1940; 121.
3	Sec HE5	Aurobindo. [*Extracts From*] Mother. 1928. (*In* Ranganathan (S R). Library administration. Ed.2. 1959. 9–10).
4	Sec PA3	Ballard (P B). Thought and language. 1934. 17.
5	Sec PD1	—. —. 48.
6	Sec PB2	—. —. 129.
7	Sec PB3	—. —. 132.
8	Sec PA3	—. —. 136.
9	Sec EC5	Blake (William). Poetical works. Ed by John Sampson. 1914. 100–01.
10	Sec VB2	Bliss (Henry Evelyn). Organisation of knowledge in libraries. Ed 2. 1939. 228–29.
11	Sec VC1	—. —. 299.
12	Sec ED1.4	Boorman (W Ryland). Developing personality in boys. 1929. 89–90.
13	Sec DF2	Brockington (A Allen). Mysticism and poetry on a basis of experience. 1934. 26–28.
14	Sec DF3	Browning (Robert). Paracelsus. Part 1: Paracelsus aspires. 1912. V1. 26.
15	Sec PD1	Butler (Samuel). Works. V19. 1925. P 118.
16	Sec EC4	—. —. —. 127–28.
17	Sec EE4	Chandogya-upanishad. Adhyaya 7. 1915. P 156–80.
18	Sec FA2	Chaucer (Geoffrey). Boethius de consolatione philosophie. Book 1. Prose 5.
19	Sec LH3	Delgorza (Flora). Machine age, the child and the book. (Children's year book. 3; 1931; 35–41)
20	Sec CA2.4	Dewey (John). Democracy and education. 1920.
21	Sec DH1	—. School and society. 1899. 95.
22	Sec EF2	Dictionary of American biography. V6. 1931. 586.

23	Sec PF4	FRANCE (Anatole). My friend's book. Tr by J Lewis May. 1923. 244.
24	Sec ED15	GIBRAN (Kahlil). The prophet. (J Nat Educ Assoc. 1939; 209).
25	Sec EC3	HALDANE (Richard Burden). Autobiography. 1931.
26	Sec EF2	HARDY (G H). Mathematicians's apology. 1941. P 85–87.
27	Sec EF2	HENDERSON (Archibald). Contemporary immortals. 1920. 8.
28	Sec PA3	HUSS (H R). Illiteracy of the literate. P 31.
29	Sec JB1	INDIAN STANDARDS Institution. Code of practice relating to primary elements in the design of library buildings. (IS: 1553–1960). 1960.
30	Sec JB1	—. Specification for library furniture and fittings. Part 1: Timber. (IS: 1829 (Part 1)–1961). 1961.
31	Sec WA3	—. —. —. Sec 6.2.
32	Sec VB3	LIBRARY ASSOCIATION record. Series 3.3; 1933; 249.
33	Sec VC1	—. Series 4.1; 1934; 98.
34	Sec HA2	LIBRARY MOVEMENT: Collection of essays by diverse hands. 1929. 1–4.
35	Sec PF2	LOCKE (John). Some thoughts concerning education. 1960. Collected works. Ed 11. V9. 1812. 1–205.
36	Sec PA4	MACLEOD (Fiana). Winged destiny P 223.
37	Sec PA5	—. —. P 223.
38	Sec PA5	—. —. P 223.
39	Sec RA3	MADRAS LIBRARY Association. Annual report. 1935 36–39; 109–16.
40	Sec ED1.2	MELVIN (A. Gordon). Progressive teaching. 1929. 29.
41	Sec PD1	MITCHELL (L S). Here and now story book. 1921.
42	Sec PC1	NEELAMEGHAN (A). Books and articles: Guiding principles for presentation of text. (Lib sc. 5; 1968; Sec B6A).
43	Sec EG4	PALMIERI (M). Philosophy of fascism. 1936. P 25.
44	Sec VC2	PHILLIPS (Howard H). Primer of book classification. 1937. P 122–26.
45	Sec EC2	POUND (Ezra). Make it new. 1934. 113.
46	Sec EC2	—. —. P 256.
47	Sec WB6	RANGANATHAN (S R). Classified catalogue code. Ed 5. 1964.

48	Sec YC1	—. —. Chap PA.
49	Sec VC4	—. Colon classification. Ed 6. 1960.
50	Sec VM2	—. —. Chap 03.
51	Sec VL0	—. —, Sec 21 to 22.
52	Sec SB1	—. Five laws of library science. Ed 2. 1957.
53	Sec YA4	—. Library administration. Ed 2. 1959. Chap 21.
54	Sec UB5	—. —. Chap 26.
55	Sec XA3	—. —. Chap 28.
56	Sec XH1	—. —. Sec 3959.
57	Sec VC4	—. Library classification: Fundamentals and procedure. 1944.
58	Sec QA4	—. Library science periodicals in India: Birth of a twin. (J lib service. 1; 1971; 7–22).
59	Sec VC4	—. Prolegomena to library classification. Ed 3. 1967.
60	Sec TG1	—. Reference service. Ed 2. 1961. Chap G2.
61	Sec HC3	—. —. Chap J4.
62	Sec TG2	—. —. Part K.
63	Sec CF6	— and Sivaraman (K M). Reference service and bibliography. V2. 1941. P 16–17.
64	Sec HA3	SAYERS (W C B). Introduction to the first edition. (*In* Ranganathan (S R). Five Laws of library science. Ed 2. 1957. 16).
65	Sec EF2	SCHOOL AND SOCIETY. 44; 1936; 590.
66	Sec ED1.1	—. —. 592.
67	Sec CA2.5	SELIGMAN (Edwin R A), *Ed.* Encyclopaedia of the social sciences. V5. 1931. P 403.
68	Sec ED1.3	T'CU HSIA monthly. 1; 1935; 273.
69	Sec EA3	TAGORE (Rabindranath). Fireflies. 1931. 215.
70	Sec BC1	TARDE (Gabriel). Laws of imitation. Tr by Elsie Clews Parsons. Ed 2. 1903.
71	Sec KC3	TENNYSON (Alfred). Ulysses. Lines 18–21.
72	Sec PB3	TERMEN (Lewis M). Measurement of intelligence. 1921. P 226.
73	Sec TJ1	THIRUVALLUVAR. Thirukkural. Chap 25. Sec 1.
74	Sec EC1	TOWNSHEND (Frank). Becoming. 1939. P 44.
75	Sec EE5	—. —. Earth 1935. P 63–65.
76	Sec ED1.6	—. —. P 106.
77	Sec CA1	WEBSTER'S NEW international dictionary of English language. Ed 2. 1934.
78	Sec VC2	YEAR'S WORK in librarianship. 6; 1933; 193.

INDEX

Note.— 1 The index number against each item in the number of the Part, Chapter, or Section of its occurrence in the text.

2 The following abbreviations are used:

irt	in relation to
qirt	quoted in relation to
r by	referred by
rirt	referred in relation to

Absorbing intellect TJ2
Abstract noun GC3
Academic staff XG3
Accelerated change CC2
Acceleration CC1
Accession
  card
    irt
      Accession number YD2.2
      New volume tallying XE1
    transmitting XE2.9
  number YD1
  numbering work YD2
  part of book number VM4
  register YD3
Account code ME2
Accuracy of fact NA12
Achievement test N
Ackley (Edith) LH33
Activity
  among students ED5
  irt Passivity ED
Adaptation, Futility of PD
Added
  entries WD/WJ
    irt Reference Service TL3
    Record of WK1
Admission to library UA2
Adult
  growth JA1
  irt
    Library civics KB3
    Overdue charge MK42
    Sense of time TD3
  psychology PD3
Aeroplane CC21
Aesop's *Fables rirt*
  Choice of words PB1
  History of students' books PF1
Aesthetics
  in students' book PC2
  of library building JA7
Age of
  dry-as-dust didacticism PF1
  experience PF4
  imagination PF3
  sugar-coated didacticism PF2
Agriculture LJJ
Ahalya EA2
Ala Valliappa PA7
Algebra, Curriculum of ED7
Alice in wonderland PF3
Alphabetical index entry WE/WJ
Alternative name entry WJ2
American
  bias of DC VB1
  book list GF3
  librarian *r by* Sayers HA3
  Library Association
    Education Committee of RA2
    irt School Libraries Division BC3
    School Libraries' Division of RC2
Animal husbanding LJKX
Annual
  anthology of inspirational passages NC3
  cancelling of students' ticket UC6

thesis *irt*
Achievement test NA4
Essay writing ME3
Anteriorising common isolates
Schedule of VF
Use of VL
Anthology
irt
Inspirational passage MG3
Recitation of inspirational passage MG1
Use of anteriorising common isolate VL5
of inspirational passage
irt Achievement test NC3
Anticipation, Pleasure of EA1
Application
card filing *irt*
Outside member UE1.8
Teacher member UD2.7
for membership *irt*
Outside member UE1.1
Teacher member UD2.1
Apprentice method of initiation TC
A priori method BD
Arabian nights PF3
Archimedes LH2C3
Architect DE3
Arnold (Matthew) DA2
Arrangement of entries
in *Essay index* MQ72
Arranging
bespeaking cards UL3
book selection cards YA4.3
books on shelf TC3
periodicals YC4.2
returned volumes XF1.2
volumes for binding XH2.8
Art books collection XB12
Artificial light JA5
Artillery, Major of DE2
Aryabhatta JH2B3
Assignment MQ22
Assistant professor DJ6
Association of children's authors PG3
Astronomy *irt*
Bowditch DJ2
Reading for information LJBX
Atlas VL1
Atomic weight LH2E2
Atomised experience EE1
Atomistic view of school life KC2
Attracting students to library HB2
Aurobindo *rirt*
Perfect perfection HE5
Qualities of school Librarian HE4
Author
index entry WE
Functions of ME3
of students' books
irt
Basic words PB2
Formation of profession PF5
Monosyllabic words PB1
Style of writing PC3
Qualities for PE2
Authority
from
corporate body BA23
powerful personality BA22
revealed book BA21
irt
Unreliability BD1.1
Why of school library BA2
Average student *irt*
Follow-up work by student LE3
Teaching technique DB4
Avoidance of duplication in book selection YB2.2
Ayodhya CC21

B group subjects BA23
Babies book or a little report of how young people should behave PF1
Bacon CA2.3
Baldwin's *On England* LH2O8
Ballard (PB) *rirt*
Language PA3
Learning of words PB2

Banaras BC6
Basic words PB2
Bay
  guide XD31
  Specification for JB1
Becoming
  Potency of the process of EA2
  Process of EA1
Beehive, Hum of EG1
Behaviour MH2
Behaviouristic psychology EE1
Bennett (Arnold) HF1
Bespeaking
  card
    forwarding UL5
    picking UL4
    receiving UL1
  noting UL2
  work UL
Bhaskara LH2B3
Bible BA21
Bibliographic classification VA2
Bibliographical
  game *irt*
    Fact finding ME1
    Supervised study MQ86
  standard PH2
Bibliography
  building
    irt Achievement test NF
    work MS
  Compilation of TF92
  irt
    Annual thesis ME3
    Initiation KA8
Biography GA5
  irt Use of anteriorising common isolate VL3
Biological force EA3
Biology *irt*
  Fact finding LH3G
  Reading for information LJG
Binder XH2.11
Bindery
  irt Reference service TL5
  Work in XH3
Binding
  collection XB6
  irt Damaged volume XF3.1
  work XH
Black list of members tickets UA75
Blake (William)
  qirt Education as becoming EC5
  rirt
    History of students' books PF2
    Inspiration LK5
Bliss (HE)
  irt BC VA2
  qirt
    CC VC1
    DC VB2
Boethius FA2
Bombardment of nucleal element DB3
Book
  and student HA3
  card UF1
    irt Volumes for binding XH2.7
      Method of circulation UF
  preparation XC2.5
  Complexity of HC4
  consulted, Statistics for UH3
  famine P
  for Indian students PE1
  Illustration in GD
  in a library, Fate of KB2
  in unusual demand UA851
  index entry WE/WG
    irt Tracing section WK2
  industry in India PG
Book
  irt
    Curiosity of student GB1
    Fire protection MN1
    Library habit KA2
    Range in school library GA
    Student HB1
    Textbook CE8
  jacket XC2.2
  Make-up of TF3

Book
  number VM
    irt
      Collection number XB12
      Stock verification XG6.3
  on education GG3
  on side interest GB3
  order
    card *irt*
      Accession
        card YD2.2
        register YD3
    section XF2.3
    work YB
  Parts of ME3
  Physical make-up of GE
  pocket making XC2.4
  Preparation of XC
  Republication of PF3
  returned after
    consultation UH2
    use XF
  review YA2.8
  section TL3
  selection
    card YA3
      Preparation of YA4.1
    Factors guiding YA1
    irt
      Follow-up work LE3
      Grouping of schools HH5
      Limitations of finance GB1
      Marketing of books PG2
      New education DH3
      Student HA2
      Teacher's work HD2
    work YA
  seller
    of St Paul's Church Yard PF2
    rirt Marketing of books PG2
  seller's catalogue YA2.4
  Socialisation of CF
  tag
    Fast sticking XD42
    Maintenance of XD43
    on the spine XD41
Books, Varieties of GA1
Boorman (Ryland) ED1.4
Born author PC3
Bosanquet CA1
Bose DH4
Boston Atheneum DJ2
Bound volume
  of periodical UA83
  Work with XH4
Bowditch (Nathaniel) DJ2
Brain capacity of student CB1
Briston VB3
British national bibliography YA2.3
Brockington (A Allen) DF2
Brown
  (JD) VA2
  (Zaidee) LL3
Brown's school days PF3
Browsing
  facility XA1
  in stack room XG1
Butler (Samuel) *qirt*
  Education as becoming EC4
  Students' book PD1

Cabuliwallah LH2O7
Calendar of the University
  of Madras CE4
Calf EA2
Calligraphy CF4
Camden's letters FA2
Camel theory of education CG
Cancelling ticket *irt*
  Outside member UE2
  Student member UC6
  Teacher member UD3
Canon of currency PB2
Card catalogue *irt*
  Imitation KA6
  Keeping diary MA3
  Physical form WA3
Care of books *irt*
  Concentric cycle TF11
  Library habit KA2

Carnegie United Kingdom Trust RA2
Carr's *Synopsis* DJ2
Casual misplacement of book MK1
Catalogue
  cabinet WA3
  card, Insertion of TC3
  irt Concentric cycle TF6
  of publisher YA2.4
  room, Hygiene in MM1
Cataloguing
  irt
    Centralisation of work HH4
    Pamphlet GF3
  section TL3
Caxton PF1
CC VC
  irt classif schemes VA2
  Main subjects in VD
Centre-hung shutter JA6
Central library
  for schools HH2
  irt Celebration of events LF3
  of schools *irt*
    Class library XB3
    Old ed of reference books GA2
Centralisation of impersonal work HH4
Chandogya-upanishad EE4
Change, Postulate of CE2
Changing future, Education for CB
Charged
  pockets filing UJ2
  tray work UJ
Charging work UH5
  irt Apprenticeship TC3
Charlie Chaplin ED4
Charm of diversity EG2
Chaucer FA2
Check card YC3.2
  irt Vigilance work YC5
Cheltenham VB3
Chemistry *irt*
  Fact finding LH2E
  Reading for information LJE
Chewing tobacco MM3
Chidambaram MD1
Chief minister of Madras GG4
Child
  centred education YE3
  psychology PD3
Children's
  authors' association PG3
  book *irt*
    Choice of words PB
    Language PA1
    Tamil PA7
  department in public library KB4
  libraries in India PC3
  song LH2O2
China CF4
Choice of words PB
Christ PF1
Cinema
  How of LH33
  reel *irt*
    Extension work GG2
    High school library CJ2
Circulation
  method UB1
  section XH2.1
  work UA0
Circumambulating the universe EA2
Citizenship MH
City father CE5
Civics-in-action MH1
Class
  index entry WH
    Functions of WH3
    irt Tracing section WK2
  library XB2
  number
    irt
      Book number VM1
      CC VC4
      Main entry WC3
  room work
    irt
      Library work KC1

Class
room work
irt
Parallel reading LD1
Role of teachers' association RC1
Teacher HD4
Topical collection XB4
Preparation for LC
Service to TH
Classification
irt Centralisation of work HH4
practice VC4
section TL3
Classified
arrangement VA1
catalogue WB6
Classifying
irt Pamphlet GF3
Steps in VE
Clerk HG4
Clippings GF5
Closed collection XB12
Coil of wire HA1
Collating
book YB3.2
periodical YC4.3
volumes for binding XH2.2
Collecting
deposit UE1.2
overdue charge UG43
volumes for binding XH2.1
Collection
by standard XB2
formation XB
irt Use of anteriorising common isolate VL5
Collection
number *irt*
Class Library XB3
Primary and secondary collections XB5
Standard XB22
College library AC2
Colon
class number *irt*
Outside-member UE1.412
Student-member UC2.217
Teacher-member UD2.311
classification *See* CC
Columbia University DG61
Common noun GC2
Communication of news CC22
Competitive examination MK2
Compilation of bibliography TF92
Completion test ND5
Compulsory
educational system FB1
library system FB1
Concentric
cycles TF
method TE2
system KA3.2
Conductivity LH2E2
Conscience box UG7
Consideration for others MK
Constitution of India DC2
Contents page ME3
Contract technique DG4
Control region UB42
Corporate body BA23
Correlation
of curriculum in book selection GB2
with experience GB4
Correction collection XB6
Cost of lost book XG6.10
Counter
enclosure, Specifications for JB4
vigilance work UH1
Counts (George S) CA2.5
Cow big with calf EA2
Crafton boys PF3
Creative
education
irt Transmissive education EE1
Vision of EE5
intellect TJ2
work in India PA3

Criminal
procedure code ME2
quality in student MK2
Cross
gangway, Width of JB1
reference entry WD
irt
Reference service TL3
Tracing section WK2
reference index entry WJ2
Functions of WJ3
irt Tracing section WK2
world puzzle CJ2
Croydon public library LG2
Cultivation of
human resources TJ1
mental resources TK
Means for TJ4
Curiosity of student *irt*
Informative book GA4
Range of subjects GB1
Currency, Canon of PB2
Curricular load CB1
Curriculum
centred education *irt*
Refresher course for teachers RA3
School library finance YE3
Sociological pressure CD3
Impact of inventions on CB3
Cutter (CA) VA2

Dalton LH2E3
Damage to library property UA5
Damaged volume
collection XF3.4
Work with XF3
Dante PD1
Darwin LH3G2
Dasara CJ4
DC VB
rirt
Basis of CC VC1
Classif schemes VA2
Dealer in a school DG4
Debate MF2
Decimal classification *See* DC
Defaulters notifying UC6.5
Definition of reference service TA
Degree in
education HF3
library science HG1
Delgorza (Flora) LH33
Deliberate misplacement of book MK2
Demand for books YA1.1
Democracy, Demand of DD3
Density
irt Fact finding LH2E2
of air ED9
Department of
education *irt*
Help from Government RA1
Library building QB2
Status of library staff QA1
geography MA4
history DG6
public instruction YE1
Deposit
collecting UE1.2
irt Lost volume XF2.2
Repaying of UE2.5
Descriptive book GA4
Deserted village PF2
Devil PF1
Dewey
(John)
and individual instruction DG
irt New School DH2
Personality of DG7
rirt
Interest in younger men DG61
New education and school library DH1
Purpose of education CA2.4
simplicity of DG8
(Melvil) VA2
Diagrammatic representation
of new school DH1

Diary
irt
Fact finding MB
Inspirational reading MD
Recreative reading MC
Need for keeping MA
Dickens (Charles) PF3
Dictation of notes DC2
Dictionary TF4
irt Use of anteriorising common isolate VL2
Didacticism
Age of
dry-as-dust PF1
sugar-coated PF2
irt Realism PF4
Directed
reading NB3
study LL3
Drector of
əducation *irt*
Auuthority BA23
Corapulsory library hour AD3
Libury idiary AD6
Result n mathematics AC4
Salary of school libraries HG6
Vacation lecture AD5
public instruction *rirt*
Influence of publisher PG2
Use of school library by public GG4
Disability from loan UA9
Discharging
non-overdue book UG41
of overdue bookUG42
work UG4
irt Apprenticeship TC3
Dıcicpline in the library CJ6
Dishonesty in student NA14
Dıisplay of
books HB4
periodicals YC6
Diversity
Charm of EG2
irt Individuality of studentsEG3
Divine curiosity EF1
Documents on library technique QA3
Donation number YD1
Double-faced stage EA2
Dramatisation MF3
Draper HF1
Dressing hair MP4
Drill master HF1
Due date label UF3
Numbering on XC3.3
Pasting of XC2.3
Dunce DD2
Duplicate ticket, Rule about UA74
Duplication, Avoidance of YB2.2
Dutt (Toru) LH2O1

Easing the back of volume XC1.2
East India Company
Directors of BB1
Eddington (Arthur) DF2
Edgeworth (Maria) PF2
Editor
index entry WF
Functions of WF2
of series entry WJ
Education
as becoming
Case studies of EB
Opinions about EC
Books and periodicals on GG3
Committee of American Library Association RA2
Degree in HF3
for
accelerated change in the universe of ideas CC
changing
future CE2
world CB
Education
Inequalities and equalities in EH
ministers of India DC4
Purpose of CA1
Teleology of CA

Educational
  code HG6
  institution AB7
  qualifications for school librarian HF1
  review RC3
  techniques DB
    irt India DC
  wastage in India DC4
Einstein (Alfred)
  qirt Def of education ED1.1
  rirt
    Divine curiosity EF2
    Supply of ferment by lib EF2
Electro-magnet HA1
Elementary
  education DA4
  school library CH
Elevating book TJ2
Emergent evolution TE1
Emerson ED1.3
Emersonian ferment EF1
Emotion TJ2
Empire Marketing Board GF4
Encyclopaedia
  Britannica CE5
  irt
    Concentric system TF511
    Use of anteriorising common isolate VL2
Engineering LJD
English
  language
    irt Students' book PA1
    Students' books in PF
  professor *rirt*
    Sleeping class EB2
    Vacation course LA2
Entertaining book TJ2
Entrance gate
  irt
    Circulation UB42
    Open access JA2
  releasing UG5
  Work at UG
Environment
  Change in PD2
  irt Students' book PD1
Environmental force EA3
Epidiascope GG2
Epitomising MF1
Equal opportunity for lower quartiles DE1
Equality
  irt
    Regimentation DA2
    Self-educability DD1
  of opportunity TA2
  of salary HG3
  of status HG2
Equipment for Library QB
Errata slip NA12
Essay
  and general literature index MQ5
  index MQ5
  writing
    irt Recreational reading MB2
    with books ME2
Etna LH33
Euclid
  irt Fact finding work LH2B3
  rirt Stimulation of nucleal element DJ2
Europe, Examination system in CG5
Evolution, Theory of EC
Exact service HC3
Examination
  irt Library habit HD2
  with book CG5
    irt Essay writing ME2
  Wrong way of CG4
Excreta MM4
Excursion LH33
Exhibition LF2
Exit gate
  irt
    Circulation work UB42
    Open access JA2
  releasing UH6
  Work at UH

Expanded metal shutter JA6
Expansive classification VA2
Expendable commodity XG3
Expenditure on school library
  in USA YE3
Experience
  Age of PF4
  Correlation with GB4
Experimental school DG4
Expression
  irt Suggestion LE2
  Medium of PA
Extension
  service to public GG4
  work GG
External stimulus LB2
Externalised memory
  irt
    Examination system CG5
    Fact finding diary MB3
    Internal memory CE3
    Reference service TJ2
  Ready reference book as CF8
Extra
  mural stimulus LF
  reading, Book for FA5

Fables
  Republication of PF3
  rirt
    Choice of words PB1
    History of student's books PF1
Facet term WH4
Fact
  Accuracy of NA12
  finding LH
    diary MB
      irt
        Achievement test NA1
        Bibliographical game ME1
    irt
      Achievement test NA
      Making it pleasurable ME
Failure in examination DB5
Fairy tales, Republication of PF3
Fallacy in school library work LA
Fascist pessimism EG4
Fast sticking book tag XD42
Fate of book in library KB2
Fatigue GC3
Faucett's *Province of England* MA4
Favoured language VM3
Feats on the fiord PF3
Festival *irt*
  Extra-mural stimulus LF1
  Interests of student BG4
Field psychology EE1
Finance
  for library QB
  irt
    Book selection YA1.3
    Teachers' association publishing
      book PH3
  Limitations of GB2
  of school library YE
Find me out
  diary MB1
  question LH2
Fire
  extinguisher MV2
  prevention MN
Fisherman boy DE2
Fittings and furniture, Specification
  for JB
Five laws of library science S
  as foundation of lib work SA
  irt Reference service TA1
  Role of SB
Floor
  level of library JA4
  of stack room, Sitting on MP1
Folder GF3
Folk method LG1
Follow-up work by student LE
Force of
  environment EA6
  phylogeny EA4
  psycheogeny EA4
  vasana EA3
Foreign medium, Havoc of PA3

Foreword AB
Formal
  education for life-long
    self-education CE7
  lesson
    as a method of initiation TE
    irt Learning library habit LL2
  library
    hour DJ1
    lesson MQ1
Formation of collection XB
Forwarding, Date of XH3.1
Foundation of library work SA
France
  (Anatole) PF4
  irt Matthew Arnold's report DA2
  Shift in human values in DA1
Franchise DA4
Franklin EF2
Frequency distribution DB1
Fugitive reading material GF
Functional library in school
  Absence of AC1
Functions of
  author index entry WE3
  class index entry WH3
  cross reference index entry WJ3
  editor index entry WF2
  main entry WC3
  maintenance section XA
  series index entry WG3
  tracing section WK3
Funeral of murdered book KB2
Furniture, Specification for JB

Game, Rules of LH32
Garland HG6
Garment DA2
Gautama EA2
Generic name entry WJ2
Geography
  Department of MA4
  irt
    Fact finding LH2U
    Reading for information LJU
  Teaching ED6
Geology LJH
Geometry, Teaching of ED8
Gibran (Kahlil) ED1.5
Glass
  cover over catalogue cards MM1
  pane JA6
Global experience EE
Gold LH31
Golden jubilee year DC5
Goldsmith (Oliver) PF2
Goody two shoes PF2
Gossiping MP2
Government
  college
    Coimbatore AC2
    Mangalore AC2
  grant HH3
  irt
    Authority BA23
    Library staff QA1
    Pedagogical inertia RA
    School library finance QB3
Grain dealer HF1
Gramophone record GG2
Grant-in-aid
  code QA1
  to school library YE2
Granth Saheb BA21
Graph ED7
Greer (Margaret R) LL4
Group study room JB3
Grouping of schools HH
Growth of library *irt*
  Building JA1
  Printed catalogue WA1
Guidance in imitating
  library routine TD1
Guide
  card in catalogue KA6
  changing UJ3
  in stack room XD
Guided excursion ED3
Gulliver's travels PF3

Habit of
  maintaining diary MB5
  using library FB3
Haldane (RB) EC3
Hamlet CD5
Hand writing WA4
Handicap in school library work LB
Hanuman CC21
Hardy EF2
Heedless Eliza PF2
High school library CJ
Himalayas CC21
Hindu CC22
  High School (Triplicane) HG6
History *irt*
  Fact finding LH2V
  Reading for information LJV
Holism, Principle of KC3
Holistic view of school life KC2
Holmes (Oliver Wendel) ED1.3
Homogeneous class DB2
Honorary work GG4
Hospitality *irt*
  CC VC2
  DC VB1
Hours of library work
  def UA11
  Fixing of UA12
  Rule about UA13
Hub of library work TL
Hughes (Thomas) PF3
  Tom Brown's school days LH2O9
Human
  agency in library HA3
  constituents of school library HA
  quality of initiation TB2
  resource TJ1
Humane quality of John Dewey DF6
Humanism
  and universal education DA
  View of DD2
Huxley LH3G2
Hygiene MM

Idiosyncrasies of periodical YC1
Illustration
  in book GD
  irt Annual thesis ME3
Imagination, Age of PF3
Imitating library routine TC2
Imitation
  by students TC1
  Force of BB1
  irt
    Why of school library BC
    Unreliability BD1.3
Income tax officer MK42
Increasingly rapid change CE2
Indemnity bond UA73
Independence, Education in India
  after DC2
Index *irt*
  Annual theses ME3
  Essay index MQ6
Indexing *irt*
  Qualification for librarian
    HF2
  Supervised study MQ84
India
  Book industry in PG
  Creative work in PA3
  irt
    Book order work YB1
    Educational technique DC
    Intensification of education CD3
    Invention of writing CF3
    Learning of library habit LL3
    Library classification VC3
    Oral education CF2
    Training of librarian QA2
  Library hour in DJ4
  rirt
    Books in mother-tongue PA6
    Library fee YE1
  Under-production of books in ND2
Indian
  national bibliography YA2.3
  schools *irt*
    Marketing of book PG2
  standards institution WA3

student
Books for PE1
irt Translation PD2
system of education AB5
Indigenous books for students PE
Individual instruction and Dewey DG
Individualism EG4
Individuating particularities DG3
Indology in
CC VC2
DC VB4
Industrial resource TJ1
Inequalities and equalities
irt Education EH
Infant, Picture book for GD2
Inferiority complex DE2
Informative book *irt*
New conception about book CE8
Range of books GA4
Information and pleasure TJ
Inherence and becoming EA
Initiation
Apprentice method of TC
Concentric cycles for TF0
Formal lesson method of TE
Methods of TB2
of student
in the use of ready reference book CF7
Requisites to TB1
Practical guidance method of TD
work, Qualities for TB
Insanity among students CD2
Inspector of schools AD6
Inspirational
book LK
irt
New conception about book CE8
Range of books in school library GA6
reading
diary MD
irt
Achievement test NC
Making it pleasurable MG
Integration of library work and class room work AC5
Intellect TJ2
Intellectual standard of books GC1
Inter-library loan I D3
Interest, Principle of HB3
Internal memory *irt*
Examination system CG5
External memory CE3
International classification VA2
Invention
irt Impact on education CB3
of paper CF4
of printing CF5
of ready reference book, CF6
of writing CF3
Investigation box XG6
Irregularity in
publication of periodical YC1
supply of periodical YC2
Issue
of book, Rule on UA64
statistics UH8

Jacket, Numbering on XC3.1
Jesperson's boy PD1
Jewett MA3
John the Baptist DG1
Johnson (Samuel) PF2
Julius Caesar LH2Q4
Juvenile library PF2

Katha-kalakshepam LG1
King
Henry V LH2O5
John LH2O6
of the golden river PF3
Kingsley (Charles) PF3
Kipling's *Children's song* LH2O2
Koran BA21

Laboratory movement EF2

Language
  irt
    Achievement test NB1
    Book number VM2
  isolates, Schedule of VF
Lantern slide *irt*
  Extension work GJ2
  High school library CJ2
Law 1 of library science KB4
Law 2 of library science *irt*
  Author index entry WE3
  Editor index entry WF2
  New education CG3
Law 3 of library science *irt*
  Editor index entry WF2
  New education CG3
Law 4 of library science *irt*
  Author index entry WE3
  Circulation method UB1
  Editor index entry WF2
Law 5 of library science JA1
Law college CC51
Law of
  parsimony WJ3
  supply and demand PH1
Laws of library science *irt*
  Circulation method UB3
  Citizenship MH3
  Class index entry WH3
  Cross reference entry WD12
  Library classification VA1
  Maintenance section XA1
  Series index entry WG3
Layout of library building JB5
Learning of library habit LL
Legal profession CC51
Letter of authorisation
  UH4.2
Librarian
  irt
    Formal lesson for learning
      library habit L12
    Parallel reading LD3
    Preparation work for class
      room work LC1
    Supervised study MQ21
    Sympathetic service to
      students HC2
  See also School librarian
  Training for QA2
Libraries
  in India YB1
  in secondary schools RA2
Library
  act FB1
  behaviour TF22
  building
    General features of JA
Library
  building
    Specification for JB
  catalogue W
    Assignment on the use of
      MQ22
    Effect of shelf card on WB2
    Functions of WB3
    irt
      Diary MA3
      Initiation KA6
      Stock register WB
    Physical form of WA
  centred education *irt*
    Refresher course for teachers
      RA3
    School library finance YE3
  civics
    in student KB
    irt Adult KB3
    Rule about UA3
  classification V
    Fundamentals and procedure VC4
    irt
      Concentric cycle TF6
      Initiation KA5
  collection
    Effect of new education on DH3
    irt True becoming EF3
  Current definition of FB
  diary *irt*
    Parallel reading LD2

Quality of school library work
AD6
Library
ethics CJ3
fee from student *irt*
Grouping of schools HH3
India YE1
Printed catalogue WA1
finance YE
irt Grouping of schools HH3
habit
in student KA
irt
Achievement test ND
School Library FC1
Learning of LL
hand WA4
hour
and new education DJ
in India DJ4
in Presidency College DJ6
irt
Cooperative effort EG3
Correct social attitude EG4
Ferment EF2
Influence of publisher LA3
Mass teaching DH3
Non-detailed hour PG2
Order by Director
of Education AD3
Teacher and librarian DJ5
Western schools BC5
Travesty of DJ6
identity card UA21
Impact of World War II on
FB1
irt
Fire MN1
Hub of educational
institutions AB7
Other social institutions
LB2.3
key LL3
lesson MQ
New function of FB2
Library
of congress classification VA2
of elementary school CH
profession, Status of AB2
property
Damage to UA5
Rule about UA4
room in elementary school CH2
routine
Imitation of TC2
irt Apprenticeship TC3
rules UA
irt
Concentric cycle TF21
Number of volumes to be
lent out MK3
scene in
elementary school CH3
high school CJ
school in India, First QA2
science
Degree in HG1
periodicals QA3
staff HE
irt
Library classification VA1
Managerial apathy QA
Stock verification XG3
Tracing section WK3
Qualification for HH6
Status and salary of HG
talk HB5
techniques QA3
work
by student AD6
Foundation of SA
irt
Class room work KC1
Diary MA2
Reference service TL
Success in examination
AC5
Life-long self-education CE7
Light in the library JA5
Line clear treatment TL5

Linguistic
capacity MF1
dictionary KA3
irt Book number VN6
standard of books GC2
Lippmann (Walter) DA1
Literature *irt*
Fact finding LH2O
Reading for information LJO
Live work shop AB6
Loan
issuing work UH7
privilege UA6
Rule about UA8
Locke (John) PF2
Locker for student UG1
London library DJ2
Long range reference service TG2
Lord Venkatachalapathi DG7
Lord's prayer PF1
Loss of books XG3
Lost
book, Cost of XG6.10
member's ticket
Rule about UA7
Vigilance about UA75
volume XF2
Lower quartiles
Equal opportunity for DE1
irt Individual instruction DG5
Problem of DE
Lucy the chatterbox PF2
Lyell's *Principles of geology* DG2

Machine age, the child and the book LH33
Macleod (Fiana) *rirt*
Foreign tongue PA5
Mother-tongue PA4
Madras Library Association
irt
Library hour AD3
Reading habit competition ME4
Refresher course for teachers RA3
Vacation lecture AD4
rirt
Books on library science QA3
First library school in India QA2
Library talk HC5
Salary of school librarian HG6
Madras Teachers' Guild *rirt*
overloading of curriculum CD5
Patrick's visit to Madras DF61
Madras University Library *rirt*
Attracting students HC5
Diary MA3
Lectures on school library AD1
Overdue charge MK4?
Queue system ML1
Spitting across window MM3
Underlining in book KB2
Magic lantern GG2
Mahabharata EA2
Mahasaraswati
rirt Perfect perfection HE5
Spirit of HE4
Main
entry WC
Functions of WC3
Sections of WC4
subject
Determination of VE1
in CC VD
of interest VE1.412
of teaching UD2.311
Maintenance
section
Functions of XA
irt Reference service TL5
work X
Major of artillery DF2
Make-up of book TF3
Malthus LH3G2
Management
irt
Library finance YE2
Provision of library equipment QB2
Role of RB
Managerial apathy Q

Manuscript book CF3
Map VL1
Margin of book GE2
Marionettes LH33
Marketing of students' books PG2
Martineau (EH) PF3
Mass
 education DA4
 teaching
  irt
   India DC2
   Library hour DJ1
   Lower quartiles DE1
   Stimulation of nucleal element DJ3
  Need for changing DE4
Mathematical gazette LH2B2
Mathematicians
 irt Fact finding LH2B2
 Picture of CJ4
Mathematics
 Excellent result in AC4
 irt
  Fact finding LH2B
  Reading for information LJB
Mayo's *Mother India* PE2
Mayor of Madras MK42
Measurement taking DE2
Measuring conductivity ED9
Medal for best students' book PF5
Meddlesom Matty PF2
Medical book KB2
Medicine *irt*
 Reading for information LJL
 Steps in classifying VE1
Medium of expression PA
Mehnert (Klaus) PE4
Melvil (Gordon) ED1.2
Membership rule UA62
Member's ticket UF2
 Rule about UA63
Membership application UD2.1
Memorabilia mathematica LH2B2
Memory
 capacity CD1
 irt
  Cultivation of mind TJ2
  Inspirational passage MG1
 testing examination CG4
Mental passivity ED2
Mind, Cultivation of TG2
Misplacement of book
 Casual MK1
 Deliberate MK2
 irt Shelf rectification XG1
Mitchell (LS) *rirt*
 History of students' books PF4
 Students' book PD1
Mnemonic in
 CC VC2
 DC VB1
Mohammud of Ghazni FA5
Monkey ED3
Mono-syllabic work PB1
Moore (Thomas) CA22
Moral tales PF2
Morte D'Arthur LH2O3
Mother
 goose's melody PF2
 India PE2
 rirt Quality of school librarian HE4
 tongue *irt*
  Medium of expression PA4
  Translation PD1
Motor CC21
Mrs Leicester's school PF2
Multi-volumed book VM5
Multiple choice test ND6
Music in story telling LG2
Muslims CF4
Mutilation of book MK5
Mystic GA6

Name of
 author, Search by MQ82
 student in member's ticket UC2.22
Narada *rirt*
 Process of becoming EA2

Transmissive education EEL
Natural
light JA5
resources TJ1
Nehru *r by* John Dewey DG8
New
books added to library XE
editions of ready reference books GA2
education
and
library
hour DJ
scene in
elementary school CH
high school CJ
pedagogical consequence EF
school library DH
irt
Camel theory CG
Library collection DH3
School and college libraries DG62
School of Dewey DG3
Role of library in DH2
Slow response to HG4
Ushering in of CG3
England primer PF1
English dictionary FA4
school DH1
volume
irt Damage XF3.4
releasing XE3
tallying work XE1
Newberry
irt History of students' book PF2
rirt Tradition of school lib BB2
medal PF5
Newspaper CC22
cutting DG8
Newton
irt Fact finding LH2B3
rirt Stimulation of nucleal element DJ2
Noise in library MP2
Nominal roll of students UC1.1
Non-detailed
study hour PG2
textbook PG2
Notation
irt Mechanisation of arrangement VA1
of CC VC5
of DC VB1
Notes taking
irt
Achievement test NE
Concentric cycle TF8
Library habit KA7
work MR
Novelty, Principle of HB5
Nucleal element
irt
Performance after leaving school DB6
Teaching technique DB3
Stimulation of DJ2
irt Personality of student DE3
Number entry WC5
Numbering
inside book XC4.4
on due-date label XC3.3
on jacket XC3.1
on tag XC3.2

Objectives of school library KC
Old overdue charge UG43
On England LH2O8
One document
many entries WB4
one entry WB11
Open access
irt
Circulation method UB2
Freedom for students UB41
Library
building JA2
habit KA4
Maintenance section XA1

Misplacement of book MK1
Multiple sequence WB12
Shelf rectification XG1
Stock verification XG3
Safeguards for UB42

Opening of new book TC3

Oral
communication CF
examination ND2
test NF2

Order preparation *irt*
Binding XH2.10
Book order YB2.3

Original poems of infant minds PF2

Outside member
irt Library indentity card UA23
Ticket work for UE

Overdue
book
Disbarging of UG42
Rule about UA66
charge
irt Consideration for others MK41
Rule about UA86
list UJ5

Overdue
sheet preparation *irt*
Outside-member UE1.5
Student-member UC3.3
Teacher member UD2.4

Overduing work UJ4

Overloaded
curriculum
Factors leading to CD
irt
Pedagogical factor CD4
Sociological pressure CD3
Way out of CE

Oversized collection PG3

Palaniappa Chettiar PG3

Pamphlet
collection XB12
irt Fugitive material GF3

Paper
Invention of CF4
of book GE2
Scrap of MM2

Parallel
movement, Principle of XB7
reading LD
rirt Inspirational reading LK4

Paramahamsa PF2

Parent's assistant PF2

Parents *irt* Annual thesis NA4

Partial comprehensions in CC VD

Parts of book ME3

Passivity
among students ED2
irt Activity ED

Paste down catalogue WA2

Pasting of due date label XC2.2

Patrick (Kirk) DG61

Pedagogical
consequences *irt*
Individual instruction DG5
New education EF
factor CD4
inertia R
Melting away of RC3
qualification HF3

Pen KB2

Penal code ME2

Perfect perfection HE5

Period of loan
irt Consideration for others MK4
Rule about UA85

Periodical
Idiosyncrasies of YC1
irt
Concentric cycle TF721
Reference Service TL5
Role of reference service TJ2
publications
irt Concentric cycle TF71
work YC

Registering of YC4
Periodicals
display
irt Apprenticeship TC3
table HC5
on education GG3
on library science QA3
Personal
manner MP
service TA1
Personality
irt Authority BA22
of
John Dewey DG7
student DE3
teacher DF1
Over-organisation of ED1.4
Pessimism of Fascist EG4
Phillips (WH) VC2
Phylogeny, Force of EA4
Physical
form of
diary *irt*
Fact finding MB1
Recreative reading MC1
growth in child XB23
make-up of book GE
passivity ED2
Physics
irt
Fact finding LH2C
Reading for information LJC
professor MA3
Physique of book *irt*
Collection formation XB12
Concentric cycle TF12
Picture
book for infant GD2
index CJ4
irt Fugitive material GF4
Plan
for school library building JB5
irt Fugitive material GF2
of stack room XD21
Playground *irt*
Library LB2.3
Rules about game LH32
Plato CA2.1
Pleasure of
anticipation EA1
realisation EA1
Police commissioner MK1
Politician HG5
Poster GF4
Postulate
1 CE1
2 CE2
3 CE3
4 CE7
5 CE8
6 CG1
of change CE2
Potency of the process of becoming EA2
Pound (Ezra) EC2
Practical
experiment ED9
guidance as method of initiation TD
work, Items for TD4
Pre
class library work LC1
historic times BA21
library days in school AC
school library days LC2
Precious stone LH33
Preface to annual thesis ME3
Prema EF2
Preparation
of
book XC
overdue sheet *irt*
Outside member UE1.5
Student-member UC3.3
Teacher-member UD2.4
ticket UC2
work of student LC
Presidency college (Madras) DJ6
President of USA DG8

Presidential election year DG8
Pressman DG8
Prevention of fire MN
Priestley LH2E3
Primary collection XB5
  irt
    Shelf rectification XG4
    Shelving of recent additions XE2.6
Principle of
  emergent evolution TE1
  equality DA4
  holism KC3
  interest HB3
  novelty HB4
  parallel movement XB7
  recency HB5
  unity of idea PC1
Principles of geology DJ2
Printed catalogue WA1
Printing, Invention of CF5
Private
  hygiene MM
  property
    custody work UG3
    irt Locker UG1
Problem project method LL4
Process of
  becoming EA1
  education EA3
Processing of book HH4
Profession of students' authors PF5
Professional
  librarian HH3
  qualification HF2
Professor of
  college MP1
  English LA2
  physics MA3
Prohibited items UA31
Project method
  irt
    Individual instruction DG4
    Learning library habit LL4
    Student's work MQ3
  Specimen for MQ4
Prolegomena to library classification VC4
Prompt service HC4
Proof reading PH4
Provinces of England MA4
Pseudonym-real-name entry WJ2
Psycheogeny, Force of EA4
Psychology of child AD3
Public
  Extension service to GG4
  hygiene MM
  institution KB1
  library, Children's department in KB4
  Establishment of CF9
  mindedness MJ
  property MJ2
  relation work LE2
    irt
      Attracting students to library HB2
      Teacher HD3
Publisher
  irt
    Library hour LA3
    Sale of non-detailed textbook PG2
    Students' books PG1
  of England PF2
Publisher's
  circular YA2.1
  weekly YA2.1
Publishers series *irt*
  Editor of series entry WJ3
  Series index entry WG3
Publishing in India PG1
Pushpakavimana CC21
Puzzle in reference question ME1

Qualification for
  library staff HH6
  school librarian HF
    irt Grant-in-aid code QA1

Quantitative standard of book
GC3
Quarterly list YA2.2
Query answering UG6
Questionnaire for fact finding LH1
Queue system ML
Enforcing of UG5.2
irt Library habit ND1
Quinquennial survey RA2
Role of management in RB1

Rain water JA5
Rajagopalachari (C) GG4
Rama CC21
Ramakrishna MD1
Ramalingaswami MD1
Raman (CV) *irt*
Fact finding LH2C3
Mass teaching DJ4
Ramana maharishi MD1
Ramanujan (S)
irt Fact finding LH2B3
r by Principal AC3
rirt
Ferment supplied by lib EF2
Mass teaching DJ4
Stimulation of nucleal element
DJ2
Rapid change CE2
Ranganathan
(Mrs) QA2
(SR) *irt*
CC VA2
Purpose of library education
CA2.6
Status of library profession AB2
Ranganathan's vision AB3
Rate of change CC1
Rational memory CD1
Ray (PC) LH2E3
Reading
for information and pleasure LJ
habit
competition ME4
irt Recreational reading NB2
proof PH4
room
irt
Bad manners MP4
Public hygiene MM2
Specification for JB2
table JB2
Ready
made class number VK
reference
book
Invention of CF6
irt
Externalised memory CF8
New conception about CE8
Range of books in lib GA2
Terminal test NA2
service TG1
Realisation, Pleasure of EA1
Realism PF4
Receipt number UE1.414
Receiving
periodical YC4.1
supply of book YB3
Recency, Principle of HB4
Recent
additions shelf
irt
New volume releasing XE3.1
Underlining in book KB2
shelving on XE2
book HB4
Recitation
irt Inspirational reading MG1
of inspirational passage NC2
Recreational reading MD
Recreative
book *irt*
New conception about book CE8
Range of books in library GA5
reading
diary MC
irt
Achievement test NB1
Notes taking NE2

Recreative
irt Achievement test NB
Rectifying sequence on shelf
XG6.2
Reference
book
irt
Absence of training CE3
Bibliographical game ME1
Concentric cycle TF52
Externalised memory CE3
Fact finding diary MB4
Range of books in library GA2
Ready reference service TG1
Use of MQ3
books, Varieties of CF6
collection XB12
method CE7
service T
Definition of TA
irt
Circulation work UA0
Equality of opportunity TA2
Five laws TA1
Other items of library work TL
School library TA3
kinds of TG0
Social role of TJ
Refractory word PB1
Refresher course for teacher RA3
irt Role of management RB2
Regimentation DA2
Register card YC3.1
Entering in YC4.4
Registering of periodical YC4
Reinforced library binding XH1
Religion BA21
Reminder
card MK42
irt Supply of periodical YC5.3
Renewal
noting UK1
of loan UK
Rule about UA87
Renewing work UK2
Replacing
returned volume XF1
shelf XF1.3
Republication of book PF3
Research, Methods of CE7
Retention of student
as customer HC
Return of
book, Rule about UA65
overdue book, Rule about UA66
Returned volume replacing XF1
Revealed book BA21
Rewett MA3
Rider (F) VA2
Rig-vedic passage EG5
Robinson Crusoe
Republication of PF3
rirt Use of monosyllabic words PB1
Role of
five laws SB
management RB
state government RA
teachers' association RC
Roosevelt (Mrs) DG8
Rote memory CD1
Routine master EA3
explained EE4
Row guide XD22
Royal mail van LH33
Rule of
queue ML1
school library UA
Ruskin (John) PF3
Russia PF4

Sacred book BA21
Safeguards for open access
UB42
Sai Baba MD1
Sakti EA1
Salary of school library staff HG
irt
Central school HH3
Grant-in-aid code QA1

Sanatkumara EE4
Sand tray CF3
Sapru DJ4
Sarada Ranganathan
endowment for library science QA3
professor of library science QA2
Sargent (John) AB
Sayers (WCB)
qirt
CC VC2
in library HA3
rirt Story telling LG2
Schedule of
anteriorising common isolates VF
language isolates VH
ready-made class numbers VK
space isolates VG
time isolates VJ
Schematic representation *irt*
Cultivation of mental resources TK
Five laws SA1
Hub of library work TL1
Scheme for library classification VA
Schofield (EB) VB3
School
and college libraries DG62
and society DG2
books in India WD21
boy EC5
building QB1
curriculum CD2
education
entry of library into CF1
irt Subject for cross reference entry WD11
going age DA31
irt Compulsory library hour AD3
librarian
irt
Annual anthology NC3
Bibliographic game ME1
Collection of informative books GA4
Directed reading NB3
Epitomising MF1
Inspirational book LK2
Library hour DJ5
Misplacement of book MK1
Promotion of public-mindedness MJ3
Service to class TH1
Terminal test NA2
Qualification for HF
Supreme position of HE1
libraries
association BC3
division BC3
in India VC3
library
and new education DH
as a live workshop AB6
Attracting students to HB2
building
General features of JA
irt
New school building QB2
Old school building QB1
Plan for JB5
Course of lectures on AD1
Evolution of the concept of FA
expenditure in USA YE3
finance YE
irt Management QB3
Human constituents of HA
in UK BC3
in USA BC3
irt
Authors of students' book PC3
Controversy at home LH31
Creating library habit KA
Details of work HE3
Development of citizenship MH
Free use MJ2
Fugitive reading material GF
Habit of using library FB3
Hygiene in catalogue room MM1

Individual way of growing
EF4
Keeping diary MA1
Library
civics KB
habit FC1
staff HE
Personal manners MP1
Preparation for class
room work LC
Principle of holism KC3
Promotion of p::blic minded-
ness MJ1
Queue system MK2
Range of
books GA
standard of books GC
subjects GB
Reference service TA3
Role of teacher LB1
Service to
class TH1
public GG4
Story hour LG.
Teacher HD
Working of ferment EF3
Look of EG
Objectives of KC
New outlook on FC
review RC3
rirt Electro-magnet HA2
Rules of UA
service, Survey of RA1
Status and salary of HG
Why of B/E
work *irt*
Children's book PA2
Role of teacher's associations
RC1
year book RA2
of library science of the University
of Madras HG6
Science, Teaching of ED9
Scott PF3
Scrap
book GF6
of paper MM2
Scripture (Elizabeth) LL4
Search by
name of author MQ82
subject term MQ81
title MQ83
Secondary collection XB5
irt Shelf rectification XG4
Secretaries of state
teachers' associations PH5
Secretary of Hindu High School
HG6
Sections of main entry WC4
Seely (HG) DJ2
Selections
irt Use of anteriorising common
isolates VL5
of inspirational passage MG2
Self
educability
irt
Individual instruction DG5
Statistical study DD1
of student DB1
education, Formal course for
CE7
Seminal book TJ2
Seminar room JB2
Sense of time TD3
Sentences in students' book
PC
Sequence of main subjects
HB5
Serial TF713
Series index entry WG
Functions of WG3
Service
in anticipation TH3
on demand TH2
to class TH
to individual student TG
to teacher GG3
Seshachalam (C) HC:

Shakespeare's
Julius Caesar LH204
King
Henry V LH2O5
John LH2O6
Shelf
arrangement XD1
card
Advent of WB1
irt Library catalogue WB2
label XD32
plank-guide XD32
rectification XG1
cum stock verification XG4
irt Apprenticeship TC3
register card *irt*
Binding collection XH2.3
Bound volume XH4.4
Damaged volume XF3.1
Different collections XE2.8
Lost volume XF2
New volume XE3.5
Principle of parallel movement XB7
Shelf rectification XG6
Worn-out volume XH2.4
Shelley LK5
Shelving
of returned volume XF1.4
on recent additions shelf XE2
Shifts in school HH1
Shutters in window JA6
Side
hung shutter JA6
interest, book on GB3
Silver jubilee year BD2
Simple sentence GC2
Sizing up new book HC3
Sleeping
class EB2
explained EB3
in reading room MP4
Smoking inside library MN1
Smritis CF2
Social
imitation BC2
role of reference service TJ
Socialisation
irt Individualism EG4
of book CF
Sociological
phenomenon DB1
pressure DA3
Soft iron HA1
Songs of innocence PF2
Sources for book selection YA2
South Indian
teacher rirt
Articles on the use of library LL4
Assignment for supervised study LL3
School library practice RC3
teachers' Association PH1
Space
for library QB
isolates VG
Spacing of formal lessons TE1
Specification for
catalogue cabinet WA3
library buildings, fittings and furniture JB
school library building QB2
Speed of transport CC21
Spirit of Mahasaraswati HE4
Spiritual
experience GA6
urge in student MD1
Spitting across window MM3
Sports-fund YE1
Sri Lanka CC21
Srinivasan PA7
St Paul's Church Yard PF2
Stack room
guide XD
irt Madras University Library HC5
Plan of XD21
Sitting on the floor of MP1
Size of JA1
Specification for JB1

Stamping in the book XC2.1
Standard
  deviation DD1
  of book GC
  student XB2
State
  government *irt*
    Library finance YE2
    Pedagogical inertia RA
  teachers' association PH1
Statesman, Appearance of HG5
Statistical study DD1
Statistics of
  books consulted UH3
  issue UH8
Status of school library staff HG
  irt Management QA1
Steam engine CC21
Steps in classifying VE
Stick UG3
Stimulation of nucleal element DJ3
Stimulus-response doublet ED5
Stock
  register WB
  verification XG2
    irt Catalogue WB12
    Problems in XG3
  verifier XG3
Stockholm airport DG8
Story
  book GA5
  corner CH4
Story
  hour LG
  telling LG1
Strength of
  book GE2
  library staff QA1
Student
  as human constituent of
    school library HB
  centred education RA3
  Individuality of EA4
  irt
    Casual misplacement of book
      MK1
    Deliberate misplacement of book
      MK2
    Formal library lesson LL1
    Habit of maintaining diary MB5
    Initiation TC1
    Library collection GA1
    Objectives of school library KC
    Pre-class library work LC1
    Queue system ML2
    Retention as customer HC
    Sense of time TD3
    Use of fire extinguisher MN2
  Library habit in KA
  member, Ticket work for UC
  Spiritual urge in MD1
Students
  Curiosity of GB1
  Differences among DH3
  in schools DA31
  Nominal roll of UC1.1
Students'
  book
    Author of PC3
    in English PF
    irt
      Qualities of author PE2
      Translation PD1
    Rhythm in PC1
  Curiosity GA4
  follow-up work LE
  Indigenous books for PE
  Parallel reading LD
  work in library lesson MQ
Stuffed monkey ED3
Style of writing
  in students' book PC
  irt Book number VM8
Stylus for writing CF3
Sub-average student DB4
Sub-lending, Rule about UA84
Sublimated emotion TJ2
Subject
  analytical entry WD
  classification VA2

entry WC3
irt Range in a school library GB
of bibliography NF1
of formal lesson TE1
term, Search by MQ81
Suicide among students CD2
Suitors of Ahalya EA2
Sun light JA5
Super
average student DB4
heater CC21
Supervised study *irt*
Individual instruction DG4
Learning library habit LL3
Library lesson MQ2
Supplementary nominal roll
of student UC1.2
Syllabus-centred education
YE3
Sympathetic
reception HC1
service HC2

Tag, Numbering on XC3.2
Tagging work XC2.2
Tagore (Rabindranath) HA2
Tagore's *Cabuliwallah* LH207
Talmud BA21
Tambi Srinivasan PA7
Tamil
Children's books in PA7
irt Children's books PG3
Tarde (Gabriel) BC1
Tasso PD1
Teacher
as human constituent of
school library HD
irt
Book selection HD
Class room work HD4
Directed reading NB3
Epitomising MF1
Force of environment EA5
Inspirational book LK2
Library hour DJ5
Parallel reading LD1
Preparation work for class
room work LC1
Public relation work HD3
Recitation of inspirational
passage MG1
Service to class TH1
Status of librarian QA1
Suggestion of books on
side interest GB3
member, Ticket work for UD
Personality of DF1
Refresher course for RA1
Rendering service to GG3
Vacation course for LA2
Teachers'
association
irt
Book famine PH1
Writing of book PH2
Role of RC
college (Saidapet) *rirt*
Lectures on school library AD1
Library facility AC1
Monosyllabic words PB1
Refresher course RA3
Teaching
profession CC52
staff HG1
technique DB1
see also Technique of teaching
Team
spirit EG3
work LC1
Technical staff QA
Technique
for illustration GD4
of teaching *irt*
Establishment of pubiic library
CF9
Initiation of student CF7
Invention of
paper CF4
printing CF5
writing CF3

Technology LJF
Teleology of education CA
Telephone number of John Dewey DG61
Temperament
of Indian boys BC5
of Western boys BC5
Temple LB2.3
tower EB1
Temporary collection XB6
Tennyson LK5
Morte D'Arthur LH2O3
Terminal
essay NA3
recitation NC2
test *irt*
Fact finding NA2
Recreative reading NB2
Tertiary collection XB5
irt Shelf rectification XG4
Test paper NE3
Text book
centred education RA3
irt
Book CE8
Limitations of finance GB2
Publishing in India PG1
Thackeray PF3
Theory of evolution EC4
Thirukkural TJ1
Thiruvalluvar TJ1
Thiruvannamalai MD1
Three R's CC3
Ticket
Loss of UA71
number *irt*
Outside-member UE1.41
Student-member UC2.21
Teacher-member UD2.31
work *irt*
Outside-member UE
Student-member UC
Teacher-member UD
Tightening of charged tray UJ1
Time
isolate VJ
Sense of TD3
Tiny research CE7
Tirujnanasambandar MD1
Tirupathi temple DG7
Title
page of annual thesis ME3
Search by MQ83
Tobacco chewing MM3
Token UG3
Tom Brown's school days LH207
Tooling XH4.1
Topical
collection WB4
sequence *irt*
Class room work HD4
Follow-up work LE3
Methods for exploiting extra-mural factors LF2
Parallel reading LD3
Service
in anticipation TH3
on demand TH2
Story telling LG3
Toru Dutt's *The lotus* LH2O1
Townshend (Frank) *rirt*
Activity among children ED1.6
Education as becoming EC1
Tracing section WK
Function of WK3
Tradition *irt*
Unreliability BD1.2
Why of school library BB
Training
college
for Women RA3
irt Help from Government RA1
for librarianship QA2
Translation, Futility of PD
Transmissive education EE1
Transport, Speed of CC21
Travel book GA5
Treatise TJ2

Trinity of library HG3
Tripitakas BA21
Tropical sun BC5
Troy, Stories of PF1
Truant boy EB1
  explained EE9
True false test ND4
Two card system YC3
Type face GE3
Typography GE3

Ubhayatomukhi stage EA2
UGC XG3
UK *rirt*
  Futility of adaptation PD3
  India's imitation BC2
  Intensification of education CD3
  Percentage of children going to school DA4
  Periodicals on school library practice RC3
  School library BC3
Ultimate class VM1
Ulysses KC3
Umbrella UG3
Unconscious hit DF
Underlining in book KB2
Undersized collection XB12
Unit book rack HB1
United
  Kingdom *See* UK
  States
    Information Service Library (Madras) HC5
    of America *See* USA
Unity of ideas, Principle of PC1
Universal
  education
    and humanism DA
    Beginning of DA1
    irt India DC3
  franchise Act DA4
Universe of ideas CB2
University
  elementary school DG3
  examination AC4
  extension lecture ED7
  of Madras *rirt*
    Course in library science AD5
    Encyclopaedia britannica CE5
    Grants Commision XG3
    Library
      school QA2
      training for teachers AD4
    Use of reference book CE4
    Vacation lecture VA2
Unknown future CE2
Uppermost quartile *irt*
  Homogeneous class DB2
  Individual instruction DG5
USA
  Presidential election in DG8
  rirt
    Futility of adaptation PD3
    Grouping of schools HH2
    India's imitation BC2
    Individual instruction DG1
    Percentage of children going to school DA4
    Periodicals on school library practice RC3
    School library BC3
User
  First reference to FA4
  irt Concept of library FA3
Uses of water EC6
Utopian purpose of education CA1

Vacation course on school library work LA2
Volcano LH33
Valliappa PA7
Variant-form-of-word entry WJ2
Vasana, Force of EA3
Vedas *rirt*
  Authority BA21
  Oral communication CF2
Venkatachalapathi DG7

Ventillation JA5
Verbal notes dictation DC2
Vernacular Book Society BB1
Vesuvius LH33
Vibhishana CC21
Vigilance
  about lost ticket UA75
  work YC5
Vijayalakshmi Pandit DG8
Viva voce NA4
Vivekananda DJ4
Vocabulary
  at different mental levels PB3
  of children PB2
Volcano LH33
Volume
  for binding XH2
  numbering work XC3

Wales PA3
Waste paper basket CE5
Water
  purification CE5
  supply CE5
  Uses of EC6
Watt LH2C3
What makes a library big HA2
Who's who TF512
Why of school library B/E
  From the angle of
    curriculum C
    educand D
    process of education E
  Lines of approach B
Wicket gate *irt*
  Open access VB42
  Queue system ML12
Wilson Lib bull GF3
Windows
  in library JA5
  in stack room JA6
  Spitting across MM3
Wood's despatch on education BB1
Words, Choice of PB
World
  bibliography VC2
  peace AB5
  War II FB1
Worn-out collection XH2.2
Writer of school HF1
Writing, Invention of CF3
Written examination ND2
Wu (John C H) ED1.3

Year of publication VM2
Yi-king BA21
Yogeshwar EC6
Youth
  in Soviet Russia PF4
  psychology TB1

Zurich PA7